British acclaim for Sebastian Faulks's

THE FATAL ENGLISHMAN

"Unusual, fascinating and interlocking in the oddest ways."
—*Time Out London*

"Superb. . . . A mystery story of rare narrative power. . . . Faulks brings to these portraits the exquisite detail which made . . . *Birdsong* so evocative. This is biography written with that revealing sense of the moment which marks good fiction."
—*Financial Times*

"This is the most wildly exciting book that I've read for a long time, and on a great theme: how the failures of Britain in the twentieth century have seeped into the souls of its countrymen. It's a classic." —David Hare, *The Spectator*

"Brilliantly described. . . . A perfectly constructed narrative."
—*Evening Standard*

"Extremely well-written. . . . Faulks describes the three heroes *manqués* with sympathy and understanding. . . . He has produced three excellent mini-biographies." —*Literary Review*

"I have always thought that good biographers could write excellent novels. Now I have to admit that an excellent novelist has written a good biography. *The Fatal Englishman* is a subtle, original and exciting book."
—Carole Angier, *New Statesman & Society*

Sebastian Faulks

THE FATAL ENGLISHMAN

Sebastian Faulks is the author of the novel *On Green Dolphin Street* and a trilogy of novels set in France: *The Girl at the Lion d'Or*, *Birdsong*, and *Charlotte Gray*, the latter two of which were bestsellers. After a period in France, he and his family now live in London.

THE FATAL ENGLISHMAN

THE FATAL ENGLISHMAN

Three Short Lives

Sebastian Faulks

Vintage Books
A Division of Random House, Inc.
New York

A VINTAGE BOOKS ORIGINAL, MARCH 2002

Copyright © 1996 by Sebastian Faulks

All rights reserved under International and Pan-American Copyright
Conventions. Published in the United States by Vintage Books, a
division of Random House, Inc., New York. Originally published in
hardcover in the United Kingdom by Hutchinson, an imprint of
Random House UK Ltd., London, in 1996.

Vintage and colophon are registered trademarks
of Random House, Inc.

The Cataloging-in-Publication Data is on file
at the Library of Congress.

Vintage ISBN: 0-375-72744-2

Author photograph © Jerry Bauer

www.vintagebooks.com

Printed in the United States of America
10 9 8 7 6 5 4 3 2 1

With love to William and Holly

CONTENTS

LIST OF ILLUSTRATIONS

AUTHOR'S NOTE

By chance I read a book about a young American who had been by so far the outstanding character of his generation – as scholar, athlete and personality of ambitious charm – that his graduation from Yale in 1957 was covered by *Time* magazine, while his contemporaries selected the jobs he would give them when, not if, he became President. Yet after a glorious start, his career stalled. The book (*Remembering Denny* by Calvin Trillin) was an investigation into what went wrong. The subject ended up committing suicide, and much of his problem seemed to stem from the fact that he could not accept his homosexual desires. Had he been born a few years later, the author implied, he would have encountered no such problems.

The book made me think that young or short lives are more sensitive indicators of the pressure of public attitudes than lives lived long and crowned with honours. The stories of young people who delight parents and friends with their talents have a concentrated significance in their beginnings, and in their premature ends there is a natural poignancy that brutally epitomises the disappointment that is also common but less evident in longer, duller lives.

Three such lives, each done at the length its span naturally required (a third of a life, a third of a book) – that might well seem full enough to take away the sense of 'so what' that would cling to a single short life. And then if perhaps the subjects actually had achieved something interesting and if they were to come from different parts of the century and so have lived against a different public background and thus illustrate the impact of changing attitudes and preoccupations over a long period . . .

This book was originally called *The Artist, the Airman and the Spy*. It is, after all, three separate biographies: the lives of three people who never met. It seemed fair that the title should not only recognise the subjects' individuality but also emphasise the defining importance of work in each man's life.

As I researched and wrote these three lives, various links between the three characters and various common themes emerged, none of which I had known about before I had started. This obviously encouraged the urge towards unity that finds its best expression in fiction, when the events can be shaped and patterned to echo the themes, while the characters can be made, within the limits of their realistic capacities, to behave in a way that adds a further level of harmony.

I tried to resist this urge. Having allowed it to dictate a new title, which stressed the characters' similarities, I wanted to remain faithful to their differences. The lives of real people, unlike those of fictional characters, seem to exert a small but constant outward force away from order. So while I attempted, as gently and as truthfully as possible, to shape the events of their lives into some comprehensible pattern, I tried also to respect their individual energies, which seemed to push in the opposite direction, back towards singularity: the artist, the airman and the spy.

I have occasionally used the words 'England' or 'English' where some readers might have expected 'Britain' or 'British'. This is not because I imagine they are interchangeable, but because I accept that there is a difference.

Christopher Wood

One day in the spring of 1921 a beautiful young Englishman set off for Paris to become the greatest painter the world had ever seen. His name was Christopher Wood and he was nineteen years old. Until he took the boat for Calais on 19 March he was working for a fruit importer in the City of London. He was the son of a doctor in the North West of England, and his sudden disappearance to France confirmed his family's worst fears. Although Christopher wore shirts from the best outfitters in Jermyn Street, was well-mannered and polite to his parents, he seemed to have no understanding of middle-class convention. Some combination of circumstances had combined with a fierce streak in his character to make him wild and ambitious. He was determined to be a painter, and the intensity of his desire was frightening to his parents.

Dr Lucius Wood and his wife Clare had two children: Christopher, whom they knew as Kit, and Elizabeth, whom they called Betty. As a child, Kit had his hair cut in a bob and wore smocks. So did Betty. The family was relatively well off; the parents believed in God and the children believed in Father Christmas.

One December Kit wrote:

My dear father Xmas, I want a new good yacht and I want it to be all hollow inside and gun and a top And Betty a big doll and a gun And I want a very sparp chissel and a good screw driver and a good peaint box and mother wants a nice comfy bed With love from Kit and Betty Wood.

He always knew what he wanted, and in his childhood he almost always had it. His mother was devoted to him and he to her. He would gather crocuses for her birthday on 25 March and she repaid him with her doting indulgence. Clare Wood came from a Lancashire family called Arthur on her father's side, and a seafaring Cornish family called Pellew on her mother's; Kit liked to think that the sea, and boats, were in his blood. Dr Wood was a general practitioner. He was a less demonstrative person than his wife and took a detached view of his son's early enthusiasms. He called him 'Snodgrass' after the would-be poet in *Pickwick Papers*. Next to Dickens, Dr Wood's preferred reading was the Bible.

At the age of seven, Kit was sent to a preparatory school called Freshfield, where he excelled at games. In 1914 he went to Marlborough College in Wiltshire. This was one of the newer public schools, lacking the history or burnish of Eton and Winchester, but respectable in its way. The aim of such schools was to prepare their pupils for the service of the British Empire abroad, as soldiers, diplomats and administrators, or to ready them for work in the professions at home. Games were as important as work, though neither was as crucial to the school's philosophy as the idea of 'independence': their claim was to turn a boy into a man, even if the evidence suggested he was still a child.

At the moment Kit Wood began his time at Marlborough in September 1914, the world changed. 'The plunge of civilization into this abyss of blood and darkness,' wrote Henry James, 'is a thing that so gives away the whole long age during which we have supposed the world to be, with whatever abatement, gradually bettering, that to have to take it all now for what the treacherous years were all the while making for and meaning is too tragic for any words.' It was as though the history of Europe had been torn up: Erasmus, Shakespeare, Michelangelo, Goethe, Mozart, Dante, Montaigne, Tolstoy, Rembrandt, Beethoven ... their work had no cumulative value any more; it was smashed into fragments that Eliot would try to reassemble in *The Waste Land*. Almost ten million men died.

While Kit Wood struggled to settle in at school, his father went as a medical officer to the Western Front, where he stayed for the duration of the War. While he was away, Kit became seriously ill. The disease seems to have started as polio but then to have been complicated by the development of septicaemia or a similar infection. One of Wood's adult friends thought it had all started with a football injury. In any event he was now forced to abandon the games field: he was unable to do his lessons in class but had to read and write in a lying position. In March 1916 he had to be withdrawn from Marlborough altogether. His mother nursed him at home, and in the long, painful hours of his illness he turned to painting. His love for her, already profound, was intensified by his physical dependence.

Dr Wood was absent from his son's life, except in the occasional letter from the Front. The progress of the War was known to Christopher Wood only from odd glimpses of his mother's newspaper during his convalescence: the 'real' world was kept at his mother's arm's length.

The illness ruined his education. He did not return to school until January 1918 when he arrived at Malvern College in Worcestershire. Like all such schools in England at this time, Malvern was in a state of grief bordering on paralysis. The school magazine that listed Wood's arrival also recorded the award of nineteen DSO's to old boys of the school and thirty-six MC's. There was no artwork in it; there was almost no room for anything but the names of the dead: a total of 457 Malvernians were killed in the War. Teachers of school sixth forms were finding it difficult to keep their nerve when the names of boys they had so carefully nurtured towards manhood and university appeared a few weeks later in the dead and missing columns of *The Times*.

After four years on the Western Front Dr Wood returned to find that his little son had become a handsome, crippled young man. His boyish beauty had remained; he had a short straight nose, a strong jaw and hair of the colour known as fair, though by no means blond, brushed back from the temples where it showed the first signs of receding. He had a clipped, rapid way of speaking, indicative of a nervous intensity that had developed in him since 1914. He limped when he walked, though he used his cane as much for conversational emphasis as for physical support.

Dr Wood had taken a job on the Earl of Derby's estate at

Knowsley near Liverpool. The family lived in a spacious house in Huyton, which was then an affluent suburb. He told Kit that he too should train to become a doctor, but among the changes wrought in Kit by what he came to call 'the War years' was a powerful indignation at anything he viewed as meddling in his affairs. Dr Wood's suggestion was briskly rejected by his son, who told him he had had enough of blood and illness: he had decided to go to Liverpool University where he would study architecture. This had the air of a compromise worked out with his mother: the subject was artistic yet respectable, the university was near home. It was as close to being a painter in an attic as he could yet realistically manage.

Wood viewed it as no more than a means to an end. One of his architectural drawings from the university survives: it is a solid piece of work, correct and craftsmanlike, but on the back of it is a highly-coloured painting of a young woman. His mind was not on elevations but on other plans.

After a year he left university and took a job in London working for an importer of dried fruit called Thornley and Felix. He lived in rooms in Bayswater and his homeward route in the evening took him past the Café Royal, where Augustus John habitually held court. Friends of Wood later claimed that he one day approached the throne with some drawings and that John was so impressed that he arranged for Wood to go to Paris and lodge with his friend Alphonse Kahn, a well-known collector and connoisseur, while he studied painting. It is possible that Wood had met John when he went to lecture to the Sandon Club at Liverpool University and was thus able to reintroduce himself, but it is more likely that the Paris connection was made by a Wood family friend called Robert Tritton, who dealt in Oriental antiques.

Alphonse Kahn had taken up attractive young men before, though there is no evidence that he required them to become his lovers in return. Kahn was an extreme example of a 1920s Parisian type whose money came from international finance but whose interests were in art and patronage. He lived in an astonishing house in the sixteenth *arrondissement* and he invited Christopher Wood to abandon his little rooms in Bayswater and to come and stay with him while he looked for a studio and more permanent lodging.

So it was that the untrained, uncertainly talented Christopher Wood took the train to Dover and crossed to Paris, where few English artists of his generation had previously ventured. The day before he left, as though in symbolic farewell to the life he was leaving, he played a round of golf with Robert Tritton at Woodhall Spa, a seaside course in Lincolnshire.

Christopher Wood was a child of the Edwardian era, born at the last gasp of imperial pomp into a country depicted by later writers, such as Philip Larkin in his poem 'MCMXIV', as criss-crossed with narrow roads and deep hedgerows, with village names from Domesday all grown-over with loving neglect, and patient football crowds with trusting, upturned faces, unresentful of their prosperous betters with their long weekends, grouse-shooting and towering blancmanges.

The England of Wood's childhood was in fact a fearful place, engaged in a battle on all fronts to keep the modern world at bay. Wood's desire to be a painter and his departure to lodge in Paris with an unmarried 'connoisseur' were deeply alarming to his father. Attempts to interest English people in new developments in painting, writing or psychology had all failed: the country not only had little appetite for knowledge of human behaviour, it had no real interest at all in the life of the mind.

Far from being imperially complacent, Britain was worried about its place in the world. After the Boer War, alarmist literature circulated about the poor physical quality of the British young: congested city conditions had produced a generation of stunted, weak, voluble children who lacked in physical or moral stamina. In the port of Liverpool, Christopher Wood's father saw just such conditions, and came to the same conclusion as the demagogues who suggested that Britain's best way forward was in increased – or as they put it 'splendid' – isolation from Europe and its modern ways.

By denying legitimacy or even publication to many of the ideas current in Europe, the conservative forces of Edwardian England managed to confuse the cranky with the serious by driving both underground. While socialism was emerging as a credible political force, anarchism occupied almost as much public attention. Many people who might have seen feminism as the most important means of social advance were distracted into anti-vivisectionism, vegetarianism or the investigation of the occult. While the country retained some adamantine self-belief, and an instinctive patriotism which found its most poignant expression in the raising of the Pals' battalions in 1915, it was morbidly sensitive to the currents of new thought that were abroad.

And abroad, in the opinion of the middle classes from which Christopher Wood came, was where they should stay. Channels to the continent were few and subversive. Walter Sickert had lived in Dieppe and studied the French Impressionists; Wyndham Lewis had been to France, as had David Bomberg and Jacob Epstein. Ben Nicholson went to Paris in the early 1920s and made some flirtation with abstract painting before retreating into figurative work for the next six years.

Christopher Wood had no historical self-consciousness and was motivated by complicated and utterly personal patterns formed in the period of his illness. He did not see himself as a pioneer, but no amount of ignorance on his part could stop him from appearing to the people he met in Paris as a very curious figure indeed.

Alphonse Kahn's house in the Avenue du Bois de Boulogne was dominated by a vast salon with a polished parquet floor and open fires at either end. About the walls were hung paintings by Turner, Rembrandt, Greuze, Poussin, Matisse and other modern painters that Wood could not immediately identify. Wood's quarters consisted of a beautifully decorated bedroom, with bathroom and lavatory attached. Kahn provided him with meals and helped him to enrol at art school. Wood had wanted to go to the Ecole des Beaux Arts, but it was beyond his means; he signed up instead at the Académie Julian in the Passage des Panoramas off the Boulevard Montparnasse, which had been made fashionable in the 1890s when Bonnard, Vuillard and fellow-painters of the Nabis group had passed through. Matisse, Léger and Derain had added their lustre to the Académie, though by 1921 it had come to depend on visiting Americans.

All these names, all these styles of painting . . . and all that Christopher Wood had was his ambition. He needed not only to orientate himself in a foreign capital, but to catch up with what had happened there when he was a child. The principal breakthroughs in painting and sculpture had been made in Paris by Picasso and others before the War. Paris had drawn in artists from all over Europe: Modigliani, Miró, Brancusi, Picasso, Kandinsky, Giacometti, de Chirico, Chagall, but still in England the most famous painter was Augustus John.

Wood never managed to form a clear perspective on the development of modern painting; and his enthusiasms were often contradictory. He admired Augustus John, even though John's work had already degenerated by this time into a succession of society portraits where his undoubted technical facility was not imaginatively stretched. But Wood also came to like Cézanne, Derain, Matisse and other French painters who were more determinedly modern. He compensated for his lack of academic understanding by an instinctive good taste, and a sensitivity to a wide variety of art.

As soon as he was settled at Alphonse Kahn's, Wood did what all well-brought up young Englishmen would have done at this time: he wrote to his mother. Almost every day a letter was despatched from Paris in his hasty, sophisticated hand, its content a rush and slither of names, places, bad spelling and half-understood developments. He negotiated an allowance from his parents of £14 a month and was grateful to them for giving him 'this chance'.

In matters of the world, in questions of politics and power, he remained vividly ignorant. In May he noticed cars on the streets of Paris being inspected by military authorities and believed this to be a preparation for war; but why, and against whom he did not know. Nor did he care. Compared to Huyton, Paris was entrancing. With Kahn's help he acquired a studio in the rue des Saints Pères, a street that runs at right angles from the left bank of the Seine. His landlord was an Englishman called Middleton, who helped Wood set himself up in reasonable comfort. He painted all morning, and in the afternoon would go to the Académie Julian, where they taught a traditional course of figure drawing. Wood's steady sketches showed a fair grasp of anatomy and perspective. They were not remarkable, but were not intended to be: his aching ambition reluctantly recognised the need for humility and apprenticeship.

In the evenings he left his student life and moved into a different world. Through Alphonse Kahn he met a number of fashionable, rich and self-indulgent people. Paris was both snobbish and democratic in its social life; gatherings might be ostentatious or competitive in their displays of spending, but the guest lists included people whose only wealth was their talent. In June Wood danced with Mme Carpentier, who was anxious about her husband George's next title fight; he watched Suzanne Lenglen play tennis at St Cloud and met Maurice Chevalier; there was an invitation from a young Clemenceau, nephew of the Tiger. Wood was open-mouthed at the beauty of such people's houses and the sophistication of their manners, but he tried to keep a level head. In his sober moments he recognised that it was useful for him to know people with money: they might make further and yet more useful introductions; they might one day buy his paintings.

He spoke little French and was not yet a proper painter. Alphonse Kahn had slipped him through the doorways of various large houses, and Wood's charm had taken him from there. He was laughably English with his hand-made shirts, his fair hair, his earnest manner; yet he was also eager, reckless, open to experience and, with his limp and his little stick to lean on, poignantly vulnerable.

Through Kahn Wood met a Chilean diplomat called Antonio de Gandarillas, a notorious figure in the beau monde. Augustus John had stayed with Gandarillas and even John, the definition of outlandish bohemianism in English terms, had been taken aback by what he called Gandarillas's 'lurid and fashionable life' Gandarillas was a man of huge financial resources but erratic solvency who claimed to be related to Catherine of Aragon. He was foremost among many South American *émigrés* in Paris who had used their wealth to patronise insolvent artists before the

War. His aunt, Eugenia Errazuriz, had supported Picasso in his early days and consequently retained a direct influence with him.

Gandarillas himself was a small, exquisite man, who looked like a spider monkey. He was exhaustingly, indefatigably social: after parties, he loved food, drink, opium, gambling, travel, art and young men. He had been educated at Cambridge and was, when Wood met him, married with three daughters. Gandarillas's life was not, however, consistent with orthodox marriage, and he saw little of his family. A family portrait done by Ambrose McEvoy in 1918 was reprinted in a book about McEvoy's work in 1923 with Gandarillas painted out and the picture retitled 'Madame Gandarillas and her children'. While he was unquestionably dangerous company for the impressionable Christopher Wood, Gandarillas had an important redeeming quality: he was capable of loyal friendship.

This was as well for Wood, because before long Gandarillas had more or less adopted him – as curio, protégé, and lover. The arrangement had an element of convenience for both men – Gandarillas gained a beautiful pet, Wood could eat – but it was underpinned by a constant affection.

Wood meanwhile continued with his studies. French girls, he complained, had large stomachs, but still on the whole, he drew women better than men. One of those he depicted was Maria, Duchesse de Gramont, a friend of Gandarillas's who sat for some sketches. The Middletons lent him a bath for his studio, and since there was a bedroom there, he was able to make 54 rue des Saints Pères his official address, particularly in letters to his mother. In fact, when he moved out of Alphonse Kahn's house he frequently spent the night at Gandarillas's house in the Avenue Montaigne.

In July Wood was invited by a couple called Whitaker to go to their twelfth-century villa outside Florence. It was a handsome place, formerly the property of the Medicis, though the party stayed only a week or so before decamping to Riva on the shores of Lake Garda in search of cooler weather. Here he met and befriended the Russian painter Michael Sévier, who gave him his first set of oil paints. Apart from feeling uncomfortably hot, Wood registered the sensations of abroad in mainly visual terms.

In late July he noticed some political unrest in Italy, but he had no interest in its causes. What he did record was a macabre incident in which two young men of about his age, who had been to dine with his party the night before, were kidnapped by terrorists and tied to the main railway line to Rome, where they lay for two hours before a train came through and cut them to pieces. The incident made a troubling impression on Wood: he never quite forgot it.

He arrived back in Paris in September. He had saved £35 in Italy, but had somehow managed to spend it on the way back and now found himself broke. He lodged briefly with a friend called Billie Shields and then with Adrien Drian, a portrait painter and decorative artist about whom he became enthusiastic: Drian was only thirty-five, but he was making, Wood could not help noticing, £5,000 a year.

In the autumn Gandarillas came to his rescue. He financed a small flat at 11 bis rue Balzac, just opposite the Carlton on the Champs Elysées, and enrolled him in a second art school, La Grande Chaumière. Wood rededicated himself to his work and was commissioned to paint some posters for the dress designer Edward Molyneux. This was a social commission, since Molyneux was one of the people he had met in the autumn season of parties, but it was the first time someone had shown any faith in his ability.

Wood was caught in a number of conflicting currents. Some evenings he would be in the company of such dubious figures as Lady Drogheda, Countess Lasocki, Princess Radziwill or Lady Idina Gordon who, though better educated, were not essentially different from what later generations came to know as 'Euro-trash'; on other nights he would be alone in his little apartment. He was still only twenty, and he found that Paris could be a harsh and unfriendly place. His dedication to his work provided a daily, albeit fitful, continuity.

At the end of 1921 Wood returned for Christmas to Huyton, which he detested. His parents wanted to know what his 'plans' were and he told them that they had not changed: he wanted to be a great painter. He had no practical details to offer them, so escaped from the stifling atmosphere of the suburbs as soon as he could and took the train to London. Gandarillas was staying at his house in Cheyne Walk and was happy to put Wood up for a few days. He introduced him to Augustus John, and Wood was thrilled. Whatever the limits of John's painting, he was still a heroic figure to aspiring English painters. Wood's enthusiastic account of the meeting, incidentally, suggests that he had not previously met John at the Café Royal or anywhere else.

Wood also met Ivor Novello, Lady Diana Manners, Gladys Cooper and and a Chilean painter called Alvaro Guevara who took a strong physical liking to him which he managed to choke off only out of respect for Gandarillas. Wood did little work. He sulked in his bedroom overlooking the Thames. What was annoying him particularly was his mother's suggestion that he take a job designing dresses for Edward Molyneux: this was not the kind of thing great painters did. Back in Paris he wrote to her extremely fiercely to point this out. He asked for her trust and promised that one day he would repay it; Clare Wood, who could deny him nothing, wrote back a conciliatory letter and the matter of Kit's 'future' was temporarily put on one side.

In January Gandarillas took him travelling to the Low Countries, where Wood had a chance to see paintings by Rembrandt and Vermeer. He was struck by the devotion of the people at prayer at Bruges and vowed that one day he would paint exactly what he had seen. His mother was anxious that he might be drifting away from the Church of England, but she need not have worried: it was the aesthetic not the spiritual aspect of Catholicism that had caught his eye.

When he was back at the studio in the rue des Saints Pères and once more attending his courses at the Académie Julian, Wood reflected on his first year in Paris and admitted to his mother that it had been very hard. He had, he told her, come close to suicide. 'I have felt lonely, terribly lonely,' he wrote. He had 'felt the lack of my Mother and home and sometimes had to do on very insufficient money . . . Paris to a young boy who knows nothing can be hell.' He was not in Paris for the rest of the year. Gandarillas took him to Menton in the South of France and thence on a long trip round the Mediterranean. Much of it was financed by Gandarillas's luck at the casino in Menton; the journey was unplanned, but gathered shape as it progressed. For Wood, as always, its purpose lay in self-education. In April they were in Tunisia and he painted a watercolour of a Moorish street which showed the early signs of a distinctive talent. It was in his use of colour that Wood first began to progress: he had clearly looked at the early paintings of Picasso, as well as those of Matisse and Derain, and learned a certain boldness.

Wood's twenty-first birthday arrived on 7 April 1922. Events had moved so quickly that he needed to pause and take stock of his position. His ambition to be a great painter was intact; the longer he worked at his painting, however, the more he understood how far he had to go. On the one hand he had to cherish his ambition, he had to keep it burning and not allow the pleasures of his new life to extinguish it; then again, he was forced to recognise that he did not yet have the technical means to convert his ability into pictures. He had simultaneously to feed his ambition and to keep it dormant.

One of the ways in which he managed to keep this awkward balance was by enlisting his mother. His great painting, when it came, was to be in honour of her. 'Some day,' he wrote, 'I hope to repay you for all your great love and kindness and the great care you took of me when I was ill. I never forget.'

Wood, who was a quite guileless correspondent, expressed with dramatic simplicity the equation that was at the centre of his creative process. His love for his mother and his gratitude towards her were genuine enough; but by equating his projected success as a painter with the 'repaying' and honouring of her, he cleverly insured his artistic ambition against failure or decrease. His love and gratitude would never fade; and now his will to paint was equally eternal. He did not make this connection from some cold-hearted calculation, but he possessed at an unconscious level the ruthlessness that art requires.

From Tunisia, Wood and Gandarillas travelled to Taormina in Sicily, then at the height of its unspoilt fame as a resort of astounding beauty, accessible, physically and financially, only to the few. Each day Wood rose early and left the villa they had rented to go down to swim in the pink shadow of Mount Etna.

The return climb of 800 feet gave him an appetite for breakfast of eggs, coffee and cherries in the garden. Gandarillas would now have risen to plan the day's enjoyment and would take coffee with him beneath the trees. In the morning Wood painted and Gandarillas read. After lunch there was a siesta, then more painting till the daily Italian lesson at five-thirty. In the cool of the evening Wood wrote to his mother. Then there was dinner laid on a little white table beneath some cypress trees on a terrace surrounded by Roman mosaics. Dinner was always an event: one day Wood was awoken by the main course when Gandarillas put two live lobsters in his bed during his siesta. Afterwards they sometimes had the town orchestra in to play for them and sometimes they read French. It was a time of almost unimaginable *douceur de vivre*, yet it was in Taormina, Mrs Wood later claimed, that Kit really began to paint. While his travels with Gandarillas took him away from his studies they also introduced him to sights, colours and scenery that were beyond the range of other students. In Taormina he painted a plate of lemons directly from above, as though he might see right through them into the plate. The perspective was actually less interesting than the brilliant yellow he achieved in the fruit.

In Taormina Wood read the letters of Van Gogh, and they left a deep impression. He had seen Van Gogh's work on the walls of Alphonse Kahn's house and greatly liked it; now he discovered that the work was produced by someone he described as having 'a beautiful mind'. He began to believe that the nature of an artist's work was determined by his moral character; and this assumption, however doubtful, fitted into his previous equation of his own success with the honouring of his mother.

While Wood placed a kind of superstitious value on his mother's affection he was happy to disregard his father altogether. He had rejected the values of Huyton and all the dullness it entailed; he came increasingly to equate his father with the forces of tedium and small-mindedness that he must escape at all costs. This was a selective view of his father, just as the elevation of his mother was unrealistic, and ignored the fact that it was his father who was paying the £14 a month. Wood, however, was not searching for a mature or a consistent system of values: he was trying to be an important painter. He believed whatever helped.

From Sicily he and Gandarillas travelled to Athens, where they hired a car and driver to take them into the mountains. This proved to be a more hazardous undertaking than they expected. The roads were not properly made, and the young driver struggled to control the car. About 50 miles north of Athens he missed a narrow bridge and plunged them into a marsh beside the road. Nobody was hurt, but they were stuck 30 miles from the nearest village. Wood and Gandarillas stayed by the car to guard their belongings while the driver set off for help.

As they were sitting by the bridge, a young Greek soldier came by. He was on his way home from the war against Turkey – what war or why it was fought, Christopher Wood neither asked nor cared. The soldier stayed to help them, and when the driver returned with some horses they were able to pull the car free and continue their journey. The next day, on a mule track, they came across a dozen eagles devouring a dead horse; one of the birds removed an entire haunch and flew off with it. The eagles were unperturbed by the sound of the car, and Wood had to fire a revolver to frighten them away. He did not explain how or why he came to have a gun with him. They proceeded by pony and spent the night in a hut belonging to a goatherd, where they dined off chicken, goat's cheese, figs and wine. They were so badly bitten by mosquitoes in the course of the night that they dosed themselves with quinine against malaria the next morning. At this stage, Gandarillas began to feel the want of fine linen, chateau-bottled wine and other necessities of life in the *seizième*. The expedition was cut short: they returned to Athens and took a boat to Constantinople.

Christopher Wood was everything Gandarillas wanted in a travelling companion: bright, appreciative, light-hearted, but sufficiently absorbed by his work to be independent for large parts of the day. In Constantinople he produced some accomplished watercolours and marvelled at the city itself. More trouble, however, was waiting for them in Smyrna.

If Wood and Gandarillas had taken greater interest in public events, or even if they had bothered to find out something from the soldier who had helped them in Greece, they might never have gone south to Smyrna in the first place. Under the treaty of Sèvres in 1920 Greece had been given Smyrna, and by 1922 the Greek army was trying to push its way up the Aegean coast. The Turks, however, had found a leader in Mustafa Kemal (Kemal Atatürk) with no regard for treaties and a committed hatred of the Greeks. He drove their army back into Smyrna, and then did what any Turkish leader would have done: massacred them.

Wood and Gandarillas, restored by their civilising stay in Constantinople, then found themselves in the middle of the slaughter. Wood viewed it with a kind of feverish detachment, though now he had a particular reason for it: he and Gandarillas had both contracted malaria. Wood's temperature descended from 106 degrees just in time for him and Gandarillas to catch the last available boat out of Smyrna. The Turks moved in the next day and killed everyone in sight, including the staff of the nursing home.

Even this sweaty brush with death provoked no more reflection in Wood than the comment that 'this fellow Kemal Pasha is a dreadful menace'. On the boat to Athens they shared a cabin with the governor of Lesbos, who smelt, and Prince Louis Alphonse, the shifty brother of the king of Spain, whom they ditched on arrival.

The pleasure cruise was now further protracted by the need for convalescence. Karlsbad in Austria had a pleasantly hygienic, Northern ring to it after the terrors of the Aegean; and Gandarillas planned a route that took them through Venice, where Wood could look at the paintings by Veronese, Tintoretto and Titian. He repaid Gandarillas's consideration by describing their brief stay in Venice as the most wonderful night of his life.

Once in Karlsbad they consulted medical opinion. The doctors prescribed arsenic injections to counter the effects of malaria, castor oil to make Wood's hair grow where his head had been shaved, and iron for his newly diagnosed anaemia. The recuperation should be completed in the mountains, they advised; Wood told his mother that this definitely ruled out Huyton.

Gandarillas also wrote to Clare Wood from Karlsbad, telling her that she need have no fear about Kit: so long as her son was in his company, whether in Paris or abroad, he would make sure he lacked for nothing. It was a charming and strategically well-judged letter, which drew a friendly response from Mrs Wood. Meanwhile Kit wrote to her again and said: 'I am enclosing to you a letter for Daddy which I wish you to read first and if you think it will ease matters should be glad if you will give it to him, otherwise tear it up.

'Remember this, that I do not wish in any way to reproach him for his curious ideas but merely to put things quite straight as they stand from one man to another. For now, although you probably never realised it, I am become a man and have to a certain extent developed during this last year.

'It hurts me to think of him being ill and worried, for at the bottom of my heart I love him, but have I, during the last few years, been able to show it?

'I shan't say more except that I love you dearly and I hope that we shall reach a good understanding.'

Wood was a slapdash writer, but there were certain suggestive phrases: Dr Wood's 'curious ideas' . . . 'I am become a man' . . . his father 'ill and worried' . . . his recognition that his mother might think it wiser not to pass the letter on to his father but to 'tear it up'. Yet somehow it is hard to believe that Wood chose to tell his father that he and Gandarillas were lovers. He could sufficiently have emphasised his independence without distressing his father further. Gandarillas's letter to Clare Wood spoke only of friendship, and it would have been foolish of Wood to jeopardise the good feeling it had engendered for the sake of some cleaving to the 'truth'.

Although he was a doctor and, thanks to his years at the Front, a man of considerable experience, Dr Wood was not the kind of father to welcome the news that his son was sleeping with another man. Homosexuality was one of the areas in which Britain had most determinedly ignored the developments of European thinking. To Dr Wood, as to most other Englishmen, the most famous instance of homosexual activity was still the imprisonment of Oscar Wilde. A writer called Edward Carpenter had proposed ideas about the instinctive nature of homosexuality in *Homogenic Love* (1896) and *The Intermediate Sex* (1908),

Christopher Wood

but they were not generally accepted in England until they appeared, only slightly updated, in the pages of a report prepared for the Home Office under the chairmanship of a Yorkshire schoolmaster called Jack Wolfenden in 1957. Havelock Ellis's great work *Studies in the Psychology of Sex* tackled the problems in 1897, but the book was considered depraved and could only be published in America. It did not appear in England until 1935.

In any event, Christopher Wood, despite his passionate, unguarded nature, had a strict Edwardian delicacy. Even at their most jocular his letters had no vulgarity and no mention of bodily functions, sexual or otherwise. The most significant line of his letter is the plaintive one: 'At the bottom of my heart, I love him, but have I, during the last few years, been able to show it?' Lucius Wood's part in his son's life was marginal, but its small tragedy was shadowed in that sad, half-stifled question.

From Karlsbad, Wood and Gandarillas returned at last to Paris, stopping en route at Munich (where they found the wooden seats in the opera house uncomfortable because they had grown so thin), Leipzig and Nuremburg, then known only as the birth-place of Dürer.

At the end of November Wood met his mother for a few days in London and introduced her to Tony Gandarillas. Clare Wood was a good-looking woman who appeared at least ten years younger than she was; nevertheless she was a provincial doctor's wife whose chief concerns, as she expressed them, were curtain fabrics and the shortage of domestic help. Gandarillas was one of the most worldly men in Europe. The meeting, however, lubricated by his charm and their common dedication to her son, was a great success. It was followed by a further cordial exchange of letters.

In London Wood also saw Augustus John, whom he continued to admire, believing him to be 'very refined and a gentleman to his finger tips'. Back in Paris he effectively moved in with Gandarillas in the Avenue Montaigne, though there was some pretence that he lived in a small hotel nearby. They had been through the wonders of Taormina and the trials of Smyrna together; whatever might happen to their sexual feelings, they were now bound close in affection and friendship. On 28

December they went to the evening service at the classical church of Saint Sulpice, the 'cathedral' of the aristocratic Faubourg St Germain. It had been a tumultuous year.

In the new year, 1923, the contrast between Wood's work and his social life became more marked. By day he attended classes or toiled in his studio, worrying about the price of paint and canvas. At night he moved with such people as Luisa, the Marchesa di Casati. She owned the Palais Rose in Neuilly, formerly the property of the exquisite Robert de Montesquiou, who had served as Proust's model for the Baron de Charlus. Her dining room was hung with black velvet, and at one end was a plate-glass partition behind which a boa-constrictor was fed with live animals during dinner. She also owned an eighteenth-century palace on the Grand Canal in Venice, which was later sold to Peggy Guggenheim. It was here that she gave a ball at which Nijinsky danced with Isadora Duncan – supremely to her satisfaction: 'It was more wonderful than making love with a negro boxer on Mr Singer's billiard table.'

Luisa Casati had red hair and red eyes, which she concealed behind a veil. She was the friend of another fantastic character, Gabriele D'Annunzio, the Italian poet-aviator who had taken the Adriatic port of Fiume by force and turned it into an independent republic. By this time, however, D'Annunzio was on the way to becoming a kind of proto-Fascist. Wood knew nothing of Fiume, which became Rijeka, part of Serbia, and cared less. He liked his new friends more than the old ones and that was all that mattered to him.

He had also understood something that escaped puritanical critics of the Parisian social circus. Many of the most colourful figures of the beau monde had good taste and the money with which to back it. Gandarillas's aunt, Eugenia Errazuriz, for instance, was a figure almost as exotic as Luisa Casati, but the two people she had chosen to finance in their struggling days were Picasso and Stravinsky, for whom she had bought a piano. Mme Errazuriz's decorative taste was for simplicity – scrubbed tiles, whitewash – and was said by Cecil Beaton to have defined 'the whole aesthetic of modern interior decoration'. Paris was not susceptible to easy distinctions between the vulgar and the valuable because the two were often co-existent.

In February Gandarillas's wife paid a visit to Paris and he chose that moment to absent himself. The doctors who had been treating Wood for the after-effects of malaria recommended a change of climate, so the two headed south. In Rome they visited Luisa Casati in her marble house whose upstairs gallery contained more than 100 portraits of her by contemporary painters, including Picasso, Boldini and Augustus John. Wood was overcome by the dramatic character of Rome and wanted to stay longer; he felt sure he could work well there. Now that the coast was clear of his wife, however, Gandarillas wanted to return to Paris.

Wood was happy enough to be back in his well-organised studio. He had made a small library and installed a vast couch in the gallery upstairs so he could spend the night if he liked. In the evening a servant would bring him dinner, and under Gandarillas's influence he had become a gourmet. On 20 April 1923 he dined alone off vegetable soup, a fresh lobster, *filet de boeuf*, asparagus, *compote de bananes*, coffee and a bottle of Bordeaux.

He worked away and felt encouraged by what he did. Alphonse Kahn told him to go and copy the paintings in the Louvre and he took this fatherly advice in good part. One of his strategies for self-encouragement was to be dismissive of the shows he visited: 'I saw the Salon today,' he wrote to his mother, 'and really there was not one picture I could not have painted much better myself.'

Like many painters, Wood had a weakness for the circus, and in June he painted a big picture with what, in the terminology of the day, he called 'two niggers', Pierrots, a gypsy, a monkey and a dog. He was not happy with the result, but the work he put into it paid dividends almost at once in another painting.

This was 'La Foire de Neuilly', one of the first paintings in which Wood's own style could be seen. It was a big, jolly, well-organised canvas. He had absorbed some naïve influence, possibly from Douanier Rousseau, but it was rendered in terms he had seen in the paintings of Matisse and Derain. The result was raw but exciting; it was a French painting with a strong English accent.

The summer season of parties was by now in full swing. The Comte and Comtesse de Beaumont held a ball in their Louis XIV house which had been decorated for the evening by Misia Sert, Diaghilev's associate at the Russian Ballet. Gandarillas wore a Pierrot outfit designed by Picasso; Wood made a Russian costume of his own. A fellow-guest was Lord Alington, one of the most remorseless pleasure-seekers in Europe. He went as the Sun King, his costume consisting of a number of rays attached to his gilded skin. As the evening progressed he gave away the rays one by one, until even his Louis XIV mask and his golden stockings were gone. When he returned the next morning to the Ritz hotel the old ladies in the Place Vendôme were taking their poodles for an early walk. The manager of the hotel rushed out to wrap Alington in a blanket, but not before Alington, on the steps of the hotel, had removed his golden fig leaf and presented it to the Ritz as a little souvenir.

Exhausted by parties, Wood confided in his mother that he was having doubts about his own abilities. 'I can no longer be content to draw things as I see them,' he wrote. 'What is the use, it has all been done long ago.' It was only a tremor. Soon he was back in his usual vein of desperate ambition: 'All I want is to succeed, and I shall do it somehow.'

Then came the invitation he had longed for. Mme Errazuriz asked him to dine with Picasso and his wife. Picasso was the king of Paris. He was at this point going through a monumental, neo-classical phase, though 'Three Musicians' (1921) and 'Three Dancers' (1925) used techniques of advanced Cubism. He was also doing figurative paintings, such as the beautiful portrait of his little son Paolo dressed as a toreador, and set designs for Diaghilev. Picasso was above the petty squabblings of rival movements; he had won the battle for respect by his Cubist pictures before the War, and by now was recognised and deferred to, far more than his great contemporaries Braque and Matisse, as the Master.

In France. In England he was regarded with distaste, except by a handful of critics led by Roger Fry. Christopher Wood, to his credit, recognised Picasso's genius. While his own painting went down different paths, he never doubted Picasso's pre-eminence. What Picasso had done, at the same time as one or two others, such as Delaunay and Kandinsky, was to break finally with the idea that a painting need represent a version of something that exists. By 1912 he had stopped trying to fix an object as the focus of a painting but was using the whole picture space itself: everything in it, whether colour or shape, contributed to the painting, but not as a representation of something in life or nature. The assumption behind this development was that images could appeal more directly to the eye if they were free of the wearisome task of trying to represent something else.

Wood did not really understand this assumption and was not much interested in it. He put it baldly: 'The old landscapes and pictures of women that looked exactly like them are no longer sought after by those who know what's what.' But he was shrewd enough both to recognise Picasso's genius and to steal from him what could be useful in his own work: 'pungency', according to the artist Winifred Nicholson; or freedom of line and boldness with figures.

The dinner went well. Picasso talked to Christopher Wood about painting and Wood believed they had become great friends. The function was probably a duty required of Picasso by his patron to please her nephew, but in any case he made himself charming to the young Englishman.

In July Wood gave his mother an unprecedented glimpse of his mental agitation. He felt lonely and unable to discuss the problems of his painting with anyone because Gandarillas was unwell and he didn't like to trouble him. 'My brain is working too hard and I don't know where the end will come . . . I have come to a certain stage, I suppose one would call it a revolution in one's mind . . . I have worked very hard and produced nothing whatever to satisfy me.' He told his mother he would give ten years of his life to be alone with her and talk. 'You are unhappy sometimes, you write and tell me so,' he went on, beginning to sound more like his mother's lover than her son. 'Have you ever loved really? Do you realise the value of it? . . . I am so looking forward to seeing Daddy again. I do so want to be very happy with him and I shall do all in my power to be so. Do you think he wants me to come home? I think a great deal about him, although I never write. I admire him extremely as a man in very many ways, but don't tell him so.'

Don't tell him so . . . Wood's exile to Paris, and the difference of opinion it revealed between his parents, caused tension at home in Huyton.

Wood worked on throughout the hot summer, standing stripped to the waist and cooled by an electric fan. In September he and Gandarillas went to London, from where they planned to motor up to Scotland with a friend called Jack Gordon. Although they went past Liverpool they did not stop at Huyton. They played golf at Inverness but gave up after nine holes, because even with his limp, Wood was too good for his companions: it is hard to imagine that a man of Gandarillas's indoor habits was much of a force on the links. From Glencoe Wood wrote to his mother: 'I am longing to see you, but I do hate Huyton.' She had to make of this what she could, knowing that he had driven almost past her door.

They returned to London, where Wood met Luisa Casati's daughter Christina, who struck him as being a more attractive version of her mother. He was beginning to be drawn to women, though he still preferred male company because women, he claimed, always kept him waiting and then required too much attention and reassurance. Gandarillas was his true friend and benefactor: they had an excellent arrangement which allowed Wood to do as much painting as he liked and, to a large extent, live the life he chose. Wood could not imagine any marriage providing such latitude. The trouble with Gandarillas was that he was so dedicated to parties: they were not a youthful indulgence, they were the love of his life.

Christopher Wood by now struck a curious figure in London. Friends of his insisted that he retained an English public school manner throughout his life. One friend, Gerald Reitlinger, said it was always possible to imagine Kit as a golfing, shooting Savile Row gentleman and that only some quirk had made him an artist; but such people knew little of his inner fury and fitful self-discipline. Meanwhile the company he kept had also left its mark on his manners, and his behaviour briefly took on a tart, impatient edge.

On 11 November he went to Westminster Abbey for the Armistice Day service. The queues were such that he could not get in; they stretched up Whitehall into a great mass in Piccadilly Circus and thronged over Westminster Bridge. T.S. Eliot had seen the same crowd and described it in *The Waste Land*, which had just been published by the Hogarth Press: 'So many, I had not thought death had undone so many.'

Wood made little of it, or of the General Election in December, which ended in a stalemate when Baldwin's Conservatives lost ninety seats to Labour and the Liberals. On Election night Wood went to a party at Selfridge's; he did not vote.

By now the shape of Wood's immediate problem was clear. He had somehow to find a way to improve as a painter, with all the toil and self-questioning that would take, while at the same time trying to keep the demands and side-effects of his social life within bounds. As he became known for his own charm and good looks and not merely as Gandarillas's accessory, the demands became greater. The potential for destruction was typified in the person of Princesse Violette Murat, an enormous drug-addicted lesbian with a hunger for company. She owned a white rat, which she believed to be reincarnated, and had a fetish for cleanliness. If she arrived to stay at the Ritz she would tie her hair up in a scarf, ask room service to send up a pail and some brushes and start scrubbing the bathroom. She had some society reputation for 'good taste' but, unlike Mme Errazuriz, left no proof of it.

With Violette Murat came drugs, though Wood had already been introduced to opium by Tony Gandarillas, and it played a crucial part in his life and death. Opium is the milk from the green capsule of the poppy indigenous to Indo-China and parts of Turkey. The European centre was Smyrna, which was possibly one reason Gandarillas and Wood made their ill-advised detour there in 1922. By the time the opium reached Paris it had the consistency and colour of treacle. A pin was dipped into it to pick up a blob of opium which was held over a small flame until it bubbled and expanded to about the size of a large pea; it was then plunged into the pinhole opening of an 18-inch pipe. The pipe was reversed over the flame while the smoker inhaled, preferably taking the entire contents in one draught.

Opium did not disable the smoker physically, like strong cannabis, or leave him feeling mentally befuddled; it gave, on the contrary, a sensation of controlled euphoria. All things seemed possible: the intellect, far from being impaired, felt regally empowered. Conversations, books, pictures and the natural world appeared charged with profound meaning and interest, all of it made magically available to the mind of the smoker; food, particularly the flavours of Far Eastern cooking, became more intriguing and more intensely enjoyable. Compared either to cannabis or to its own derivative, heroin, opium was refined, civilised and intellectual.

Above all opium lived up to its Homeric name – *nepenthe*, the destroyer of grief. Graham Greene recorded that after four pipes, 'unhappiness and fear of the future became like something dimly remembered which I had thought important once.' Thomas de Quincey, who took opium in alcohol as laudanum, wrote: 'Here was a panacea . . . for all human woes: here was the secret of happiness about which philosophers had disputed for so many ages, at once discovered: happiness might now be bought for a penny, and carried in the waistcoat pocket: portable ecstasies might be had corked up in a pint bottle.' Opium was a princely drug – flattering, powerful and enriching. While many native Chinese had learned how to live with it over generations, nervous European types like Christopher Wood found it difficult to control the euphoric genie they had released from the pipe.

The morning after, he would be back in his studio in the rue des Saints Pères. In the spring of 1924 he was working on a large nude in oils as well as copying drawings by Raphael, Leonardo and Titian. He was struggling also with what he called the 'almost suffocating influence of modern art'. He both appreciated what had been done, and knew, as a proper artist, that he had to make some accommodation with it; yet his own strength was not in Cubism, Dada or Surrealism. He had to find a way of absorbing the modern without disturbing the originality of his own distinctive, but essentially old-fashioned talent. And this in turn had to be achieved with Violette Murat laying out lines of cocaine in the bathroom.

At this time, despite the drugs and the bad company, the tensions of Wood's life still resolved themselves as comedy. He sat on the Louis XIV *lit de repos* in his little apartment within Gandarillas's house on the Avenue Montaigne and looked about him. There was a big open fireplace in which a fire burned all day. The room was panelled, with one wall entirely taken up by books. Outside there was a courtyard from which he could hear the splashing of a fountain; it made him think of home, and how happy he had been as a child, before everything was spoiled by the War years. He did not pine for England any more; he believed that the only possible life there for a young man was to 'stagnate or become a merchant and the owner of a small villa on the outskirts of some provincial town'. While he regretted that he had had no choice but to separate himself from his family, he did not doubt that he had made the right decision.

In February Tony Gandarillas was offered the Chilean ambassadorship to Paris. He refused, much to Wood's relief, on the grounds that the entertaining would cost him too much. In March the two of them set off once more on their travels. Wood had wanted to return to Rome because he felt he would be inspired there, and Gandarillas was happy to oblige. They travelled by way of Corsica, Leghorn and Pisa, and once in Rome Wood found himself thrilled by the Coliseum, the via Appia and the Villa d'Este. He enthused about almost all the places that he visited with Gandarillas, but Rome was the one with which he had the truest affinity.

He noticed that a man called Mussolini was much admired by the Italians; in fact they knelt down when he went past them in the street. One morning as Wood and Gandarillas were driving through Rome their car was stopped in the traffic. Wood looked out of his window and found himself face to face with Il Duce, whose car was going in the opposite direction. It was a momentary glimpse, a single tableau, before their cars rushed onwards into the Roman traffic, but it was typical of the way Wood glimpsed politics and public affairs as they worked themselves out into history. The process by which world events in their turn eventually affected his private, self-absorbed life was longer and more subtle.

The stay in Rome was again shorter than Wood might have wished, and after a visit to Florence, where he saw paintings by Titian, Leonardo and Botticelli, they returned to Paris. Wood's sister Betty was visiting, and although her parents had made other arrangements for her accommodation she was allowed to see Kit a couple of times: he in turn spared her the attentions of Violette Murat.

In May Wood visited Princess Radziwill at her chateau near Paris, in the grounds of which Jean-Jacques Rousseau was buried. She told him how she had witnessed the death of Rasputin, and how neither poison nor the revolver bullets that thudded into his body seemed able to kill him. There were a number of Rasputin bores at large in Europe at this time, though the Revolution had also driven to Paris some of the most cultured and attractive White Russians, as Wood later discovered to his delight.

Neither he nor Gandarillas had fully recovered their health since the malaria episode; Wood complained that he had been ill constantly since the age of fifteen. He was receiving injections for anaemia while Gandarillas was having problems with his lungs. In the early summer Wood tried to escape the demands of society by reading in the evenings. He found it hard to remember in detail what he read and wondered whether this was a sign of a basic intellectual weakness – the side-effect of his abandoned education. Something he had read which did remain with him was an epigram from Lamartine: *'La vie doit avoir un courant, l'eau qui ne coule pas se corrompt'* – 'Life should have a current; water which doesn't flow becomes stagnant.'

The current of his own life swept him down to the south of France in the summer, to Le Canadel, a resort in the Var, where Jean Cocteau and Moise Kisling were also staying. Wood was so tired by Paris that he showed little interest in either of them, though both were substantial figures. Kisling had come from Poland but acquired French citizenship by fighting in the Foreign Legion. His painting had developed from his early days with Bonnard and Vuillard through his membership of the Picasso-

Braque-Max Jacob group, and had had enviable commercial success.

At the end of August, Gandarillas took Wood down to Spain, where he was impressed by the Goyas in Madrid and a bullfight in Malaga, the birthplace of Picasso. But they then returned to Le Canadel, which Wood thought a 'godforsaken little spot'. Although he claimed to be uninspired by it, his painting did progress there. He was set on further simplification of colour in the manner of Van Gogh, who became a visible influence at this stage. His confidence began to seep back. 'I know I can be a great artist,' he wrote to his mother, 'because I understand and feel the things I like so much if I can only be left with them.' The paintings by now had style and feeling, but they were still awkward: the influences of other painters were not fully assimilated.

The coming of autumn softened the colours of the countryside and Wood's hostility to it, but at the end of October they moved to Villefranche, a fishing port on the Riviera, whose modest quayside inn, the Hôtel Welcome, became for a few years in the mid-twenties a legend of tawdry glamour. Villefranche was a medieval town with small streets and big stone archways, with a bay in front and mountains behind, whose steep slopes were covered with olive and cypress trees. The Hôtel Welcome was dominated by the figure of Jean Cocteau, who had a corner room with balcony on the first floor. He attracted many artists and musicians from Paris who were delighted to be joined by the rougher trade from the American naval ships and the prostitutes from Marseille and Nice who came down to service them.

Among the visitors to the hotel were the musicians Honegger and Milhaud (two of the group known as *Les Six* that also included Poulenc and Georges Auric), Picasso, Stravinsky, Hemingway and Fitzgerald. The corridors stank of opium and the dining room was filled with the sound of self-conscious artistic conversation. The elements of talent and pretension were, as in Paris, indissoluble. Isadora Duncan, who had first prompted Diaghilev to bring his Russian Ballet to Paris, now just made scenes. The English writer, Mary Butts, a devoted opium smoker with tangled red hair, wrote regional novels of the English West Country with mystic overtones.

In addition to the creative, the narcotic and the ridiculous, the Hôtel Welcome could offer more: religion. A sinister young seminarist called Maurice Sachs was the subject of frenzied ogling when he danced on the table in cassock and pink socks. Max Jacob, the poet and friend of Picasso, found that his new Catholic faith was not enough to keep him from the terrible draw of the Hôtel Welcome and its troupe of handsome young men, most of whom had been brought down for the delectation of Jean Cocteau. One of these youths, called Jean Bourgoint, habitually wore the uniform of the French army. Other regulars were the delicate artist and decorator Christian Bérard, known as Bébé for his cherubic expression, and the writer René Crevel. It was a circus of dubious taste whose clashing elements were united by sexual self-interest.

It was not Huyton. Even after three years in Paris Christopher Wood seemed gauche. He had brought some watercolours to show Cocteau, and another English visitor, Sir Francis Rose, himself only a teenager at this time, described Wood's anxiety about his work. To Rose he appeared a 'lame and timid young man, with his strange, handsome English schoolboy's face'.

Wood was overwhelmed by Jean Cocteau. He believed him to be a genius in drawing, writing and conversation: he was simply the arbiter of what was elegant or worthwhile. Wood believed he had made friends with him and was proud to have done so.

Cocteau was a man of great gifts, many of them on permanent display. He had burst into Paris at the age of sixteen at a ball given by Madame de Chavannes at the Opéra. He appeared dressed as Heliogabolus, the most dissolute of all Roman emperors, carried on a litter by two Nubian wrestlers. It was an entrance to which he had lived up as poet, draughtsman, librettist, talker, impresario and self-publicist with a lifelong passion for what he had to sell.

Edith Wharton remarked of Jean Cocteau that no one had ever made her understand better the lines of Wordsworth 'Bliss was it in that dawn to be alive/ But to be young was very heaven.' Cocteau was thirty-five when Wood met him in 1924 but had made a fetish of his own youth. He ran away to sea at the age of fifteen and published his first poem in 1908 when he was nineteen. The financial support of his mother allowed him to indulge his talents. He brought out a magazine called *Schéhérézade* in 1908 which belonged in essence to the *fin de siècle*: its little drawings had a touch of Decadent mascara. When Modernism burst on the world shortly afterwards Cocteau was swift to adapt his ideas; but in the 1920s the fact that he could trace a line back to the old days helped him to rise above the competing manifestos of Dada, Futurism and Surrealism. As well as being a perpetual *enfant terrible*, he was old enough to know better.

Cocteau infiltrated himself behind the scenes of the Russian Ballet. He liked everything about it – the snobbery, the glamour, and particularly its principal dancer, Vaslav Nijinsky. Diaghilev hired him to work as a publicist, but forbade him access to the showers. In 1915, Cocteau made up for this by joining an ambulance unit run by his friend Comte Etienne de Beaumont, one of Paris's greatest party-givers. The unit included shower-baths in which Cocteau took numerous photographs, celebrating the experience in a poem called '*La Douche*'. He recalled the bodies with sensual pleasure, particularly the part that fascinated him all his life – '*Je ne crois guère aux hommes de petite verge*' ('I can't really believe in men with a small prick'). Throughout the war he commuted back to Paris, where he struggled to stage a ballet called *Parade*. When the ballet opened in 1917 he called it 'the greatest battle of the War', a tiny provocation to the French army, then in full-scale mutiny over the epic loss of life on the Chemin des Dames.

Cocteau befriended the aviator Roland Garros and flew with him on several occasions. Garros was involved with trying to develop a machine gun that fired through gaps left as the propeller rotated. Cocteau claimed that Garros had solved the problem by watching an electric fan in Cocteau's mother's flat in the rue d'Anjou. Garros was killed on a mission in 1918 and Cocteau dedicated his book of poems *Le Cap de Bonne Espérance* (*The Cape of Good Hope*) to him. The figure of the airman had caught his imagination, just as it had appealed to Proust, who visited the aerodrome and in *Albertine Disparue* compared some wheeling, looping angels in a Giotto fresco to 'the young pupils of Roland Garros'.

The best and worst of the period, the brilliant and the cheap, the beautiful and the spurious, met in the person of Jean Cocteau. He appropriated a bar called Le Gaya, initially as a snub to the Dada movement, but then found he liked being a night-club manager. It was succeeded by Le Boeuf sur le Toit, the definitive bar for visiting Americans.

When Wood met him in 1924 Cocteau was in mourning for his lover, Raymond Radiguet, a boy comet he had met at Max Jacob's house when Radiguet was only sixteen. Radiguet produced a novel called *Le Diable au Corps*, which was widely acclaimed as a masterpiece, but died of typhoid, apparently contracted from bad oysters, in December 1923, still only twenty years old.

Cocteau's ostentatious mourning led Parisians to apply to him the word '*veuf*' (widower), usually in the vicious sobriquet '*le veuf sur le toit*'. A friend called Louis Laloy suggested his grief might be assuaged by opium and Cocteau took to the drug so readily that he smoked it for the rest of his life. He was shrewd enough to buy only the best and to treat it with the respect it required. He went through two cures for smoking, though the literary benefits that accrued, both in the books he wrote about it and in the quiet that the sanatorium gave him to consider other projects, led Stravinsky to comment that 'the chief purpose of the drug-taking came to be book-making'.

The impressionable Christopher Wood sat in Cocteau's first-floor room watching him at work. From Picasso he had learned the trick of making a drawing with a single line, without taking the pencil from the page. Wood, who often struggled with his line, was suitably awed. Cocteau talked to Wood about opium and shared his delight in the ritual aspect of smoking. The pipes were best prepared by Chinese 'boys' while the smokers lay back and awaited their pleasure. 'People talk about the "enslave-ment" of opium,' Cocteau wrote; 'but taking it at regular hours is in fact not only a discipline but a liberation . . . It reassures by virtue of its air of luxury, its rites, the elegance of its non-medical lamps, flames, pipes and by the secular ritual of its exquisite communion.'

Most of what Cocteau said was true, but with the weighty provisos that the smoker should be rich enough to buy the best drug, self-disciplined enough not to abuse it, and should come to it in a state of mind that was not vulnerable or unbalanced. None of these serious reservations would have counted with Wood, who was in the first rapturous glow of hero-worship. Under Cocteau's influence, Wood's use of opium, which had been an occasional indulgence with Gandarillas, became a regular habit.

Cocteau left Villefranche at the end of November 1924 to travel to London with Diaghilev's ballet for the opening of Milhaud's *Le Train Bleu*, decorated by Henri Laurens with a curtain by Picasso, for which he had written the libretto. By December he was back in Paris, smoking heavily, and seeing Christopher Wood. He encouraged him in his painting and promised to bring Picasso to come and look at it. In return Wood offered to share his studio with him. Cocteau accepted, and the arrangement worked well because Wood was a morning worker and Cocteau seldom left his mother's house before noon.

Wood was thrilled by his own life and confused by public events. He believed that there was panic in Paris because everyone was expecting a revolution, but he was too absorbed by his work to find out what it was all about. He told his mother that 'I hope to goodness there is not' a revolution; but having escaped the massacre of Smyrna he felt no particular need to take any precautions against mobs in the *seizième*. He returned to the easel.

Cocteau arranged for him to go to classes with André Lhote, who was regarded as the best teacher of composition in Paris. He also took him to a doctor who diagnosed acute anaemia and put him on a further course of iron and arsenic injections. Cocteau told Wood he had more talent for painting than anyone he had ever met.

It was almost enough to turn a young man's head; though there is no evidence that it did. One of the ways in which Cocteau kept himself youthful was by taking young lovers, and Wood's handsome naïveté was exactly what appealed to his taste. At about this time, however, while Wood's regard for Cocteau's achievements in no way diminished, he formed the opinion that he was a 'most jealous and selfish person'. If some sexual incident took place it made no impact on either man, or on their relationship, in which Cocteau for all his selfishness continued to encourage, and Wood to learn.

In February 1925 Wood saw his old friend Drian, who, to his hilarious disgust, had taken to painting people's ceilings with a picture of the owner, his house and a map of the surrounding countryside. Wood meanwhile invited his mother to come and stay in his studio in the rue des Saints Pères, where he still officially lived. She came in March, and the visit passed off in perfect harmony. It was what Wood most wanted: to paint all day long with his mother in the background and his father several hundred miles away. When Clare Wood returned to Huyton Kit wrote to her as though they were adulterous lovers, waiting for the day when the impediment to their happiness would be removed. He did not say how he expected this to happen, but quoted his favourite proverb: *'Tout s'arrange dans la vie.'*

At the same time Cocteau was persuaded to take an opium cure at the Thermes Urbains, a clinic in the rue Chateaubriand. His disappearance from Wood's life and studio ended a tense period in which Wood's loyalty to Gandarillas had been tested. That it passed off without major incident was largely due to Gandarillas's decision to let Wood's hero-worship run its course.

Shortly afterwards Wood and Gandarillas set off for their customary spring break. Gandarillas had been anxious to escape a visit to Paris by the president of Chile, accompanied by Mrs Gandarillas. They went first to Marseille, where, like many others, Wood painted boats in the harbour; then they moved to the Bristol and Majestic hotel at Monte Carlo where Picasso had taken a floor to accommodate his wife, their baby and several servants. Also at the hotel were the principals of the Russian Ballet. Wood felt flatteringly at one with what he called a 'big family of artists.' Picasso said he would like to see his paintings, but Wood had nothing of sufficient interest with him. Picasso gave him a sketchbook but no dedicatory sketch; he was notoriously mean about giving drawings to his friends and preferred to throw away the ones that did not please him. Only Mme Errazuriz was regularly given his work.

From Monaco Wood and Gandarillas moved on to Rome, where Wood returned to the Villa d'Este with Lord Berners ('a musician and an intelligent man') and saw the Sistine Chapel. Gandarillas had a fever, which prevented him from going out, and Wood sat with him. After lunch the shutters were closed against the heat of the afternoon, but Wood was unable to join the general siesta. They were building an extension to the hotel and there was the sound of hammers, pulleys and shovels; behind that was the noise of unsilenced car exhausts, to say nothing of motor horns and the regular Roman background of churches tolling the hour while women shouted to each other across the narrow streets.

Wood did some drawings in red chalk, even though Picasso had told him one should always draw in pencil. He coloured them in with what he saw as the characteristic grey and brown of Rome, being careful to avoid the prettiness of the amateur water-colourist.

Back in Paris Cocteau was sufficiently impressed by the drawings to suggest Wood might try to exhibit some of them. This was guarded praise, but Cocteau was nervous enough of his own reputation not to want to be associated with anything of whose value he was not certain. It was the first real indication that Christopher Wood was on the verge of leaving his student days behind and becoming a painter whose work people might admire and buy.

Drian's absurd exhibition, meanwhile, was a predictable success. Wood spent more and more of his time at Gandarillas's house and began to feel some remorse for his little studio. An innocent but intense passage of his life had been lived there, a schoolboy dream of bohemian life with four-course dinners miraculously thrown in. But the studio was too hot in the summer months, even if he stood stripped to the waist. At Gandarillas's house he could paint all day in his pyjamas while the lunch provided by the cook was much better than that in the restaurant near his studio. He was getting more work done this way, yet he remained wistful about the rue des Saints Pères. He felt that an era was coming to an end. 'The time goes terribly quickly,' he wrote to his mother with a strange fatal note. 'I hope the rest of my life won't pass so fast as this.'

Later in the summer he and Gandarillas went to London, and within days of his arrival there was talk of an exhibition. The talk came from Frank Dobson, who was then at the height of his considerable fame as a sculptor and was also president of the London Group. Augustus John admired a screen that Wood had painted at Gandarillas's house in Cheyne Walk and paid him the compliment of buying a small picture of two girls sitting on a bench. Dobson introduced him to the Redfern Gallery in Cork Street; John told Gandarillas that Wood's work showed huge natural talent and had, indeed, the makings of greatness.

It had happened. Rather suddenly, in a way, but now there was no denying that Christopher Wood, who had left England in 1921 with nothing more than a perverse and earnest ambition, had returned as an artist. His success was at this stage only with other artists and not yet with the public; but he valued their opinion more than that of dealers or buyers. His position was roughly comparable to that of a writer who has had his first book accepted for publication. However minor, and however embarrassingly recollected in later years, it is a breakthrough.

Wood handled his success badly. He was so afraid of losing it that he was superstitious even of admitting it to himself. This fear could be quelled only by little rushes of conceit: 'There are one or two modern French people, two painters amongst them,' he told his mother, 'who think I am already a better painter than anyone in England except John, who doesn't come into it at all and who is too old-fashioned now.' He had said it, and perhaps it was better to be frank: a young painter could not be faithful both to Picasso and Augustus John.

The young Spanish painter Pedro Pruna wanted to swap drawings with him; most of the others Wood had brought with him from Paris were accepted by London galleries. Wood made himself a bedroom at the top of Gandarillas's house on the Embankment, where he sat amid the silver and black decorations, taking stock of what he had done. He noted soberly that Augustus John had sold his portrait of Luisa Casati for £12,000.

Some equilibrium returned. For all his superstition and his vanity, he kept a grip on his ambition. He did not allow his small success to satisify it; in fact he made sure it only served to feed it further. He was to be, after all, not just a painter but the greatest painter that had ever lived.

In November Wood approached Diaghilev with an idea for a ballet called *English Country Life*, to be based on a story by Victor Spencer. Diaghilev encouraged him and Wood worked at some initial designs. He thought it would be both a great honour and an excellent advertisement for his work. The music was to be written by a then unknown English composer called Constant Lambert, who had worked on another ballet with designs by Augustus John. However, Spencer's work was disappointing. Diaghilev was first indecisive, then discouraging. Wood blamed Spencer and Lambert for the reverse. His fragile new pride was seriously hurt by the rebuff and he wrote to his mother a letter of considerable *de haut en bas* condescension about Constant Lambert. He concluded: 'All the pictures I paint now will be fatal one way or another to my career. They must be personal, quite different to everyone else's and full of English character.'

Lambert, much to Wood's irritation, came to stay with him in Paris in January. He had been commissioned by Diaghilev to write the music for *Romeo and Juliet* and consequently considered himself, according to Wood, a 'perfect little genius'. However, he sat for a very satisfactory portrait, so Wood felt he had to some extent served his purpose. Lambert was portrayed with bold assurance; the simplified lines and colours owed more to modern French painting than to the school of Augustus John. It was not a deep painting, but it was a confident one, and incidentally fulfilled Wood's own idea that a painting should be a portrait of the artist: it showed both his irritation and his agitated self-belief.

For some time Cocteau, Gandarillas and Picasso himself had been saying they would arrange for Picasso to come and see Wood's work. This laying on of hands by the high priest of modern art, which had acquired a vatic significance in Wood's mind, eventually happened in an informal way. Picasso was lunching with Mme Errazuriz in early February 1926 and asked what she was doing afterwards: 'Visiting Kit Wood's studio,' she answered, and so left herself no choice but to invite Picasso too. He seemed to like what he saw; he 'said a lot by his standards', according to Wood, who was greatly encouraged by Picasso's approval. His emotion was less one of exhilaration than one of relief: he had received the visitation and had not been found wanting.

The other major development in Wood's life at the start of 1926 was that, for the first time, he acquired a girlfriend. She was not the kind of sensible girl Clare Wood might have hoped for; she had no potential as a wife or mother. Her name was Jeanne Bourgoint and she was the sister of the muscular boy in army uniform, Jean Bourgoint, who had been such a source of pleasure to Cocteau at the Hôtel Welcome. Jeanne and Jean were to be the models for the main characters in Cocteau's novel of disaffected youth, *Les Enfants Terribles*. They lived in isolation, sharing a bedroom in their mother's flat. Jeanne had a twin brother who disapproved of the closeness of the *enfants terribles*; she had once been married for a year to a businessman, but her bond with Jean proved too strong for an outsider and she found her way home. Their emotional closeness and the similarity of their names sometimes made them seem like two halves of the same person, but Jeanne's distinctive female grace was what attracted Wood. She worked as a mannequin; she had a much-admired body and a powerful erotic presence of a feline, bisexual kind. Wood kept their relationship quiet for some time and made no record of how it began.

In February Wood and Gandarillas once more headed south to Monte Carlo, where Gandarillas resumed his preferred nocturnal rhythms, sleeping all day, and drifting from party to casino and back again through the night. Wood mixed with the dubious company that was on offer, though with a more hard-headed sense of purpose than before. He was bored by Lady Cunard, but she did buy a harbour view for 2,500 francs. He rationalised the situation by promising himself that one day he would have no further need of these people; meanwhile he needed (like Picasso and others before him) to get on. His parents thought the beau monde was the enemy, a dangerous distraction, but it was not as simple as that. Although the effort of keeping a balance drove Wood almost to distraction, he was often successful in having it both ways.

Diaghilev was also in Monte Carlo, and began to flirt again with the idea of using Wood as a designer, this time for his *Romeo and Juliet*. Although the *English Country Life* project had foundered, Wood had not come out of it too badly. His sketches had been widely seen and appreciated, and by the time he saw Diaghilev again in Monte Carlo he was able to swallow his disappointment sufficiently to make himself amenable.

Diaghilev, typically, toyed with him. There was the possibility that he might use Augustus John for the designs; then again he might use someone else altogether. Back in Paris, Wood had lunch with Diaghilev and Tony Gandarillas. They seemed to talk about everything except *Romeo and Juliet*. It was only over coffee, after considerable prompting from Gandarillas, that Diaghilev revealed his decision: in a line of designers that included Bakst, Matisse, Picasso, Rouault, Utrillo and Derain, his new ballet would be designed by . . . Christopher Wood.

It was only five years since Wood had left his golf bag in the clubhouse at Woodhall Spa; and of those five years almost three had been spent travelling. For an Englishman who was supposed to have been working at Thornley and Felix, filling in dockets for the import of Syrian prunes, it was a triumph he was entitled to feel in a quite personal way.

And so he did, though he did not forget what he owed to others. His good manners compelled him to admit how much he was indebted to the support and friendship of Tony Gandarillas and to the influence of Jean Cocteau. In the succeeding days Wood learned how the commission had come about. It was Picasso, apparently, who recommended him to Diaghilev, after coming to his studio. Diaghilev had intended to use Augustus John, but was persuaded that John, although a greatly superior draughtsman, was too old-fashioned.

The collaboration between Wood and Diaghilev was not, alas, a happy one. Diaghilev was a great figure, but no one had ever suggested that he was easy to work for. He had been unable to pursue his chosen career as a singer because his voice was too harsh; he had had no success as a composer, and therefore brought a sense of grievance and disappointment, as well as vision and energy, to his third choice of career, as an impresario. One of his favourite injunctions to performers was 'Astound me'; and he had himself astounded Paris by introducing to it previously unknown Russian composers such as Rachmaninov and Rimsky-Korsakov. The dancers he brought – Fokine, Pavlova, Nijinsky – opened new worlds to the French, whose own ballet, despite the loving chronicle made of it by Degas, had long been artistically stagnant.

Christopher Wood was not really sufficiently developed as an artist to take on such a trying commission. Diaghilev had decided to set his *Romeo and Juliet* in the rehearsal room of a ballet company preparing a performance of *Romeo and Juliet*. Wood's scope for design was drastically limited, and within days he was emitting signals of distress. Cocteau helped him considerably with the designs; both he and Picasso advised Wood to stand up for what he believed and not to compromise. (This was easy enough for Picasso to say, but in 1920 when Diaghilev had ripped up his designs for *Pulcinella* and ground them beneath his foot, Picasso had meekly started again.)

Wood took their advice. He told Diaghilev he must have a free hand or nothing. Diaghilev was astounded, though not in the way he preferred. He told Wood in a rage that if that was how he felt he would have no scenery at all. Wood resigned, and Diaghilev commissioned Joan Miró and Max Ernst in his place.

Wood's reaction to this setback was much tougher than his pettish response to the *English Country Life* episode the previous year. He ground his teeth and pressed on. The ability to do so came from his increased self-belief, which was based on the good opinion of such people as Picasso, Frank Dobson and Augustus John. Dobson and Gandarillas told him he had done the right thing. Wood had the strength of mind to digest his disappointment and convert it into something like resolve.

In London and Huyton the General Strike got under way. Troops appeared on the street; Winston Churchill, with the help of other believers, including a keen young man called S.R. (Roy) Pawley, brought out a magazine called the *British Gazette*; most working men obeyed their trade union leaders as unquestioningly as they had obeyed their officers at Arras, Beaucourt and Passchendaele.

In Paris Christopher Wood saw more of Picasso by day and Jeanne Bourgoint by night. 'I have a charming little girl friend to amuse me,' he confided in his mother. Picasso paid him the honour of showing him all the paintings in his studio. Diaghilev's *Romeo and Juliet* at last opened to the public. The Surrealists Louis Aragon and André Breton had organised a demonstration against the involvement of two of their number, Ernst and Miró, with the gangster-capitalist Diaghilev. Stamping and booing greeted the final scene in which Romeo, in flying goggles à la Roland Garros, swept Juliet off to elope in an aeroplane.

Wood reported joyfully that the production was a complete disaster, but in fact the interruptions gave it a certain *réclame*.

In London volunteers from the universities offered to drive the trams and buses; in Paris Tony Gandarillas ordered a new Delage for £350. The General Strike eventually collapsed, with the miners returning to work in similar, or in some cases worse, conditions. 'How glad I am to hear,' wrote Wood on 16 May, 'that the strike is over and that everything will be normal again in England.'

It was from England that his principal encouragement was coming. Frank Dobson told him he had the greatest talent of any painter since the young Augustus John and Wood believed as much of the praise as his superstitious self-defences would allow. In Paris he had come to terms with the Diaghilev disappointment and was feeling happy with his domestic arrangements. Gandarillas did not feel threatened by Jeanne Bourgoint, and Wood valued Gandarillas's friendship, which was still worth more to him than the considerable delights of his new girlfriend. Wood identified steadiness of domestic life as a prerequisite for hard creative work: he was seldom able to acquire tranquillity, and if he had had to struggle with small children as well as with love affairs, opium and parties, he might never have got to the easel at all.

His work in fact stagnated briefly in the summer of 1926. On a visit to London he allowed himself to accept a tiresome commission from Lady Cunard to paint some drawing-room panels. His mother came to visit him and told him that Dr Wood had been offered a practice near Salisbury. Kit urged them to leave the North West as soon as possible; 'Huyton,' he told her with grave but apparently unconscious understatement, 'has no natural attractions.'

Then everything moved forward again. In August Wood went to Cornwall with Tony Gandarillas. There was a small but undistinguished artists' colony already established at St Ives, a town Wood thought beautiful but austere. For six weeks he painted continuously, and the results were recognisable as an early version of his mature style. He learned how to finish a picture properly, and he had the feeling of illumination: much that had previously confused him was made clear. The sensation filled him with confidence. 'I was born an artist,' he wrote, 'and have not just become one.'

Meanwhile he wrote passionately to Jeanne Bourgoint. He called her his 'adorable little hare', his 'dearest little friend', his 'dear little Jeanne'. 'I love you terribly,' he wrote, 'I do not hesitate to tell you that you are the only woman for me.' For all the talk of her body, 'so perfect and firm', however, Wood felt he had to make it clear that he was not in a position to make what Huyton would have called an honest woman of her. 'I prefer to tell you frankly that it will be several years before I can really support two people', and therefore, 'to prove my limitless love I do not want you to hesitate for a moment if by chance you find someone who can make your life more beautiful or easier'.

The obvious, i.e. mildly paradoxical, interpretation is that Wood was unconsciously signalling the limits of his devotion. In view of the guileless, literal way he wrote, however, it may be that he meant no more than he said: that he was short of cash.

On his return to London in the autumn Wood was taken by Cedric Morris, a painter he had encountered in Cornwall, to a flat in Chelsea that belonged to two then almost unknown English painters: Ben and Winifred Nicholson. It was a decisive moment. If the drift in Christopher Wood's life towards drugs, danger and

Christopher Wood

frivolity could be exemplified in his acquaintance with Luisa Casati and Violette Murat, then the Nicholsons could be said to offer an exact counterweight – personal austerity, country living and a puritanical dedication to work. Ben was the son of the painter William Nicholson and Winifred also came from an artistic family. Their own work, and their marriage, were at a fragile point of development.

From the outset, Wood's friendship with them appeared momentous. Winifred Nicholson recalled the first meeting in almost apocalyptic terms: 'I was dressing in a little white room I had at our flat in Chelsea . . . and somebody was talking with Ben and Cedric down in Ben's studio. I had no idea who it was but they went on talking and talking, with a voice that moved me strangely . . . And I sat and cursed – for half an hour – and I cursed and cursed. I did not want something to come into my life, as big as my love for Ben, and to come like this with fire . . .'

Winifred Nicholson, who was pregnant at the time, was a woman of powerful religious and emotional convictions. She formed a passion for Christopher Wood that was the more harrowing for being chaste. Self-sacrifice was at the core of her life, and the scope for it in the triangular relationship that developed between Wood, her husband and herself only strengthened her feelings for him. She was a Christian Scientist with firm beliefs in purity and the after-life; she seemed to see in Wood from the first day some intoxicating spiritual innocence.

It led her to exaggerate the strength of the paintings Wood had done in St Ives, which she saw at Tony Gandarillas's house in Cheyne Walk. 'He was showing us his summer's work . . . Crowded together in his small bedroom were an amazing array of canvases. He produced masterpiece upon masterpiece . . . dark with adventure and imagination. We walked home in the high skies. Here was England's first painter. His vision is true, his grasp is real, his power is life itself.'

England's first painter . . . his power is life itself . . . However much of Winifred Nicholson's euphoria is discounted, there remains in it the recognisable effect that Wood's paintings had on those who appreciated them. In the world of English painting, a world reduced in French eyes to Sickert's grim interiors and

John's banal society portraits, Wood was on the verge of doing something different. If Sickert had been an honorary consul in Dieppe, bringing news of the commotion that had bypassed England, Wood was able to offer something of its spirit in his work. Winifred Nicholson was too quick with praise that the pictures did not yet deserve, but what she wrote captured the visceral effect of the best of Wood's pictures: sophistication in simplicity, Modernism in an English idiom, the exhilaration of something bright and joyful achieved in a mysterious and oddly menacing way.

Whatever happened at St Ives in the late summer of 1926, Winifred Nicholson and Kit Wood were both right to see it as a turning point. In Winifred Nicholson's mythology of Wood's life it was the first of a succession of summers in which he created the body of his work. Wood, who did not see his own existence in such an organised way, responded to the change in the only manner he knew: more ambition, more work. His life was full of breakthroughs, new beginnings and moments when he believed he had at last discovered something durably exciting; as such it was typical of the lives of artists. Its peculiarity lay in the ferocity with which he drove on from each new departure.

At the end of 1926 Tony Gandarillas was given notice to quit his house on the Avenue Montaigne, and at the beginning of 1927 he moved to a sumptuous apartment in the rue des Marronniers in Passy, on the south-west outskirts of Paris. Wood was assigned a bedroom and a small studio, which he furnished with a low sofa made of mattresses and cushions, an easel and two tables – a long one he had brought from his old studio in the rue des Saints Pères, and a smaller one on which to draw. There was a terrace with a view of Paris and the barges moving slowly down the Seine. Wood found it all rather cramped, but the confined conditions suited the mood of self-denial he brought to what he increasingly referred to as his 'struggle'.

'I have never worked so hard before,' he wrote to Winifred Nicholson, 'and am really having a life and death struggle with it never as I knew before . . . So many ideas crush my brain that I seem never able to contemplate one than a thousand others disturb it.' The intellectual weakness – an inability to order his thoughts – that he had previously diagnosed in himself made it more difficult for him to know which avenues to follow. One good painting did emerge from this period, and this was a self-portrait. It showed him standing on the balcony of his room with the roofs of Paris behind him. He was wearing a tight, multi-coloured sweater, and his clean features glowed with uncertain pride. It is the picture of a man who, as Gerald Reitlinger remarked, could just as easily have been a golfer: his huge red hands look swollen by the seaside winds, as though he had just won the President's Putter at Rye.

His own pleasure in the picture led Wood to tell his mother how much he would like to paint a Wood family portrait, with his father depicted reading the Bible. His parents had confirmed their move to Wiltshire and Kit was enthusiastic; he thought that his father was 'just the sort of man for country people who don't like gushers': no Diaghilev he.

The Nicholsons invited him to go and paint with them at Bankshead, their farmhouse in Cumberland, but Wood decided that, though he envied them the rustic idyll he imagined, he ought not to disturb the creative tranquillity he was enjoying in Paris. It was in fact a confused decision, because although he was spending many hours at the easel, he was too frantic to produce much that was worthwhile.

One of the things that was agitating him was the question of money. His increased renown as a painter had made little difference to his income. While Gandarillas gave him lodging and shared his meals if he was in Paris, he did not actually give him money, and his own finances were erratic. There was a temporary slump on the Paris stock market that foreshadowed a bigger cataclysm. While Wood paid no attention to such matters, the movement of capital did not leave him out of its considerations: it was hard to sell pictures to rich people worried about falling share prices.

The fruits of Wood's frenzied spring in Paris went on show at the Beaux Arts Gallery in Bruton Place off Bond Street in April, though by this time he was mainly exhibiting with the Seven & Five Society, of which Ben Nicholson was chairman. The Seven & Five had begun in 1919 as a refuge from the war of competing styles: their cautious manifesto felt that 'there has of late been too much pioneering along too many lines in altogether too much of a hurry.' From its non-doctrinal beginnings the society grew to give a fair reflection of the progress of English art. Under Ben Nicholson's influence it eventually, in the 1930s, refused to show any more representational work.

The Beaux Arts was a joint show with the Nicholsons and the potter William Staite Murray. Cocteau wrote an introduction to the catalogue in which he spoke of Wood's innocence, comparing him to a puppy that had not yet had distemper. Just before the show opened Winifred Nicholson fell through an open trap door and broke her back; her Christian Science beliefs denied her the usual medical treatment and she herself ascribed her recovery to a miracle.

There was little miraculous about the show. Wood's best work was not in it; the pictures he did show left no impression even on Winifred Nicholson. For all the 'life and death struggle' he had put into them, the street scenes he had painted at Passy were unremarkable. Wood told his mother the show was a success, though he sold only three pictures. He sent six to the Leicester Galleries, the rest to the London Artists' Association and reckoned that, when one took framing into account, the thing had just about paid its way. Winifred Nicholson's verdict was terse: 'No one noticed the exhibition.'

From May until the end of 1927 Wood was in the Mediterranean. He told Winifred Nicholson that he could not go to England because it was the time of year that he always went to Rome with Gandarillas, 'whom I love the best in the world'. They hadn't managed to make it the previous year because Gandarillas had lost all his money at the casino in Monte Carlo on the way.

Wood had by this time developed an intimate friendship with Winifred Nicholson, based on his appreciation of her abilities as a painter and the fact that she was what he called a 'real woman'. There seemed much more to her than to Jeanne Bourgoint, of whom he had started to tire. He told Winifred Nicholson that he had 'the misfortune to love if one can call it so a Tom Boy who is wonderfully beautiful physically but that is all and a person who doesn't create anything, not even a thought and who won't be created in any form. If I had allowed myself to love her I should have been very unhappy.'

Winifred Nicholson changed Wood's views of women. He had thought of them previously as people who kept him hanging about but might, as in Jeanne's case, provide sexual pleasure. His feelings for Winifred Nicholson were ardent but pure – exactly the kind of emotion she wanted to feel for him, though there was a sexual element in her fondness for Wood which, by denying, she intensified. She was not Wood's preferred physical type, but his admiration for her, coupled with the memories of the pleasure Jeanne Bourgoint had given him, made him eager to find a woman who might combine both roles. His ideal might have been a gifted and spiritual artist, like Winifred, a loving admirer, like his mother, with a hard, boyish body like Jeanne Bourgoint.

Meanwhile he went with his friend Tony Gandarillas to Naples, Athens and Monaco before, after a brief return to Paris for Luisa Casati's fancy dress ball in June, they went south to Cannes in July. Gandarillas was detained at Vichy to 'get over all his debauchery', as Wood rather frankly put it to his mother, adding with all the confidence given by a liver still at its peak: 'I eliminate mine by painting.' A fortnight later, however, even Wood's youthful constitution was feeling the strain and he took a water cure at Cannes.

Cannes had been 'discovered' for the English by Lord Brougham and was popular with the wealthier elements of London as well as of Paris. In August 1927 the town was almost as full of Chelsea and Mayfair as of the *seizième* and Montparnasse. Wood liked it because it was beautiful without being obviously picturesque. The mountains opened up before him like a Chinese fan, and the air, so soft beneath the deep blue skies by day, was filled at night with the mysterious sound of tree frogs.

Wood was able to put behind him the memory of his fruitless spring in Paris. Such passages of unrewarded labour were necessary, he convinced himself, to a painter's development. He believed that in Cannes he might do some work of real substance, provided he could escape from the rackety claims of 'society'.

When the major development that Wood was expecting finally arrived, it was not in his painting. He fell suddenly in love. Everything was emotionally propitious; in fact, from the new interest in women he had developed since knowing Winifred Nicholson it might almost have been inevitable. The woman in question, however, raised as many questions as she answered: she was called Meraud Guinness, and he had met her at Lord Alington's and at a party given by Augustus John in Dorset.

Meraud (pronounced 'Merod', though she preferred to be called by her second name, Michael, given in honour of her godfather, the Russian Grand Duke) was the daughter of Benjamin and Bridget Guinness. Even by the standards of the family they were rich, with houses in London, Pittsburgh and New York as well as in Cannes. Meraud was a painter and had studied at the Slade, then with the sculptor Archipenko in Paris, before attaching herself to the Surrealist Francis Picabia. She insisted that she was a serious artist some of whose subjects happened to come from the beau monde; critics viewed her as an ex-debutante who dabbled in painting.

She had large, heavy-lidded eyes, a short nose and a fleshy mouth. A portrait of her by Alvaro Guevara in 1929 minimised the breadth of her jaw and width of her lips, but showed her candid, gamine sexuality, at once more feminine and less pretty than Jeanne Bourgoint. According to her mentor Picabia, she had 'eyes full of sighs'. Kit Wood spoke of her with childish glee: 'I see her pretty often, she has a lovely sailing boat.'

He was so wrapped up in her that for ten days he even forgot to write to his mother. When he did so he was full of apologies for his neglect, reassuring her, in a way that was certain to alarm, that she was still his greatest love. 'Don't forget,' he concluded, 'your old friend of the war days.' The reference to his illness showed how seriously Wood was taking the affair with Meraud: he invoked this intimate and painful passage in his life only when something of comparable significance was happening to him.

The romance began in mid-August and within a month was being widely savoured by the gossip-hungry population of Cannes. Speculation focused on the likely reaction of Meraud's parents. Wood had no illusions about his desirability; he thought

Meraud's parents were snobs who 'would like her to marry a duke'.

One night he was woken from a troubled sleep in his hotel room by the sound of laughter outside. He stumbled to the door in his pyjamas to find Prince George, the Duke of Kent. Awash with champagne, the Duke's party had come to see the young painter whose love life was the talk of Cannes. Wood was not at his best and made a note to send round his apologies the next day.

At this delicate moment Tony Gandarillas left for Nice, where he was to have an operation on his haemorrhoids. His parting advice to Wood was that he should marry or elope. Wood valued his old friend's approval because Gandarillas had made no secret of his dislike of Jeanne Bourgoint. It was an awkward time to be alone, however, with his opium, his painting and his uncontrolled feelings for Meraud.

Meanwhile, Bridget Guinness, Meraud's mother, moved into action. She told Meraud she could not throw herself away on Kit Wood but must wait for someone suitable. It was not just her daughter's happiness for which she was concerned but her own social ambitions. Although she was a generous patron of the arts there were limits: Kit Wood, after all, was penniless, he smoked opium; and, with the exception of a liaison with a decadent tomboy mannequin, his tastes had been homosexual. To the mother of a nice young girl in 1927 these objections counted for something.

In separate conversations with Wood himself, Bridget Guinness pointed out that her husband would not consent to the marriage. As a mother she disliked the gossip that had been attached to her daughter's name and now expected Wood to see a good deal less of Meraud. She presented Wood with a choice: either he could elope with Meraud, in which case she would be disinherited; or he could finish the romance with dignity and in his own time. But if he had come to the Guinnesses looking for a way to finance his opium and his painting he had chosen the wrong family.

It made Wood reconsider. What exactly was he after? The model of the Nicholsons – that of two painters working devotedly side by side – exerted a powerful attraction. Could he picture himself and Meraud as such a couple? Her paintings leant heavily on the example of her mentor Picabia, who had been an important figure in successive movements from Post-Impressionism, through Cubism, Dada and, by 1927, Surrealism. The trouble was that where Picabia's work was authenticated by proven talent and experience, Meraud's paintings had some of the more dubious trappings of Surrealism – shock tactics, bits of string – without the proof that she could even really draw. Wood had no interest in Surrealism and felt particularly suspicious of it since 'his' commission from Diaghilev had gone to Miró and Max Ernst; and where Winifred's homeliness and spirituality offered a good anchor for an artist husband, Meraud was headstrong, dangerous and twenty-two. Wood doubted whether she was really what he called 'enough of an artist' for him; he wondered whether her principal motive in marriage was not merely to escape from her snobbish family.

But he was in love with her. The relationship was of the enclosed, self-regarding kind that makes parents uneasy: they are convinced on one hand that such feelings in their children are comically short-lived, but wistful on the other that they themselves can no longer aspire to such passion. Wood told his mother: 'I worship the very ground she treads on, and am proud to be capable of so great a love.' Even the worrying narcissism of young love was there.

Bridget Guinness's campaign to 'save' her daughter was successful. Meraud told Kit she would have to see less of him because 'people' were talking. It would be different if they were engaged, but since her father was in America that was impossible. Wood thought that if she really loved him none of this would matter, but he was convinced by her submission to her mother that Meraud was 'a baby at heart'.

He left Cannes and took himself to Arles, a sacred place for him because of its association with Van Gogh. He wrote letters of bitter despair to Winifred Nicholson. The anguish of his thwarted love for Meraud was intensified by a suspicion that she was not, *au fond*, the right woman to share the artistic life he planned. On hopeful days he ignored this suspicion; on days when he wanted to get on with his work, he exaggerated it. By

October he had persuaded himself that Meraud was too 'girly' and empty-headed for him. 'I must say,' he wrote, 'that French women once they care for you nothing can drag them off'; English women by contrast, 'are decidedly undeveloped sexually and mentally.' His experience of Jeanne and Meraud scarcely entitled him to such grand generalisations, and he knew it. He was temporising. He did then what he always did when he was confused: first he wrote sentimentally to his mother, then he went to join Tony Gandarillas.

This meant going to Marseille, where Gandarillas was looking after René Crevel, an old hand from the Hôtel Welcome, who was suffering from tuberculosis. He had been on the point of leaving for Egypt, but had been too ill to travel and had almost died in the hotel. Wood and Gandarillas spent an anxious ten days while Crevel's condition gradually improved. In intervals from nursing, Wood painted in Marseille. He did some landscapes, some flower paintings and two self-portraits. He wanted to work at his waterfront hotel, but it was too busy. He vowed to return one day because he liked the traffic of the port: 'All the bustle of this great place makes one want to do some very ugly pictures,' he told Winifred Nicholson. 'I see everything ugly here. The women with hideous faces and bodies, enormous legs and fat arms, holding pig-like babies, the men who slouch round are the worst dregs . . . I only like ugly things now, as what I thought beautiful before, it does not last . . . I shall never marry anything but a hideous wife if ever I do this foolish thing. I have forgotten almost about my lovely lady of Cannes this summer.'

As Crevel's health improved, Gandarillas and Wood took him up to the village of Vence in the hills behind Nice, where the air was reputed to be good for the lungs. Wood's instinctive reaction when in trouble – to go and find Gandarillas – paid dividends in an unexpected way: in his painting. He was pleased with Vence. He painted pictures in dark colours, experimenting with shades of black. His mood of petulant post-Meraud gloom may have been a facile starting point for this new darker colouring, but he developed it into a subtle and important way of giving depth and doubt to his mature paintings.

Wood stayed with Crevel until December when he went back

to join Gandarillas in Paris. Gandarillas had been diagnosed as having consumption and had experienced a minor haemorrhage in Vence. Wood was upset by the news but thought it would give him the chance to show his devotion by nursing Gandarillas in some remote mountain sanatorium. But the illness, whether TB or not, neither developed nor prevented Gandarillas from resuming his old ways, beginning with a New Year's Eve party in Berlin.

At Christmas Wood wrote to his mother: 'Daddy talks of my not sticking to my arrangements. I never make any on purpose but I don't think he need worry about my place in the world, I think that will be all right.' The ambitious optimism recalled Keats's more well-founded claim, made at an even younger age: 'I think I shall be among the English Poets after my death.' Wood resembled Keats in many ways: in the desire to live a life of sensation rather than of thought, the almost reckless devotion to work, the spasmodic development that came swiftly from the ruins of temporary failure, and in the boyish eagerness that felt weighed down by admiration of past achievement but quickened by its appreciation of the modern.

As far as his 'arrangements' were concerned, Dr Wood's captious view was vindicated in the most spectacular way a few days later when Kit announced that he and Meraud Guinness were about to elope.

Meraud arrived in Paris in preparation for leaving the country and marrying abroad, since no ceremony could take place in France without her parents' consent. There was one small piece of grit in this plan: Meraud had left her passport behind. Wood was not upset by such a minor administrative detail. He was happy and exhilarated beyond anything he could recall. The long months of separation, thinking that she didn't care; the dull weeks nursing René Crevel and painting with a black palette . . . all could be forgotten now, because it was Meraud that he loved, and had done all along, ever since he had first seen her almost four years ago. Meraud's father was furious, but what was a father's anger at such a time? 'It is wonderful,' he told Clare Wood. 'All the world is at my feet.'

Figuratively, perhaps, it was; but without Meraud's passport the world in fact remained crucially distant. While Wood basked in the justice and rapture of love won, others took swift and practical steps to prevent matters going further. Bridget Guinness came to Paris and gave the performance of her life. Although the things she most objected to in Wood were his past homosexuality, his drug habit, his poverty and his middle-class background, she mentioned none of them. Instead she appealed to his deeper nature. She gambled on the possibility that no number of masked balls with Luisa Casati or lines of cocaine with Violette Murat would quite have eradicated a schoolboy sense of fair play. If he could prove himself a suitable husband, Bridget Guinness proposed, then all might yet be well; but even Christopher himself must admit that he was not on the face of it everything a mother might look for in a husband for her beloved daughter. So what she was proposing was a compromise: he and Meraud should not see each other for a year, and if at the end of that time he had proved his devotion, then they should be married.

Wood at last saw the significance of the missing passport: if they had already been married none of this bargaining would have mattered. As things were, he was made to see the justice of Mrs Guinness's plan. If he really loved Meraud then a year was not very long to wait; and then she would have her full inheritance and the blessing of her parents. It was fair enough.

Then Bridget Guinness began negotiations with her daughter. She explained how much Meraud owed them in return both for the education and the latitude they had given her. Bridget Guinness played on Wood's drug problem, knowing that her daughter was also worried by it: Meraud had in fact thrown Wood's opium pipe into the Seine. She pitched her appeal subtly, arguing more from love than anger, and Meraud, like Kit, found her sense of justice touched.

She found it 'dreadfully hard', but she did what she was asked and returned with her mother to Cannes where she was promised the run of her father's flat in the grounds of the Majestic hotel and given an allowance of £400 a year. She was determined to see out the year, as was Kit. Of the three principals only Bridget

Guinness understood that once such a break has been made the stipulated time makes little difference: one year, five years . . . Whatever telegrams of panic and congratulation passed between Cannes and Pittsburgh, she had proved herself a formidable modern mother.

Wood was left in the wretched state of the lovelorn, feeling he had contributed to his own misery and exhausted the sympathy of his friends. He met Meraud's sister Thanis on a train and she merely asked him, 'Why didn't you do it properly?' Gandarillas meanwhile considered the matter closed. Although he was always game for gossip and intrigue, he was too world-weary to care about the travails of love once the plot had failed.

Wood went to London where, using some money left to him by his grandmother, who had died a few weeks earlier, he set himself up in a flat on the King's Road. He saw a good deal of the Nicholsons, who had at least not been bored by the saga of Meraud. Winifred made curtains and chair covers for him, while he painted hard, though none of it, in her view, was any good. It was the worst month of his life. He had wanted the romance with Meraud to prosper because it would bring into harmony all the different urges of his sexual and creative life: he saw its failure as an indictment of his unformed personality.

The Nicholsons were kind to him, and even in his distress he showed his habitual sense of gratitude. In February there was another show of the Seven & Five Society in which he exhibited two of the pictures he had done in Vence while nursing René Crevel. Winifred Nicholson, quick to damn his inferior work, was impressed by them; she thought they had the 'profound resonance of organ music'. The exhibition, however, made little impact, and afterwards Wood went to stay with his parents at their new house in Broad Chalke, near Salisbury. Here, quivering in the different force fields exerted by his parents, he tried to reorientate himself.

Stays with his parents, tense at the best of times, were complicated by the fact that he was always in enforced withdrawal from opium. At such moments he needed to express himself on paper, and since he could not very well write to his mother, he had to find another confidante. Winifred Nicholson was his choice. She was happy to oblige, and found new scope for self-sacrifice in the role assigned to her. Winifred wrote to Meraud, more or less on Kit's behalf, but in the end he did not post the letter in case Meraud should feel that he and Winifred were asking for her pity. The trouble was, he told Winifred, that he had come to despise himself; but now he had determined to make a new start.

The mental toughness he had learned in dealing with the Diaghilev setbacks was now applied to his emotional life. He determined to forget the past and look only to the future. At some level he was letting go of Meraud, even as he planned to keep her. She became subservient to his artistic ambition. She was a failure from which, with enough determination, he could learn. In fact the emotional and artistic became confused in one strange fatalistic commitment: 'Now for evermore I don't talk of myself, for if you knew how sincerely I loathe myself . . . but I feel freer, happier and with my face in the wind, which is a real exhilaration and ready to start on the biggest journey one can make. I will get there and I do trust that it will be quick.'

In March Wood went to stay with the Nicholsons in Cumberland. Winifred Nicholson was willing at the time to be his confidante, his helper and his critic, but she did not reveal her true feelings for him till many years later, when she recalled his visit to Bankshead.

'He came in March. His arrival was like a meteor. The wild country delighted him. The dark forests took on a mystery and magic as he looked at them . . . Inspiration ran high and flew backwards and forwards from one to the other . . . he painted some pictures from nature, carrying an enormous box of paints and an easel over the rough fields and hills, and walking at his usual swift pace . . . He came up from the valley with the springing step of eternal youth.'

In his 'swift pace' and 'springing step' she did not even see his limp.

In Wood's mind the visit was only a partial success. He did like Bankshead and he enjoyed the chance to paint with two such dedicated people. However, he found conditions 'Spartan' and he was missing Gandarillas. At the end of April he returned to Paris where his troubles seemed to crowd in on him again. Someone had told Gandarillas that they couldn't see why Wood did not marry Meraud regardless of her parents' wishes; people found it hard to understand how two such unconventional characters had given in so meekly. Meraud's sister Thanis believed they would still marry. He had one piece of good advice from a friend of Meraud's: 'If you really want her, you can have her, but if you are not sure, leave her alone.'

He was not sure. Paris was close and thundery; storms rocked the house and tempers were strained by the heat. Wood kept thinking about Meraud and kept comparing her with Winifred Nicholson. He asked himself what he needed from a wife. He thought about love as an abstract idea; in mystic terms he had borrowed from Winifred, he contemplated love's purifying force. And then, if he was really honest, part of the problem was this: he had met someone else.

Frosca Munster was one of the many Russians who had been swept to Paris by the Revolution. Boris Kochno, Diaghilev's secretary, described her: 'She was a young Russian woman whose serene face had the strange beauty of the models painted by Piero della Francesca; she was an impenetrable but captivating character.' She had separated from her husband, a Polish count, a year earlier, though it was some months before Wood even considered there might be a Mr – or a Count – Munster.

Frosca was unusual among Russian *émigrés* in having managed to bring out a reasonable amount of money. She lived on the Boulevard de Lannes, on the edge of the Bois de Boulogne, whose tennis courts, picnics and other gentle relaxations were visible from her house. Although she moved in the same social world as Wood and Gandarillas, Frosca was sceptical of its worth. She had discernment, taste and a stable temperament. She was shy about her feelings, particularly about her fondness for Wood, whom she rechristened 'Kit of the Woods' because she felt he was so untamable. She was by most people's standards an exotic creature, and it says a good deal for the co-ordinates of Christopher Wood's world in 1928 that what he valued most in Frosca was dependability.

He compared her in his mind to Meraud, from whom he had just received a letter and a photograph 'which made her look such a silly little girl. It made me look at dear old Frosca and think "you do look more solid with your head well planted between your shoulders and feet on the ground." ' The role of 'dear old Frosca' was therefore the one that Wood assigned her, and she was sufficiently glamorous and self-confident not to mind.

She became the biggest love of his life, though her influence crept up on him and had to defeat his frequent insistence that she was more of a friend than a lover. This was never the case, but Wood still liked to think of women as either the Meraud-type or the Winifred-type. It took him a long time to understand that Frosca had over-ridden this distinction and was capable of being his lover as well as his friend. When he finally surrendered to the depth of feeling that she had engendered in him, he admitted it was the strongest he had ever known.

Late in 1928, however, before this transformation was complete, Wood was still haunted by Meraud. 'I am a little frightened to see her now,' he told Winifred Nicholson, 'as I am so fond of Froska [he usually spelled her name with 'k'] and am happy and so is she, very, and I'm terrified that M has some extraordinary power or attraction for me which is destructive . . .'

The year of separation was coming to an end and Wood felt humiliated by the fact that Bridget Guinness had plainly outmanoeuvred him. He did still want Meraud, but only in a half-hearted way. He did not think they could be happy together, and in any case he now had Frosca to consider as well. It had all worked out exactly as Mrs Guinness must have planned: he had been her dupe. To concede as much by not going back to Meraud, however, would be tantamount to admitting that their affair had not amounted to much in the first place, and that was not the case. On the contrary, his feeling for Meraud – whatever reservations people, including him, might have about her character – had been frighteningly intense.

As if this were not complicated enough, Wood had not fully broken off with Jeanne Bourgoint. He continued to think wistfully of her and occasionally to give in to temptation. There was then the more substantial figure of Tony Gandarillas, though here there had been a curious development. Gandarillas had begun an affair with Maria, Duchesse de Gramont, Wood's very first sitter in Paris. Wood loyally believed they had been in love for years, and felt no jealousy. His problem was that he was not sure how much Gandarillas still needed him. He did not know whether he should continue to live in Gandarillas's flat out of politeness, in order not to hurt his feelings, when the old atmosphere was changed and the rooms were filled with the presence of Maria. Worse than this was the fact that Wood was secretly sorry for Gandarillas. He thought that his endless partying was, *au fond*, pathetic; he pitied him because he had no purpose to his life. His pity was misplaced because Gandarillas was able to function quite happily without a serious sense of purpose; he was a survivor almost as charmed and tough as Jean Cocteau.

Meanwhile, as Bridget Guinness's one year neared its end, a crystalline pattern formed about Wood. Tony had backed Meraud but hated Jeanne. Jeanne thought Meraud was despicable. Tony loved Maria. Kit pitied Tony and feared Meraud. Winifred tortured herself to be kind to Frosca. They all loved Kit.

And he was really less interested in any of them than in his painting. The tensions of his emotional life, while complicated, had reached a temporary equilibrium. It was good enough, anyway, for him to be able to paint and to feel himself at a point when his full talent was about to be realised.

In August he took the train to Cornwall and the real work began.

From the moment he had arrived at Alphonse Kahn's house more than seven years earlier Wood had been certain that if he could find the time alone, in the right circumstances, then he would be capable of producing pictures of the highest quality; that he could be – and he didn't feel shy of the term – a great painter.

He had no obvious reason to believe this. Picasso and Matisse, for instance, could not only draw much better than he could, they had a sense of composition and an understanding of traditional and modern forms that was far beyond his. Lesser painters than those two were still more obviously accomplished than Wood.

What had he done anyway? He had shown himself to be deft at copying others, at taking useful tricks and mannerisms from them. He was also good at digesting what he took so that within two or three paintings, the borrowed style became part of his own vocabulary. Cézanne, Matisse, Vlaminck, Derain, Braque, Picasso, Rousseau, Van Gogh and Utrillo were among those he had raided: Wood's paintings of the mid-1920s made the head hurt with the number of associations and references they triggered. For all their high points – 'La Foire de Neuilly', the portrait of Constant Lambert, the brilliant early watercolours, the developing single-line drawings à la Picasso, the red ink sketches in Rome, the self-portrait in the bright sweater – they lacked grandeur. They were often impressive, but they remained the work of someone finding his way.

At the beginning of his painting career Wood had had temporarily to divert his ambition to paint great pictures into a determination to improve his technique. Since both long-term ambition and immediate determination were controlled by a common willpower this was not as difficult as it appeared. As his study and practice developed he came to the stage in August 1928 when he believed he had the technical means to do what he wanted. This then was the moment for him to recall exactly what it was that he had planned to do with his work; this was the time to look back inside and see what driving force, temporarily diverted into learning, had made him want to be a painter in the first place.

Wood believed his painting had an autobiographically expressive purpose. This was unfashionable as a premise then as now, and Wood's painting partner in 1928, Ben Nicholson, particularly disliked the sentimental idea that pictures 'tell us' something of the artist. The feelings and ideas Wood had were the product of the mingled emotional forces of his English childhood, youthful illness and the determined, unreciprocated, ignorance of the public world.

It was in painting that England had fought its most dogged battle for insularity. Augustus John was a draughtsman of rare talent and some of the paintings he produced in the first decade of the century were touchingly beautiful. However, he chose not to accept the challenge laid down by Cézanne, by whose work most of the Modern movement in France was shaped. John turned his gifts instead to society portraits; by the time Wood met him in 1921 his work was already beginning to look meaningless. Sickert had understood both the Impressionists and the Realist painters such as Courbet and Millet, yet found his bluff agonisingly called by Roger Fry's Post-Impressionist exhibition in London in 1910. Though he admired individual paintings, Sickert's heart was not in it; his response was generous but it was not warm. Even such tepid respect as this was unusual amid the general outrage that greeted the show.

The story is familiar now, but it was significant at the time of Wood's early formation as an artist. The show, entitled 'Manet and the Post-Impressionists', was mounted by Roger Fry in November 1910. The principal exhibitors were Cézanne (21 pictures), Gauguin (36) and Van Gogh (22). There were also eight paintings by Vlaminck, three by Derain, two by Picasso, and three paintings and three sculptures by Matisse. It was England's first full-frontal view of the new French art and the response was seismic.

Pornography . . . the work of lunatics . . . a practical joke . . . of no interest except to the student of pathology: these were the reactions not of the editorial column of the *Morning Post* but of professional painters and liberal critics. Paul Nash recalled that the exhibition 'seemed literally to bring about a national upheaval'. His own teacher at the Slade told the students that although he could not prevent them going to the Grafton galleries, he would much rather they stayed away. And these were not the canvases of Rothko or Jackson Pollock, not bricks or found objects, not action paintings, pickled sheep or used sanitary towels: these were figurative paintings – Matisse and Derain in their Fauvist period, Picasso at his most sweetly lyrical, Gauguin and Van Gogh in the popular colours that are today on sale as birthday cards even in the post offices and gift shops of Huyton.

The public of all countries was slow to accept the new painting of the late nineteenth and early twentieth century. The French reviled the Impressionists and the Fauvists (literally 'Wild Beasts'). The response of the United States to the Armory Show in 1913, when it was given its first view of modern European art, was also hysterical: the Illinois senatorial vice commission mounted an inquiry; Matisse was moved to tell an American interviewer: 'Please tell the American people that I am a devoted husband and father, with a comfortable home and a fine garden, just like any man.'

The difference in England was that it was not just the public that was outraged; it was the artists. They proved it by turning their back on Modernism until it was almost a quarter of a century old. Roger Fry's second Post-Impressionist exhibition in London two years later was dominated by Matisse and Picasso, but also included some paintings by English artists. This may have been intended to show that the new art had 'taken' in England, but the quality of English paintings was inferior. Sickert's influence declined after the first show, and while Fry's Omega Workshops provided a focus for the avant-garde, the body of English painters had looked the other way.

The exceptions were singular. Wyndham Lewis showed the influence of Parisian Cubism only four years after Picasso had painted 'Les Demoiselles d'Avignon', usually cited as the first Cubist picture. Lewis was also abreast of the Italian Futurist movement, and even anticipated it in such paintings as 'Smiling Woman Ascending a Stair'. Jacob Epstein studied in Paris from 1902 to 1905. He kept pace with Modigliani and Brancusi and arguably outstripped them both in his dramatic 'Rock Drill' in 1913. But Epstein was *sui generis*; he was also, like Britain's foremost Modernist poet, T.S. Eliot, an American.

By the time Christopher Wood emigrated to Paris at the age of nineteen, the direction of painting and sculpture had been changed by the War. Wood's own 'War years' were what gave him the time and the urgent desire to be a painter; but for the artistic generation before him, the experience of the War itself had two devastating effects. In France it drove many of the most experimental artists back on themselves; and in England it cut off the first attempts, notably those made by Wyndham Lewis, to build bridges across the Channel.

David Bomberg, a student at the Slade, had done what Wood did as early as 1913. He went to Paris and met Derain, Picasso and Modigliani; he picked up some of the rush and clamour of Futurism and showed elements of Cubism in his pictures. But when the war came and he was asked to depict the work of a Canadian tunnelling company, his pictures were rejected. Only when he redid them in a traditional style did they find favour, and he never resumed his pre-War experiments. C. R. W. Nevinson, also strongly Futurist in style before the War, struggled to express the flesh-and-blood aspect of what he saw in such a machine-dominated idiom, and his pictures became old-fashioned, almost journalistic. Even Wyndham Lewis, shaken by the death of his friend Gaudier-Brzeska, had qualms about trying to express the destructive force of military machinery.

The only English painter who appeared to flourish was Paul Nash, who initially enthused, in letters that are shocking to read, over the pictorial aspects of trench warfare. By the time of Passchendaele in 1917, however, he was sick to his soul: 'Sunrise and sunset are blasphemous,' he wrote, 'they are mockeries to man.' He continued in his own way after the War, out of touch with the mainstream of Modernism as it eventually developed in England in the 1930s when its most important early figures included Wood's painting partner in 1928, Ben Nicholson.

The French painters enjoyed a remarkable rate of survival, but found their lives and their art changed by the War. The Cubist movement ended on 14 August 1915 when Braque, Gleizes, Léger, Lhote, Villon and Duchamp-Villon were mobilised. Braque was wounded but was able to resume his work after the War. Léger served as a sapper and was so impressed by his fellow engineers and the materials they handled that he forsook the abstract art towards which he had been moving and vowed never again to 'let go of objects'. André Breton worked in a hospital where the use of psychoanalytic techniques laid the basis for the unconscious or automatic elements of Surrealism. Juan Gris and Picasso, the Spaniards, stayed behind, and Picasso mocked the War and its effects. 'I took Braque and Derain to the station,' he wrote, but 'I never found them again.' This epigram, spoken for effect, contained some truth about the ending of the first phase of Modernism. After the War, Braque concentrated on consolidation. Derain rejected experiment to become a classical, at times almost wilfully old-fashioned, painter.

By the time Christopher Wood emigrated to Paris in 1921, the city had become a different place. The greatest holocaust ever seen in Europe had been enacted within earshot, and twice within gunshot, of Montmartre. Paris was depicted, largely by Americans, as a rodeo of reckless novelty, of sex and drugs and the frilly underwear of the Folies Bergères, but in fact it was a quieter place than before the War. Picasso, while scornful of his former Modernist confrères, had himself shown an interest in neo-classical forms. Matisse had left Paris for Nice where he was painting in a sensuous, highly coloured style. The new movements of Dada and Surrealism made noisy claims on an artist's attention, but there was no obligation to sign up.

When Wood arrived he was making a move less bold than Bomberg in 1913. But while he might be said to be in the second wave of English, the first one had been extraordinarily small: even as Paris began to fill with American students and bohemians, a nineteen-year-old boy from Liverpool still looked like a pioneer in 1921. The other remarkable fact of Wood's move was that he did not have much personal interest in the artistic movements that were forming in Paris. His own interests included the early work of Picasso, but stopped short of Cubism. He was a figurative painter, and while he took little tricks and calligraphic details from Cubism, he never tried to paint in that style. His alliance of himself to Picasso and what he represented was quite a humble recognition that this was where the talent and the future lay. If he did not copy it, he had to be near it; and this knowledge, amid all Wood's ignorance and confusion about public affairs and even about art, showed a shrewd instinctive judgement.

This surprisingly sure-footed decision was connected to the emotional certainties of his ambition to be a painter. His polio, and the three-year convalescent period of being nursed by his mother, had coincided with the absence of his father at the Front.

His illness changed the course of his life: from being an athlete he became a cripple. He was shamefully removed from the world of other children, and was in continual pain. At the same time he became handsome and attractive; puberty came to him as he lay prone.

He turned his frustrated physical and sexual energies to painting, which became an acceptable vehicle for all the unassimilated emotions of this harrowing period. He continued in later life to see his painting in this way, as when he viewed the ending of his affair with Meraud Guinness in the same way as the rejection of his designs for Diaghilev and used them both merely as a spur for his ambition. When he found as a crippled adolescent that he could paint, that he actually had some natural ability for it, he clasped the talent to his heart. In his life there was only one other emotion that counted, and that was the storm of enduring gratitude he felt towards his mother. She had saved him and nursed him; by encouraging him to paint she had helped release in him some tender, appreciative feelings towards the world he saw. It was natural that he should then make the one further step and lock together the two most important aspects of his emotional life: his painting would become a way of thanking and honouring his mother. The little paradox was that to accomplish this, he had to leave her. He had to go where the real art was and to escape from the influence of 'Huyton'. Always there was the half-formed idea that he would one day return when he had sufficiently proved himself and made for her a monument that could never be tarnished or destroyed.

Clare Wood encouraged him to believe he had a special mission and that she was its presiding deity. She once wrote to a friend of his: 'I adore him, as you know, and he must make a big thing of his life and use his talent conscientiously. I feel very seriously about that, as it is a thing that has been given to him to use.' Clare Wood's support of her son against the judgement of her husband took courage, but her emotional investment in Kit's career as a painter was almost as great as his own. Kit was enabled by his gift and by the fact that he was a man to live and enjoy those aspects of life and feeling that she had had to subdue to the requirements of her unimaginative husband. Lucius Wood was a decent man, but despite all he had seen at the Front from 1914–18 he lacked the ability to imagine the inner lives of those nearest to him. Clare and Kit were bent on some mission of their own, and she loved him with the unforgetting passion of a mother who had nursed her only son back from death.

In the Paris of the 1920s Wood was a rarity: an Englishman who painted. In a world of doubtful glamour his clean-cut innocence was a quality to which everyone could respond. He was always well dressed, usually in English clothes, though the cuffs of his Jermyn Street shirts were often frayed. He looked clean, even if he had been working all night and smoking opium; his clear complexion seldom betrayed the excesses of his life. He spoke briskly and simply, and had a streak of gallantry which often made him choose to dance all evening with the plainest-looking woman at a party. Younger women, such as his friend Gerald Reitlinger's sister Winifred, thus felt flattered by his attention. He courteously warned her that his and Gerald's parties became wild after midnight and she should make arrangements to go home.

His charm was qualified by his unreliability. He often failed to turn up at dinner parties if he thought someone who bored him might be there. His opium smoking also made him moody, though he warned friends not to worry if they called on him and found him distracted. He was quite punctilious about his louche habit.

A Parisian friend, Jacques Porel, claimed that 'He never uttered a cruel word. His presence alone was enough to save any gathering from vulgarity. At the same time he made you feel at ease in the order of things his delicacy had imposed.' Porel also noticed a certain boyish playfulness: 'His eyes looked down to the ground, his schoolboy pout was fixed, then would turn into a shy smile as he suddenly took out of his pocket – with exactly the same air of surprise – a thousand franc note or a pair of twenty-five centime coins, and said, "Look how rich I am. Georges, Jacques, listen, my dear chap. I'm asking you to dinner." ' According to Porel, 'one half expected him to clap his hands and jump up and down with glee.'

Wood's unreliability could be hurtful and alarming. Lucy

Wertheim, a friend and supporter, waited for two hours at her flat for Wood to come to dinner as arranged. At ten o'clock a friend rang to say Wood was unwell. The next day he arrived unexpectedly at her birthday lunch in a restaurant in Piccadilly, thrust a picture into her arms and borrowed half a crown for the taxi. He had a black eye, spoke as though in a trance, and hardly ate. Lucy Wertheim believed that, 'a restless energy seemed to impel him to keep moving whilst the knee that troubled him obliged him to take frequent rests.' Yet she, like Winifred Nicholson, was powerfully affected by his presence from the first meeting onwards. She sensed something in him that was almost frighteningly dynamic.

Wood sat on the train to Penzance in August 1926. He was ready to make the big push forwards. His private life had reached a fragile equipoise, his technique was sufficiently developed. In Ben Nicholson he had an ideal painting partner: quiet, dedicated and appreciative. Although Nicholson's own painting would shortly embrace abstraction, never to return, he was at this time painting in a figurative style so similar to Wood's that some people found their paintings hard to distinguish. Despite Wood's social life and nervous character, Nicholson found him the most generous and inspiring companion he ever had. In analysing how Wood tried to emulate the Nicholsons it is easy to overlook how his painting inspired them at a difficult time in their lives.

Wood's only obstacle to high achievement was his increased reliance on opium. He told Frosca that he would try to do something about it for her sake as he did not wish his appreciation of her to have any narcotic element. At the same time he invited her to come and stay with him at Porthmeor Beach, in St Ives, and preferably to bring some high quality drugs with her. The trouble was that Tony Gandarillas was now seeing so much of Maria de Gramont that Wood could not get access to his supply.

Frosca duly arrived at Wood's little cottage, and to begin with all went well. His painting reached a new level and he felt happy with Frosca. He painted the sea, the boats and the local people with what Winifred Nicholson called 'imaginative reality'. She believed his painting was now back on track after the frustrations caused to it by city life and the upheavals over Meraud. 'I too,' Winifred Nicholson recalled, 'painted with keenest delight. My little boy [Jake] ran with bare feet by the sea.' Like all Wood's bright idylls, this one was short-lived. Frosca Munster was not a woman easily upstaged, but cliques of friends are always irritating to outsiders. Frosca did not feel threatened by Winifred as a sexual rival, but she felt uneasy about the artistic and personal intimacy she enjoyed with Wood. She made one or two comments to Winifred Nicholson which hurt her grievously. Winifred took herself off to walk along the seashore, turning them over in her heart.

She would not admit to herself that she had the interest of a lover in Kit Wood. Her feeling, she told herself, was all spiritual. 'My love for him,' she later wrote, 'was severe discipline, severe sacrifice, and meant going through fire, but fire purified it . . . and gave it that element that neither death nor sorrow can come near.'

Whatever state of purity it reached in her recollection, she decided in the autumn of 1928 that she was not welcome at St Ives and had better leave. She said it was the hardest thing she had ever had to do. Nevertheless she managed to subdue her own feelings sufficiently to take some pleasure in the happiness that Frosca had brought to Kit. She had seen the look of joy on his face when Frosca had arrived at St Feock with all her 'lovely, glistening frocks', and she had seen the new strength of purpose that came into Wood's life as a result, she believed, of Frosca's influence. She believed Wood had found the arrangement he had long sought: a relationship with a woman who was a friend as well as a lover, and who consequently gave him the peace of mind to be fully creative.

Wood and Ben Nicholson were out walking one day when they went past the door of a fisherman's cottage. They looked inside and were amazed by what they saw: an array of primitive paintings they both believed to be bordering on genius. The painter was a retired fisherman called Alfred Wallis. He painted on old cardboard boxes, bus timetables, anything that came to hand. The pictures, which he had started to paint after the death of his wife in 1922, were of the sea and ships: they had a foreshortened perspective and crude lines, but an intriguing sense of form and colour. Wallis was a kind of picturesque original who might appeal to someone who had been to too many of the Comte de Beaumont's fancy dress balls. He lived in a single room, where, much to his neighbour's irritation, he played improvised melodies on a battered accordion that he kept beneath a purple spotted cover. He had once been a rag and bone man and had once run a shop, but had not been able to balance the books. He had a gruff attitude towards his painting and to such of Wood's and Nicholson's as they subsequently showed him.

His effect on Wood's work was considerable; in fact Winifred Nicholson thought that, after Picasso, Wallis was the most important single influence. His naïveté inspired Wood to develop an aspect of his style that had first become apparent in the days of 'La Foire de Neuilly'. Wood was not a true naïve like Wallis, and did not try to be, but he combined the naïve with other elements of what was emerging as his mature style. Some critics commented that Wallis gave Wood an excuse for a certain clumsiness – that he gave a fancy vindication to a basic lack of technique – but Wood could have authenticated an unfinished element in his style by reference to any number of other painters, including the more respectable Picasso and Van Gogh. Wallis's work persuaded Wood to narrow his range of colour and to experiment with house paint and board instead of oils and canvas, but what he really offered him was a renewed childlike directness: 'I want a good new yacht . . . and a good peaint box.'

On 15 October Frosca returned to Paris and Wood cried himself to sleep. He invited his mother to come and keep him company, but bad health prevented her from making the journey from Wiltshire. Alone again, he resumed his work and was excited by what he was doing. 'It is a great moment in my life,' he wrote. 'The studentship has passed, my work is forming something quite personal and mature, unlike anybody else's, and I don't think anyone can paint the pictures I am doing.' It was a fair comment on what had happened to his painting. St Ives did represent a genuine advance, a real breakthrough. Wood responded to it with the note of fatalistic desperation he found on such occasions: 'This time of quiet has come at the right moment . . . now it is essential as it is now or never and I am making a big dash for it.'

He worked hard by day, his needs taken care of by a local man: 'My servant is a hunchback, and very quick and good tempered. We eat blackberries like golf-balls and fish that are still flapping about when they are served.' By night he smoked opium. When Frosca got back to Paris, Winifred Nicholson returned to St Ives, but by this time Wood was going so deep down into himself that he found her and Ben irritating with their self-sacrifice, their vegetarianism and their noisy child.

Wood stayed on alone as the winter set in. St Ives was giving him something important, of which he had inadvertently given a good description in a letter. 'When someone dies here, they burn the mattress, the clothes and even the bedstead of the defunct on the beach. The male folk, these darkly dressed men, carry it all down on their shoulders and make a huge fire among the rocks and stand around with paraffin cans in hand musing on the life of the dead person. It is rather impressive with the huge green waves like horses bounding and pounding in on the sand.'

What he was describing was what became a typical Wood picture: the sea, darkly dressed fisherpeople, drama, strangeness, something primitive; the homely human figures set against a background of wildness and mystery, expressed in misleadingly simple terms.

It was in the human figures that Wood was distinctive. He was the only serious English painter between the two wars who continued to believe that a picture could deal with the lives of people. The dogmatic concerns of modern art as it developed in England ruled out the appearance of human beings at all, unless in some non-representational way, a mere occupation of the picture space, like a pipe-cleaner in a Cubist collage.

In his cottage by the sea Wood was by this stage smoking five or six pipes of opium each evening, and the drug was of poor quality. He promised Frosca he would begin treatment for his addiction as soon as they were together again, but asked if she would, in the meantime, try to get hold of some better quality opium from Gandarillas.

The euphoric effects of opium were real enough, and deeply appealing to Wood. De Quincey noted that 'the moral affections are in a state of cloudless serenity; and over all is the majestic light of the intellect.' Cocteau put it tersely: 'Alcohol provokes stupidity; opium provokes wisdom.' Wood was aware of his intellectual failings and prized opium's ability to give him at least the semblance of power. But there was another aspect of the drug's effect that was important to him. In a test at the Harvard Medical School in the 1950s a Dr Lawrence Kolb came to the extraordinary conclusion that, 'the intensity of pleasure produced by opiates is in direct proportion to the degree of psychopathy of the person who becomes an addict.' Millions of non-psychopathic Chinese over hundreds of years proved the finding to be false, but Dr Kolb's footnotes were relevant to Wood: 'Opium produces in these cases a feeling of mental peace and calm to which they are not accustomed and which they cannot normally achieve.'

It was not just the 'majestic light of the intellect' and the banishing of even the notion of unhappiness that opium offered Wood, it was access to a quite normal state of mind – mental peace – which in Dr Kolb's unintentionally poignant words people such as Wood 'cannot normally achieve'.'

The effect of all drugs depends to some extent on the character and mood of the person who takes them. This is particularly true of hallucinogenic drugs, such as LSD, when the mental state of the user seems in fact almost entirely to dictate whether the chemical has a euphoric or terrifying effect. But it is to varying degrees true of all drugs. Graham Greene was unexcited by the way that opium extinguished the possibility of unhappiness; his narrative passed quickly on from this revelation to the story of a dream in which he met the Devil dressed in a deerstalker and a tweed motoring coat on the steps of a club in St James's Street. Greene was not interested in a world without grief because he could not write about it: he would rather retain unhappiness if losing it meant forgoing material for his next novel. De Quincey, on the other hand, was rapturous about the same sensation because he was what he called a 'eudaemonist', by which he meant he was too much attached to the sensation of happiness. Wood's response was somewhere between the two: he shared De Quincey's romantic eudaemonism and and in that way he was weak, but he had also a splinter of Greene's icy ambition in his heart, and this made him resentful of his dependence on the drug.

At the end of November he packed up and left St Ives. It had given him a great deal: boats, the sea, people, menace and joy. It seemed to have almost everything his painting needed.

Back in Paris Wood moved into Frosca's apartment on the Boulevard de Lannes. Frosca's relative wealth set her apart from most of the Russian *émigrés*, of whom there were more than 50,000 in Paris, mostly of noble stock, working as porters, labourers, taxi drivers, bank clerks or floorwalkers in the big department stores. A typical Russian enterprise was the Restaurant Moskou near the Etoile, a modest little place with a canvas awning that was run by Colonel Narishkin. The number of taxis parked outside led strangers to suppose it had been discovered by Paris society, but in fact it was the taxi drivers who were eating there. The customers tucking into borscht, shashlik and kissel included generals, barons and princesses. Narishkin himself wore a blue denim tunic buttoned up to the chin on the grounds that until he could return in dignity to his estates he didn't wish to ape the manners or clothes of a gentleman.

Although Wood loved Frosca for her earthbound qualities – the concision and clarity of her letters, for instance – she had by most people's standards a high degree of wilfulness and worldly desire. Like Wood she could negotiate her way through the salons where art and money had their doubtful meeting, though she also shared his ambivalent feelings towards Paris society and was often glad to accompany him to more austere places. He was proud of the fact that Cocteau and Georges Auric referred to Frosca as Madame Récamier and played charades at her house till four in the morning. He himself became so bored by it that he went off into the night on his own.

Wood received an invitation to the opening of Meraud Guinness's show at the Galerie van Leer and had dinner with her afterwards. The experience troubled him. He told himself that he was no more than fond of her and that he had definitely done the right thing in not proceeding with her. She had no serious conversation, her looks had gone off; she was quite empty-headed and lacking in the qualities that he loved in Frosca. And yet she frightened him. He believed that she still wanted to marry him, and since the year was all but up they could do it easily enough. A part of him still wanted her, but as he told his mother, 'I feel she is without knowing it rather a dangerous influence to someone who has a very serious life to lead for the next few years as I will.'

Bridget Guinness heard that Meraud had been seeing Wood again and despatched her friend Mrs Patrick Campbell, the actress, accompanied by her cook, a Mrs Danveral, to keep an eye on Meraud in Paris. Meraud's other principal suitor was the Chilean painter Alvaro Guevara, who had previously been more attracted to Wood himself. Guevara saw what was going on and made himself pleasant to Mrs Campbell, who consequently took back favourable reports of him to Bridget Guinness.

Wood meanwhile repaired to his parents' house in Broad Chalke for Christmas where he spent a painful time trying to detoxify himself from opium. The difficulties of family Christmas were intensified by the symptoms of his withdrawal: everywhere cold turkey. Upstairs in his room he scribbled a note to Frosca, begging her to write to him, not in her usual terse style, but giving him the details of her inner life.

Wood survived the festivities and in January 1929 set himself up in a small house in Minton Place, off Bury Street in Chelsea. The Nicholsons and Tony Gandarillas had their London homes nearby, so he was not alone, but the move showed that he no longer thought of Paris as his base.

On 23 January at the Henrietta Street register office in Covent Garden Meraud Guinness, having given up on Kit Wood, married Alvaro Guevara, with C. R. W. Nevinson as the chief witness. While Mrs Guinness had fought and won the battle of Meraud's hand against Wood in Paris, she now found herself giving her blessing to a man who was famous on both sides of the

Channel as a drunk, a poser, and a bore. Known as 'Chile' Guevara for his habit of beginning almost everything he said with the words 'When I was in Chile', Guevara also turned out, by an irony that pleased Kit Wood if not Bridget Guinness, to have been devotedly homosexual and a regular user of opium.

Wood was well set up in his house in Bury Street, with a housekeeper called Mrs Illesley who filled the place with fresh flowers and cooked excellent dinners. In March Frosca came over from Paris to stay with him while he prepared for an exhibition of the Seven & Five Society at Tooth's Gallery in Bond Street.

The show, once again, was disappointing. Wood and Ben Nicholson had decided to exhibit Alfred Wallis at the same show and some critics thought Wallis's genuine naïveté showed theirs to be bogus. At the beginning of April Wood had his first one-man show in London, also at Tooth's, and this too failed to make the impression he had hoped. Even Winifred Nicholson was disappointed; she believed that there was something either in the gallery or in the way the pictures were hung that failed to give a fair idea of what Wood had achieved or of what lay ahead. Gandarillas threw a party for him in Cheyne Walk, Frosca was on hand to encourage him, and afterwards his mother also came to stay. But however good the pictures had become and however loyal their support, he was failing to make enough money to support either a small house in Chelsea or a regular opium habit.

Wood was unable to think clearly enough to find a way out of his predicament. His inability to plan clearly was made worse by his drug habit and the way that his nervous ambition made him reluctant to stop painting long enough to take stock. He did sense, however, that a change of scenery would help, and in April he went to Dieppe with Frosca. She reported a frenzy of activity: 'Kit is working like a mad thing. He never puts down his paint brush for a second . . . never has there been such a profusion of pictures.' The results were of a high quality. Although the subject matter, boats and the harbour, was commonplace, Wood was now painting in his mature style, which gave charming depth – what Winifred Nicholson called the 'resonance of organ music' – to his best pictures. Some of the Dieppe pictures were ravishing: tightly controlled compositions with powerfully rich colours.

In May he returned to Paris, where the early summer passed in the state of semi-agitated torpor the city now seemed to induce in him. To produce a good painting seemed to require twice as much effort in Paris as elsewhere. He went to see the new Diaghilev ballet, which had been designed by Georges Rouault and de Chirico, the Italian metaphysical painter whose great days had been during the War. Wood admired the scenery, but could not help agreeing with Cocteau, who had remarked: 'One is too old to see de Chirico discovered by Diaghilev.' The parties started up again in earnest. Tony Gandarillas now went everywhere with Maria de Gramont, but Wood still managed to attend a fancy dress ball given by the Vicomte de Noailles, who had covered his garden with a wooden hall 60 feet high, invited 1,000 guests and commissioned ballets with music by Poulenc and Auric. Even this was surpassed by Henri de Rothschild's party with its moving stage and 3,000 guests.

The morning after, Wood played tennis with Frosca at the Racing Club in the Bois de Boulogne and lunched under the trees. In the evening they went boating on the lake where people rowed with red Chinese lanterns slung from the bows. By the beginning of July he had begun to feel agitated by his life of luxury, and by the end of the month he was in Brittany.

Brittany had appealed to painters before. Gauguin's residence at Pont Aven near Lorient on the west coast was so fruitful that a 'school' was named after it. Matisse was powerfully affected by a visit there in 1895; the intensity he achieved in his Brittany painting led the English critic Herbert Read to suggest that he had approached a point of rapture. More recently Kisling, whose presence had made little impact on Wood at Le Canadel in 1924 but whose paintings did find echoes in Wood's work, had visited the westerly fishing port of Douarnenez. So had Derain, whose early paintings considerably influenced Wood's treatment of landscape.

Brittany regarded itself as more Celtic than French and had had great difficulty in integrating itself with the Republic. It had ethnic links with Cornwall, which in some ways it resembled, though its rustic Catholicism was more wild and more picturesque than Cornish Nonconformism. British holidaymakers throughout the century found that, despite the demands of tourism, parts of the long Brittany coast retained a weird and forbidding character. In 1929 these had not been developed at all.

Wood approached it crabwise, with no clear intentions. He went first to Dinard, which he hated, then to St Malo, which he liked but found unmanageably large. In St Servan he watched the fishing boats disappearing into the Atlantic while the sailors' wives, dressed in black with white headdresses, sat and waited in a small rowing boat. He did not linger there, but he had seen the image that was to recur in his work that summer: the mysterious sailing boats vanish on their fraught voyages while the black-clad women wait.

At St Malo he was joined by Christian 'Bébé' Bérard, the painter and designer who had been a regular at the Hôtel Welcome, and a twenty-two-year-old picture dealer called Pierre Colle. They drove to Douarnenez, which Colle knew because his parents had a house in the area. Douarnenez was a fishing port known for its prodigious catches of sardines. The bay it overlooked had the pleasant Breton characteristics of wind-whipped trees and whitewashed houses, but with its long wharfs and warehouses it was too much a commercial port to be picturesque. It sat on the eastern side of a long sea inlet; on the western side, reached by an iron bridge that had been erected about forty years earlier, was the village of Tréboul. The railway station was on the Tréboul side so that the track could be taken on into the western peninsula without the need for a second bridge. Despite the commerce of Douarnenez passing through the railhead, Tréboul was a small and undeveloped village. Its livelihood was the sea, but its fishing boats put out from a tiny harbour. In 1929 the Breton peasants were still in the traditional dress they had worn for centuries, uninterested in life on the other side of the inlet, let alone in 'France', a country to which they were most reluctant to belong.

Douarnenez reminded Wood of St Ives, though the boats were

bigger. At the end of August he rented a small house opposite the Hôtel Ty-Mad (Breton for 'good little house') in Tréboul and Frosca came to join him. The hotel was set just above a sixteenth-century church, the Chapelle St Jean. A narrow path led down to a small sandy beach. Fishermen came and went to the little whitewashed houses in the village behind the hotel; women dried nets against the walls: otherwise the solitude by day was undisturbed. Yet although this corner of the village was quiet, it was not dull. The proximity of the old chapel in its little sandy square gave a spiritual, but not particularly comforting, atmosphere. The tall, narrow hotel with its simple rooms and Breton-speaking waitresses had a powerful ambience of its own. The village of Tréboul was entirely inward-looking and visitors were left to make of it what they wanted.

Wood initially viewed it as wholly tranquil. 'I have a little sailing boat,' he told his mother, as though Father Christmas had at last delivered. 'I sit in it and glide along and look at all the things I love the most. I see the lovely fishing boats with their huge brown sails against the dank dark green fir trees and little white houses . . .'

He painted steadily, but was not particularly excited by the results. Although he was usually the first to claim great progress for his work, he was not immediately aware of it in Tréboul. Perhaps this was because he was relaxed.

These were the happiest days of Christopher Wood's life. He was with Frosca, whom he loved; he was painting well; he was in a place that agreed with him. He found the balance he required: there was no Violette Murat waddling through the bar with her bag of cocaine, no Napier Alington plastering himself with gilded costume, no Luisa Casati unwinding her boa constrictor and laughing with her terrible red eyes. There was instead the plain, spiritual life of the ancient Breton coast, with its historic kinship to Cornwall, the country of his mother; there were sailing boats with sails of deep and gorgeous colours; there were silver, dazzling fish on the quayside; there was a terrestrial paradise of dour beauty ringed by transcendental, frightening horizons.

Yet there were also diversions enough in the evening. As well as Frosca, Pierre Colle and Christian Bérard, there was the Breton poet and painter Max Jacob and the precocious English exquisite from the Hôtel Welcome, Sir Francis Rose. Jacob and Rose were staying in the Hôtel Ty-Mad, rechristened by Jacob 'Ty-Mad de Cocayne'. Francis Rose had a portable gramophone on which he played Stravinsky and negro spirituals until the others begged him to stop. Bérard was not inspired to paint by Tréboul: he lay in his hotel room with the shutters closed and smoked opium.

Max Jacob had shared a studio with Picasso in the already legendary days of the Bateau Lavoir in Montmartre when each was still hungry. Picasso slept by day and worked by night, vacating the studio's lone bed for Max Jacob in his turn. Jacob had eventually won renown as a poet, and was a writer of fine and intelligent irony. Though born of Jewish parents, he had felt no religious attachment until he embraced the sacraments of the Catholic Church with all the alarming fervour of the convert. He was an incurable lover of young men, who daily and extravagantly repented his lust but was incapable of controlling it. Though flayed by guilt and anguish, he was a kindly man, much loved by his friends, generous and gentle in his manner; he wrote powerful *Méditations* on his new faith and his human failings.

The unsustainable claims made for Jacob in the name of Breton nationalism, which eventually replaced sardine-canning as the principal industry of Douarnenez, paradoxically made it difficult to take him as seriously as he deserved. He was unfortunate to be upstaged by the Surrealists in the mid 1920s when the poetry he had been writing, such as *Cornet à Dés* (*Dice Cup*), was arguably Surrealist before the fact. His painting never developed sufficiently to compensate for this disappointment. It was in his struggle with himself, with his desires and beliefs, that the measure of the man became visible. Francis Rose thought him a saint; the more dependable evidence of Jacob's own *Méditations* showed a profound and generous thinker. He remarked of himself: 'The cross I have to carry through my life is being born a Jew, being homosexual, and still being a practising Roman Catholic.' His conversation was playful, but in his missal he kept the names of the living and the dead for whom he prayed each day.

Max Jacob was involved in a car accident with Pierre Colle and broke his leg. It was while he was recovering that Wood painted his portrait, a bold, witty painting of a Breton Mr Punch that was given to the Quimper museum. Francis Rose recalled the summer of 1929: 'Kit, from a fishing boat, painted pictures of other fishing boats. He used ripoline house paint, thinned with turpentine, and his colours were clear and pure. No real sail held as much of the brown and orange of a sun-lit sail as did those of his paintings. His "Mackerel" and "Sleeping Figure" shone with the blue deepness of the sea and the silvery glitter of a wet fish. His lobster baskets were as wet in colour and as well drawn in pattern as the real ones, and there was never a suspicion of the decorative in his work. Kit was good, handsome, simple, deformed; with a masculine build, a delicate nature, and the terrible fears of the poet. I loved him deeply . . . I spent most of my days with Kit and Frosca in a whitewashed villa on the seashore. He, too, smoked opium, and loved collecting opium pipes in bamboo and ivory when he could afford it. We found them at an antique dealer's near the Galeries Lafayette in Paris, where Cocteau and all the other smokers went to buy lamps, pins, and equipment for smoking opium.'

When Francis Rose was on the beach one morning a postman brought him a telegram from Serge Lifar. Diaghilev had died in Venice. Christopher Wood was sufficiently moved to believe that Diaghilev 'will be terribly missed by everyone'. But the news did not really disturb the calm surface of his mood. 'I sit on the green grass banks above the sea each evening which becomes like a lake, pale grey blue like milk and lovely ivory-coloured sailing ships go past very slowly,' he wrote to his mother. 'I can't tell you the beauty of this place with dark fir trees and the little white houses like jewels, the curious faces of the people like Holbein's drawings, there is such dignity and compactness about everything.'

Even so, he still, at this stage, preferred Cornwall. Tréboul did not exert its full power on him during his first visit, and in view of the fury of that eventual power, he should perhaps have been glad of the tranquillity at first given to him by the 'dignity and compactness' of the village. The minute he returned to Paris, the effect on his paintings was remarked by others. In October he was approached by Georges Bernheim, who ran an important gallery in the rue du Faubourg St Honoré. Bernheim offered him a one-man show for the following May. This show, Wood told his mother, would make him the first English artist to be exhibited in Paris since Whistler. As Whistler was in fact American, the honour was perhaps even greater than Wood supposed. Perhaps in the excitement of the moment he could be forgiven for overlooking the fact that Meraud Guinness had exhibited the previous year; or perhaps he discounted her on the grounds that her show was more or less sponsored by Picabia.

Boris Kochno, who had been Diaghilev's secretary, asked Wood to do the scenery for a revue he was putting on for Charles Cochran with the remains of the Russian Ballet. The music would be by Lord Berners, whom Wood knew from Cannes. Like the *Romeo and Juliet* project, this was a show about a show: called *Luna Park*, it concerned the life of freaks or *phénomènes*, who followed a ballet company round Europe. Wood might well have felt disdainful about receiving the commission now, when he had already been offered a show in Paris, but he could not afford to turn down any chance of making money. He wrote simply to his mother: 'I was very happy about [the Kochno commission] after the unfortunate affair of four years ago when I was not really competent enough to do it.' He asked Clare Wood for money. Usually he was reluctant to do so, and often returned her cheques with assurances that he had no need of funds since everything was about to work out fine. At about this time, however, money or the lack of it, became more than an inconvenience for Wood: it became a major destabilising factor in his life. The bailiffs seized his house in Minton Place.

He had not officially been 'kept' or given an allowance by Tony Gandarillas, but nor had he been expected to pay the bills, either at home or when they went travelling. The looseness of their arrangement, however, was demonstrated by the way that, as they saw less of each other, Wood found himself in trouble: no arrangement could be made to continue when they were apart, because none had existed when they were together.

Wood told his mother about the bailiffs repossessing his house on 25 October 1929. He characteristically made no mention of the fact that the day before had seen the collapse of the New York Stock Exchange in the events known as Black Thursday. In Paris, most of Christopher Wood's rich friends were burned. Frosca had to take a job introducing rich clients to a picture gallery in return for a commission. A month later Wood claimed that Violette Murat had lost five or six million pounds. Maria de Gramont was having to work as an interior decorator (a consultant rather than actually going up a ladder) for £100 a month. Gandarillas was broke, and his aunt, Eugenia Errazuriz, had, according to Wood, 'lost everything'. Clare Wood suggested that her son should do more work, but an artist, he told her tartly, was 'not a machine': the greatest painters – Degas, Cézanne, Renoir – had left no more than 300 or so canvases. Whether this was a sufficiently urgent response to a crisis that had convulsed the world, Mrs Wood was free to wonder.

Wood never dreamed of taking a job. The Duchesse de Gramont might have to dabble in decoration; the exiled dukes of Russia might be slicing up beetroot for the borscht in the Restaurant Moskou, but he would carry on searching for a way to make his paintings capable of expressing the ambitions he had for them. He would do the ballet designs for Cochran: that was, after all, a commission; it was a 'job' of a kind. Then in the New Year he would have to prepare his paintings for the exhibition at the Galerie Georges Bernheim.

'Everyone wants money and thinks of little else at the moment. C'est une belle horreur,' he wrote in November. Tony Gandarillas had urged him to marry Frosca, but he felt he did not have enough money. Cochran was to pay £25 for the revue designs in January and a further £25 a month later. Mrs Wood suggested he come and work at Broad Chalke, but he declined her offer. 'It's not my atmosphere and kills my work and me. I love your part of it, and if you lived there alone I should love it and be there a good deal.' But she was not alone; 'Huyton' was there too.

On 13 December Wood told his mother he had caught sight of Meraud in a restaurant, 'looking very changed and not at all happy'. Any agitation he felt about Meraud was swept away by the terrible news that came on Christmas Eve: Jeanne Bourgoint had committed suicide. She had been behaving more wildly than usual after becoming the object of Violette Murat's unwanted advances. The hard-bodied tomboy had become dishevelled and drug-addicted; she lived in squalor, seldom bothered to wash or dress, and was said to have had an abortion and a failed drug cure. She died of barbiturate poisoning in the family house in the rue Hippolyte-Lebas. Her desperate end was discovered by her brother Jean, the surviving *enfant terrible*.

Wood worked hard through January to finish the ballet designs, and this time there were no reverses. He painted more pictures, but saw no chance of selling them. The revue opened in Manchester in March – 'a great success', Wood told his mother – before transferring to London. Frosca, whose financial reverse was not as serious as she had feared, had a skiing accident in St Moritz and was in hospital for several weeks with torn muscles in her leg. Wood went to Mousehole, in Cornwall, in March, and painted hard to give himself enough representative material for the Bernheim show in May. Bernheim himself helped by finding Wood a house in Paris where he could work quietly. Two of Wood's best paintings – 'The Little House by Night' and 'The Little House by Day' (sold at Sotheby's in June 1994) – were depictions of this house in the rue Singer, in the *seizième*.

Back in Paris, Wood did something extraordinary: he persuaded Georges Bernheim to let Ben Nicholson share his show. On 16 March he wrote to Bernheim: 'I won't have enough pictures to really fill your two enormous rooms, since I don't have any outsize pictures like Max Ernst' – the word he used for outsize was '*grosses*', an interesting adjective for the work of the man Diaghilev had preferred to him. Wood offered twenty-five or thirty pictures of his own and recommended that the rest of the space be occupied by Nicholson, whom he described as the painter he most admired in England and whose work had something of the same character as his own. He even proposed that the show be titled '*Deux Peintres Anglais*'.

Although there was a practical consideration – filling the space – this was a magnanimous gesture, which shows that Wood's self-absorption did not always make him selfish. He was not slow to complain about the difficulty he had in persuading Bernheim to accept Nicholson, but the fact that he was aware of his own achievement in being offered the show made it more remarkable that he was prepared to compromise the glory by sharing it.

Ben Nicholson, alas, was 'simply beastly'; he was unhappy with his work and could only offer ten paintings. Nicholson was also by this time seriously worried about Wood. In a postcard to Winifred on 8 April he wrote: 'Kit needs our help. I think that he is trying to stop his opium and drinks instead, or mixes the two . . . I am doing all I can to make Kit stay in Paris and chuck London and that awful life he was living there.'

The show, which opened on 17 May, was dominated by Wood. It was a qualified success. Wood sold about eleven paintings, but for the modest prices that were all the post-Crash world could manage. A further panic on the New York Stock Exchange just before the show opened had made matters even more tense. He had in fact only two buyers: Winifred Reitlinger bought a picture of a fishing boat in Dieppe harbour; the other ten canvases all went to Lucy Wertheim, a collector from London who had taken a passionate interest in Wood. He himself seemed indifferent to the impact of the show. This may have been an affectation, but it may also have been caused by his restless determination to continue with his painting. He knew that his best work – or the work that he believed he could do – was not in the show. It was in his mind, and he needed to go back to Brittany to release it.

Winifred Nicholson believed the Bernheim show had at last done Wood something like justice. 'His work in that exhibition was fine, dark and blocked. It was hard to see what his next move would be. One picture was different from anything he had done. It was at Tréboul, of a woman mending nets against a white cottage. This was simple and mystic.'

Money worries pressed him still harder. He asked Clare Wood to pay the rent on the house in Minton Place; Frosca's affairs had undergone a reverse because she was subsidising her brother-in-law. And so, with the threats of creditors and the praises of Cocteau and Georges Auric humming in his ears, Wood left Paris in early June to return to Tréboul.

He stayed this time in the Hôtel Ty-Mad itself, looking over the sea. In a period of about six weeks, from early June to late July, Wood painted in a frenzy. He completed almost forty canvases, about one a day.

Later accounts of Keats's extraordinary summer of 1819 – scraps of paper, birdsong, coughing – were burdened with significance they cannot really have had. Christopher Wood's summer of 1930 seemed to have the makings of myth even as it was being lived.

The Ty-Mad was completely unlike the *hôtels de grand luxe* he had frequented with Tony Gandarillas along the shores of the Mediterranean. Its writing paper was headed 'Pension G. Cariou', with the name Ty-Mad in small letters underneath, and in most respects it was no more than a *pension*. A painting Wood did of Francis Rose at his toilet showed the simplicity of the rooms, furnished with iron bedsteads, bare table and chair, and walls decorated by a single picture of a woman in a Breton headdress. The Ty-Mad was plain to the point of austerity; it was a corrective to the Vicomte de Noailles and his fancy dress balls, and it was also, to Christopher Wood, a liberation.

Tréboul was not merely a convenient and quiet place to paint; it provided subject matter, inspiration and the atmosphere in which Wood finally brought together his technique and his ambition for it, with the result that he was able to plunder his emotions – something which until then he had been able to do only with frustrating inconsistency. Once he had unlocked this power, he exploited it relentlessly: he worked by day and by night, using postcards to prompt his memory of a scene when the light had gone.

The paintings that resulted were basically landscapes and seascapes, characterised by the presence of sailing boats, Breton peasants, whitewashed churches and cottages, dark grass, fir and cypress trees on the cliff's edge and the day-to-day objects of the life of fishermen and their families. Within this framework, however, he introduced remarkable variations. Some of the figures were, as he intended, like drawings from Holbein, but in other paintings he worked in more modern ways. In the foreground of 'Building the Boat, Tréboul' the face of the old woman seems to foresee the drownings the finished boat would bring: her head recalls 'The Scream' by Munch.

In the painting known as 'La Plage, Hôtel Ty-Mad, Tréboul' (in fact it depicted the hotel at a neighbouring beach, Les Sables Blancs), the foreground is occupied by monumental characters who might have come from an undiscovered period of Picasso. In the magnificent 'Sleeping Fisherman, Ploaré' (also wrongly catalogued: it was set on the Plage St Jean, Tréboul), the huge figure of the title seems less like a peasant than a Greek god, slumbering on the sands where he has stopped to rest. A French critic, Françoise Steel, commented: 'Kit Wood was often a nostalgic witness to the rootedness of these Breton men and women who seem to have sprung up spontaneously out of their own patch of earth.' This seems right. The ribs of the boat in 'Building the Boat, Tréboul' appear to be part of the same notional body as the skull of the old woman in the foreground: she nurses in her arms what first appears to be a baby but turns out to be a piece of timber from the boat. In the paintings of women drying the nets or decorating the inside of the church, Wood portrayed a mystical union between people and place. They were one and the same: they had 'sprung up spontaneously from their own patch of earth'. Wood understood and realistically depicted this autochthonous quality of the people; yet he also made them look like gods.

The results were at best, as in 'The Sleeping Fisherman', powerfully moving: strange, beautiful, unsettling, with a taste and character not quite like those of any other painter. The naïve elements, developed from Rousseau and Wallis, were now settled down into the painting; the landscape techniques taken from Van Gogh and Derain had been assimilated. The result was that Wood's own vision at last came blazing out in all its curious and contradictory forms.

The landscapes without people had a similar sense of precarious harmony: the wild and the familiar, the romantic and the quotidian, set side by side in unsettling colours. The painting of the Chapelle St Jean, done from his bedroom window in the Ty-Mad, has a characteristic mixture of these elements: it is certainly beautiful, restful and realistic – all the pieties and reassurances of rustic Catholicism have been observed; but it is also edged with menace. There is the sea behind; there are voyages to be made beyond the horizon. While the picture is faithfully Breton, it is also otherworldly. The achievement of it was that the transcendent aspect did not have to be read into it in some literary way: it was present in the actual manner in which the church was painted. This was finally painting of a gorgeously expressive kind; it was not what Modernism was concerned with, but it was what Wood had striven to do all his life.

Although Wood had tried to stop smoking for Frosca's sake, he had not been successful. He relied on her to send him supplies from Paris, but she in turn depended on Tony Gandarillas, who was frequently out of town. In the creative frenzy of June and July 1930, Wood gave up any pretence of moderation: he smoked all night if he had opium to smoke, and failing that, he smoked the leavings or dross. His physical state therefore varied between intoxication and withdrawal. He didn't care. He had risked everything to get this far; he was driven by forces he did not even wish to control.

This was what it had all been for: all the 'progress' he had so eagerly reported, all the 'struggles' he had so boyishly endured. He sensed that he had to make a 'dash' for it; there was a compelling urgency: it was as though he believed that he might lose what he had searched so long to find – that if he did not paint as much as he could while all the elements of his life were in propitious harmony, they might shift into a new configuration and he would have lost his dream or his ability to paint it. 'It's extraordinary,' he told his mother, 'how I have to hurry, hurry from one thing to another, but it's just the one moment or chance I have to get on.'

Frosca came to stay but did not distract him. He was too tired to write letters; he had a wardrobe full of unanswered mail. He was painting one, sometimes two pictures a day and was obliged to rent a second room in the Ty-Mad because the smell of drying paint was so overpowering. Some of the painting showed recognisable scenes from Tréboul; some were fanciful mixtures, taking a building from one place, a beach or seascape from another. At night he smoked opium and sometimes still painted, consulting his stock of local postcards. 'I was always called hasty but I can't work otherwise,' he wrote. 'It nearly kills me, the effort to get it done.'

At the beginning of July Frosca returned to Paris, because her mother had died. Wood worked on in unabated fury. The only other occupant of the hotel was Max Jacob. The two men met at mealtimes, then returned to their work. Jacob was charmed by Christopher Wood and by the innocent frenzy that gripped him.

On 10 July Wood wrote to Lucy Wertheim, whose purchase of his pictures, coupled with small loans, was helping him to exist: 'I have quite run out of paper and have got into such a state with my work and the fact that I have not been out of my room for over a week that I can't possibly go downstairs to get any more. My life is terrible here . . . When I have worked at one end of the room for four hours without stopping even to make a cigarette and go and lie down on the bed at the other and smoke perhaps a pipe of opium which is the only resource of quietness which takes my mind for the moment out of that awful turmoil of ideas and colours that go on in my busy head . . .

'I have painted a good deal of architecture, churches in a curious lonely country by the sea, very restful but very strong, and determined. Max Jacob said that I paint *"des arbres pleins d'oiseaux"* which is a very beautiful way of expressing fullness and feeling and yesterday he saw a large picture I had done. He said *"C'est meilleur que fait mon vieil ami Derain"*.'

Better than Derain . . . such praises goaded him on. 'I am enjoying my work enormously,' Wood told the Nicholsons, 'and I haven't the least idea of what is going on anywhere else, whether my house still exists or whether Paris is still in the same place as it was before.'

There were occasional visitors to Tréboul. One of them was a Swiss writer called C.A. Cingria, who was on a bicycling tour of Breton churches. He was astonished by Wood's self-absorption. On Midsummer Day a celebratory bonfire was piled high in the square between the Chapelle St Jean and the Hôtel Ty-Mad. A light breeze made the flames surge through the dry branches and the resulting blaze was so powerful that onlookers feared it would engulf the hotel. But as the uncontrolled fire crept up the sides of the building, Kit Wood lay stretched out on his bed by the open window, indifferent to the mounting blaze, drifting on the private fumes of opium.

A moderate opium habit can be sustained, with money and care in preparing the drug, with no adverse effects. The problems begin when too much is taken for too long, when a drastic reduction is attempted or when it is not properly prepared. It was in the state of withdrawal that De Quincey experienced his appalling dreams and visions, which, despite his careful explanations to the contrary, many people take to be a description of the effects of the drug rather than of unsupervised withdrawal from it. Jean Cocteau was disintoxicated in hospital at St Cloud in 1929, as was Tony Gandarillas, with the help of sedative drugs and close medical supervision. Even so, it was not easy, and much of what Cocteau wrote at the time (in *Opium*, 1930) had a bearing on Wood.

'You cannot trifle, or mess about with opium. If you do, it will forsake you. You will be left with morphine, heroin, suicide, death.' This was melodramatic: there was no absolute connection between opium and its less pure compounds, but it showed Cocteau's respect for the drug's power.

'If you ever hear someone say "X killed himself by smoking opium" you can be sure it's not true and that the death was caused by something else,' he wrote. This was true, though Cocteau did not mention that 'something else' could include the side-effects of withdrawal.

'Opium is a substance which defies analysis – living, capricious, and capable of suddenly turning against the smoker. It acts like a barometer for a weak personality. In humid weather the pipe leaks. The smoker arrives at the seaside and the drug swells up, refusing to cook. The approach of snow, or storms or strong winds makes it ineffective . . .' Cocteau might almost have had Wood in mind when he was writing.

Cocteau was not always clear about the question of the 'dross' – what is left in the pipe after the smoker has inhaled. Graham Greene spoke disparagingly of its bitter taste, but Cocteau thought mixing dross with the raw drug might increase the chances of getting a good smoke in difficult circumstances in which the drug for some reason would not 'behave'. However, the addition of dross changed the nature of the pipe, and, as Cocteau warned, 'It's impossible to foresee the results.' He came down against dross: 'Some people tell you: "Experts throw out the dross." Others say: "Experts make the boys smoke opium and only smoke the dross." But if you ask a boy about the dangers of the drug he'll tell you: "Good opium makes you fat, dross makes you ill." The sin of opium is to smoke the dross.'

By the sea, however, the drug was hard to handle. On his own, Wood didn't have the social aspect of opium-smoking to keep him respectful; nor did he have a supply that was equal to his craving. In these circumstances he was tempted to smoke the dross or even to eat it. The results of either would have been, as Cocteau emphasised, dangerous and impossible to predict; instead of offering increased intellectual control, the drug could become hallucinogenic. But Wood had no regard for his own safety: he was reckless, impatient and addicted; he was also in the midst of a creative storm.

'Opium,' wrote Cocteau, 'becomes tragic only in as much as it affects the nerves which govern the personality ... It is dangerous to smoke it if you are unbalanced ... Never confuse the opium-smoker and the opium-eater. They are quite different things.'

The first, he implied, is civilised, desirable and, in the 'majestic light of the intellect', superior to his fellows; the latter is crude, inferior and self-destructive.

New, surreal elements appeared in some of Wood's late pictures. He had shown almost no interest in Surrealism proper until this stage; in fact since his rejection by Diaghilev in favour of Miró and Max Ernst his attitude had been hostile. Yet strange figures wandered into the dark backgrounds of these paintings and, in the case of 'The Yellow Man', came striding to meet you. He appeared to be a *saltimbanque*, perhaps liberated from the tents of the freaks where Wood's designs for Cochran's *Luna Park* had first imagined him. 'The Yellow Horse', stranded in the mid-ground of a moonlit landscape, was a fantastic creature, unrelated to the burly drayhorse of 'La Foire de Neuilly'.

Some saw in these exotic additions to the late pictures the defining stamp of Wood's achievement. Those who, like Winifred Nicholson, loved the simple emotions of his more earthbound landscapes, saw them as brilliant, but aberrant. In Winifred Nicholson's eyes they were also signals of Wood's increasing mental disorder. She described what she admired in the rapturous paintings of 1930: they were 'very much more inspired than any he had done previously. He worked at high pressure painting forty pictures in a month ... There were pictures of churches, of the sea, of women praying, the colour was very simple and of the utmost purity like Hope itself. Human passion is at its highest tension, thought is mystic, and the theme of travel beyond the horizon which had constantly recurred in all his work now reached a pitch of utmost intensity beyond which it is not possible to go.'

This assessment had a characteristic element of wishful thinking: Wood showed no interest in the spiritual life, and if there was a 'mystic' quality it was concerned not with a wordless union of people and god, but of people and place. But the minatory, fearful note struck by Winifred Nicholson at the end was justified: 'Beyond which it is not possible to go'. It had taken Wood almost seven years to reach this stage, but when he got there he painted in such a way that he seemed to close off most logical avenues of development.

At the end of July Christopher Wood returned to Paris. He showed his summer's work to Christian Bérard. The paintings were wrapped in packets. Bérard knelt down and cut the strings that tied them. He separated them and looked at them one by one. He was astounded. He saw landscapes of such light and purity that he felt as though all around him were in a deep fog.

While in Paris, Wood painted two of his best-known paintings: one depicted a tiger in front of the Arc de Triomphe, the other was called 'Zebra and Parachute'. Both showed a mastery of composition he had not always achieved before, though the original unsettling elements of the Tréboul paintings were here exaggerated into outright incongruity. A tiger from the deepest

Rousseau jungle lay peacefully before the realistically painted Etoile, not far from where Wood had first stayed with Alphonse Kahn and then with Gandarillas. The background of 'Zebra and Parachute' was the Villa Savoye, Le Corbusier's famous Modernist house near Paris. A placid zebra gazes left in the foreground; the diagonals of Le Corbusier's design give a desolate air to the middle ground, reminiscent of some of de Chirico's forlorn quays; and in the top right-hand corner a slumped figure, apparently already dead, floats to earth on a parachute.

On 19 August 1930 Wood set off for England to meet Lucy Wertheim, who was to mount an exhibition of his pictures in London. He took the train from Paris to Le Havre in order to cross to Southampton, from where he would travel to London.

An encounter on the boat made him believe he was being followed by members of the Guinness family or their agents. He felt so sure he was being watched that he threw his pipe and opium overboard. Although he loved Frosca, he had never been able to extirpate Meraud from his thoughts; he was frightened of her family, with whom he had been on bad terms ever since the affair had ended. There was no doubt that the affair with Meraud – although he forced himself to view it, and her, as immature – had troubled him in a way that related to his sexual identity and to his whole idea of himself. But the development of Wood's anxieties to the point of paranoia can only be explained by the unsettling effects of the last few months. He was mentally and physically exhausted by his work, and his system had been abused by alternate indulgence in, and withdrawal from, large doses of opium.

When he arrived in Southampton he sent a telegram to his mother asking her to meet him for lunch in Salisbury the next day. He then caught a ferry to the Isle of Wight.

No one knows why he decided to go to Salisbury before London; Frosca understood that he wanted his mother's advice about something that was troubling him. At any rate, it is possible, thanks to the inquiries made some weeks later by a private detective, to recreate Wood's movements with a certain plodding precision.

He arrived at the Pier Hotel in Yarmouth at eleven o'clock on
the morning of 20 August. He had three suitcases with him and
three large packets of pictures. He said he would have lunch at
the hotel if they could reassure him there was no one else around.
Lunch was served to him, but he was too agitated to eat. He was
out for most of the afternoon, took no dinner, and went up to his
room at nine. He was heard walking about until eleven o'clock,
soon after which he went to bed.

At 6.30 the following morning he appeared in the dining room
and asked for a whisky and soda. He was told that the bar was not
open. He said he wanted breakfast at once but the waiter told
him the chef was not up. Wood paced up and down the dining
room. He told the waiter he had been out all night; that although
he had initially gone to bed in his room he had then left the hotel
and slept on a quayside. The waiter went to hang up Wood's coat,
which he had left on a chair. Owing to the weight of it, he looked
in the pockets. There he found a six-chamber revolver. Perhaps it
was the same one with which he had frightened off the eagles in
Greece.

Wood went upstairs and had a bath. He came down at 8.15,
had breakfast and left in a hurry. The boat for Lymington was due
to leave at 8.30, but fortunately for Wood it was a quarter of an
hour late. He just made it. Although the Guinness family was
well known in Yarmouth there was apparently no trace of them
there at the time. They had a yacht, which they sometimes
brought over for Cowes week, but various 'yachting people'
interviewed by the private detective stated firmly they were not
there. Wood was imagining his persecution.

That morning he took a train from Lymington to Salisbury. At
about 11.30 on the morning of 21 August Wood walked into the
bar of the County Hotel in Salisbury and accosted a Major
Beckley, who was staying there. He said, 'Can I have a little
interview now, as I expect my mother in about half an hour.'
Beckley explained that there must be a mistake: he had never
seen Wood before and had no business with him. Wood paced
about the lounge until a woman's voice was heard outside. He
went out and spoke to her. She asked how he was; he replied that

he was very well, and said they would 'settle what we will do in half an hour'.

He had lunch with Clare and Betty Wood in Salisbury. What passed between the three of them is not known. Frosca later wrote to Winifred Nicholson (presumably on the basis of what Clare Wood told her) that Wood told his mother that he was being pursued and that he had heard voices telling him to commit suicide. Afterwards Betty drove all three of them to the station, where Wood bought a ticket for Waterloo. A porter called Alfred Hibberd saw the car pull up at about 1.40 pm. Wood jumped out and the car drove off. Hibberd saw him say goodbye to Betty, but was not sure if he said goodbye to his mother, as he himself then went into the station. Hibberd was told that a passenger in the cloakroom required a porter. This turned out to be Wood. He took his luggage on to the Number Two platform for the Waterloo train. A newsboy called Leslie Smailes, employed by Smith and Sons, sold Wood a book for eight shillings and sixpence. He said Wood appeared agitated and flushed; he sat on a seat near the bookstall but seemed too distracted to be able to read. He shut the book, stood up, and walked up and down the platform. He was standing only two feet from the corner of the bookstall when the train was coming in.

At this point, according to Smailes, Wood 'sort of ran and jumped and dived and screamed'. He jumped right in front of the engine.

The driver of the engine, Charles Davie, was on the point of pulling up in the usual way, on time, when his fireman, who was on the platform side of the engine cab, called out: 'Whoa! A man's jumped in front of the engine.' Davie applied the brake fully and the train pulled up quickly.

A Mr F.L. Buttar, a medical practitioner and police surgeon, said he was telephoned by the police and asked to go to the Southern Railway Station. When he arrived he saw the body of a man on a stretcher. He had received severe injuries to his trunk and legs. He was dead. The upper part of his body and head were uninjured. Buttar believed death to have been instantaneous, caused by shock following the injuries.

Buttar, Hibberd, Smailes and Davie all gave evidence to an

inquest in Salisbury conducted the following day by the City Coroner, Mr A.M. Wilson, sitting with a jury. They were told by P.C. Berryman of the Salisbury City Police that on searching Wood's body he had found a bloodstained envelope with the County Hotel's stamp on the flap. Wilson read what he could of the message; he said it appeared to him 'perfectly senseless' and evidence of the fact that Wood was not in his normal state of mind. As far as he could decipher them, the words were: 'Are they positive', followed by a word that might have been 'though' or 'through'. Then it continued: 'Are they positive as to who they are. Throwing away is not a big enough proof.' The coroner believed the words had been written by a man 'out of his senses'.

The jury returned a verdict that Wood died from shock following injuries sustained from his throwing himself in front of a train while of unsound mind. The coroner expressed deep sympathy for Dr Wood and his family on the loss of one he believed to have been a brilliant artist.

The last word was spoken with the controlled politeness of the English upper-middle classes into which Wood had been born. Dr Lucius Wood, veteran of the Western Front, embodiment of Huyton and good sense, rose to his feet and thanked the coroner for the sympathetic way in which he had conducted the inquest.

Christopher Wood's life was finished.

Across Europe, in apartments and hotels, in galleries and houses, there were detonations of private grief. News reached Wood's scattered friends at different times, awkwardly, sometimes from the wrong people. Frosca first heard when Winifred Reitlinger wrote to console her. The pathetic letters Wood's friends exchanged conjured the terrible shock, the stricken intake of breath, the slamming doors. The scribbled lines revealed the hellish despair of Frosca Munster, Tony Gandarillas, Winifred Nicholson and others who had loved him; what remained beyond reach were the feelings of Clare Wood as she surveyed the ruin of her fallen Icarus.

One of the last letters Kit wrote to her concluded: 'I love you so dearly and think of you as my best and dearest friend, and I shall never forget how perfectly sweet and understanding you have been towards me, and when I think of all the sacrifices you have made for me it makes me very ashamed, and makes me think you must care for me very much. Goodbye my sweet. All my love and I'll write as soon as I get back to Paris. Your loving Kit.'

It was appropriate that his final words should be of thanks. In the confused mesh of his motive and ambition, a desire to improve his painting, to realise his talent to the utmost, had become synonymous with his feeling of gratitude. His wish to please her led him indirectly to the strain that made him do the thing that in all imagining would hurt her most.

Clare Wood showed herself to be a woman of great resource. In the days between the death and the funeral she was so composed that friends worried for her. When Winifred Reitlinger wrote to offer her condolences, Clare Wood replied magnificently: 'Dear Miss Reitlinger, Thank you for your letter full of kind thoughts. I feel so sorry for you to have lost such a good friend as I know Kit was . . . Will you give Frosca my love and tell her I am thinking of her all the time. I am glad she will soon be seeing you.'

Lucy Wertheim telephoned Clare Wood on the evening of Kit's death. Mrs Wertheim, who was subsequently to enter a tense relationship with other parties over the possession of Wood's work, had bought a large number of his best paintings at advantageous prices: 'The Yellow Man', for instance, became hers for only £30. Wood had liked her and enthusiastically supported her proposed gallery; he borrowed money from her on account during the summer of 1930 against future work. Nevertheless, it was not tactful to telephone a house that had received such news only hours before.

Clare Wood's letter to Mrs Wertheim the following day was remarkable:

My dear Lucy,
Thank you for all your dear sympathy, of course I should love to see you but don't feel like talking to anyone until after tomorrow. The funeral is tomorrow at three. As I said in my wire I could see you on Sunday and love to or any other time you might choose. The telephone was so bad last evening and we were so upset that

Betty could hardly understand what you were saying. Thank you so much for telegraphing. You will understand dear why I can't write more now, my heart is too full but there is one thing I want you to do and that is if you know where Kit has sent his new pictures to, were they addressed to you?

I am so sorry to trouble you about it but we think we ought to know where they are, as Kit told me yesterday they were all packed up and sent off, but where to I don't know. Could you let me know this by return in case you cannot come to see me just now.

Very much love, dear Lucy. Ever Yours, Clare.

The lines of Clare Wood's character – her love and ambition for Kit, her altruism and politeness – were starkly laid out.

Frosca, meanwhile, was alone in Paris when she received Winifred Reitlinger's letter. She wrote to Winifred Nicholson (in French, though for once her terse and beautiful style fell apart):

Dear Winifred,
I beg you to write to me, speak to me of Kit. I know how much you loved him and what the loss of a man like him means. I am suffering terribly and the only consolation I have is to talk to the people he loved and who loved him like you. Teach me, tell me everything that is your idea of good, or of the hope you have in life. Perhaps that will bring me some consolation. I am appalled, I just cannot accept this injustice. I find it terrible to have to live on this earth if such atrocities are allowed to happen ... Dear Winifred, tell me something, write, I can think and speak of nothing but Kit. What an angel, what a marvellous being – and how will I be able to accept life without him, how can I carry on, start again. Life will never again give me something as perfect as Kit was for me. I am very unhappy, I need help. Write to me. I embrace you with all my heart. Frosca.

Winifred and Ben Nicholson replied, but Frosca was still almost demented: 'I cannot tell you what a state I am in. I don't even know if I am alive . . . Nothing I say can explain to you the state of my heart.'

Tony Gandarillas was in Biarritz. He wrote a postcard to Winifred Nicholson: 'Kit will always be alive between us – We must do all we can for his memory – I am so frightfully unhappy that I can't write yet and tell you all I want – He meant to me more than my children and all my family, a friend like Kit is very rare in this world. I didn't deserve his friendship and great affection . . . Don't leave me quite alone – I must be near Kit's friends.'

In a letter from Madrid he wrote: 'I also see exactly like you in most of his paintings that journey to the far horizon and the longing for which is beyond this world. He is gone and I can't part with him. I think I could have saved him and I feel more miserable each day.'

Wood had once described Gandarillas as a 'chittering, charming, childish and always cheerful small monkey'. He was irresponsible, but he was irresistible. It was probably with him that Wood first smoked opium, and this knowledge added to Gandarillas's torment. Both he and Cocteau had had the money and the sense to undergo cures; if only he had stayed closer to Wood he might have seen the danger signs and financed some treatment. Gandarillas was tormented by the feeling that he might have prevented the catastrophe. He wrote to H.S. Ede, the curator of the Tate Gallery, who had become a friend of Wood's in London: 'It is marvellous of you to have done all that work in Minton Place. I couldn't have done it. I think I would have died. I couldn't have seen so many things of the past, the memories of the last ten years of my life. I can't have any serenity over Kit's death. I know it is wrong but I can't help it. I feel I should have saved him.'

By the end of September, Gandarillas's anguish was no better. He wrote to Ede: 'You know what it means to me, his work. It is all my life as I have been waiting for the day he will become great. Whatever I do I can't think of anything else but Kit and I feel more and more unhappy each day.'

The days of Taormina, the lobsters in bed, the terrace with the Roman mosaic; the lovely earnest Englishman out painting all morning then back for lunch beneath the trees . . . it was hard for Gandarillas to believe that this was the ending to which the treacherous years had all the time been leading. His anguish led him into a nervous collapse.

'I can't have any serenity . . .' This was the agony of Wood's

Christopher Wood

death for both Tony Gandarillas and Frosca Munster. Apart from
the pain of bereavement, there was in his case the feeling of
impotent frustration, the sense that he could have helped; and in
her case there was a raging resentment of what she saw as a
terrible injustice.

If anyone were to have serenity it would be Winifred
Nicholson; at least she had religious faith. In her short memoir,
'Kit', she expressed her feelings in the conventional language of
her Christian Science; she concluded on a note of radiant
optimism. But this was later. At the time she, too, was distraught.
Her marriage to Ben was coming to an end and she went to the
Isle of Wight, then to Paris, as though to be near Kit.

Beneath the clouds of her rhetoric, she had her characteristic
moments of insight. 'Besides the awful greatness of the universe,
its solitude, its silence, its power, the vast deep unknown, there is
only one thing as awe-inspiring, and that is the soul of a man who
is inspired by a purpose that risks all to scale the high skies, to
aspire to abstract beauty herself.'

'Risks all' did accurately suggest the recklessness of Wood's
pursuit of his artistic vision in the last summer of his life. He was
not willingly self-destructive, but it is clear that he did not care
whether the pursuit destroyed him: he was indifferent. And
according to Winifred Nicholson, in a letter to H.S. Ede, Wood
was aware of the possible consequences of his single-mindedness:
'The tragic element was always hard upon his heels. What the
tragic element was, I, not being God, do not know, but I felt that
fear of it always from the moment I saw him . . . I have never felt
fear like that – I remember it when we were walking along the
quay in Paris at night under the quivering poplars, beside the
quaking river – and he turned of a sudden and said, "I must enjoy
every minute of this springtime in Paris – You know it might be
one's last." '

Such scraps of conversation, even if only preserved in scribbled
letters no one sought to publish, made fertile ground for a
romantic myth. Wood's physical beauty, the mystery of his awful
death, his bisexual glamour, the parties of the beau monde, the
drugs, the frenzied work in a 'curious lonely country by the sea',

(97)

the beautiful boy as victim of a cruel world . . . It is not surprising that Christopher Wood became in the 1930s a minor cult hero.

Much of the interest in him was of the kind that always attaches to such figures. Yet at the core of Wood's life and work there remained something that was not so easy to dismiss. Winifred Nicholson was always a partial witness with an evangelical view to propound, but she was also a distinguished painter who knew Wood well. There was almost always something true in what she had to say. This is what she wrote in a private letter to H.S. Ede:

> Those last pictures are to me at the passport office of madness. Of course I don't value those last pictures as his highest work. It is a swan song, but like a swan song carries with it the haste, the doom of the end . . . not because his song is complete but because he knows it is his last chance – and he'll put his soul into it to the last ounce. Not one of those pictures carry in them a bud – a new life for other pictures – I mean that no one who is creating would want to have one in his room – as one would his earlier ones. Any Cézanne, however late and complete, carries that bud – like all images of the Buddha carry the tiny image of the next Buddha to be, in the circle of their halo . . . High courage, daring is the key word of his painting – something flaunted in the face of suicide.

To Frosca Munster she wrote: 'I consider, you know, that he practically gave his life for those pictures. He put everything he knew and every force he possessed into them, and then had nothing left to battle with his opium difficulty – which he could have coped with quite easily, like Tony and other people can, if he had not put his whole soul with that whole-hearted strength and impulse which was his more than anyone's . . . Anyone who has painted knows that such work can only be done at great cost – incalculable cost.'

'He practically gave his life for those pictures . . .' This was the peculiarity of Christopher Wood. His own letters from Tréboul made it clear that he was prepared to ignore all danger in order to get his vision on to canvas. His determination for his art was stronger than his attachment to his own survival. Although such a choice may be central to romantic myths, it is extraordinarily unusual in reality. What does it mean?

It implies, to begin with, a disregard for self, for the meanest animal instinct of self-preservation. Wood did have, periodically at least, that disregard. Although he was proud of his work, he was not proud of himself: he was not at ease with his nature, his impulses or his crippled body.

Winifred Nicholson wondered in her letter to Frosca Munster what it was that made Kit so unhappy, so eager to grasp the moments of calm and sunlight when he had stayed with her at Bankshead. She did not know, but thought it went back to his childhood, to his parents, to his illness and the pain it brought him.

At the end, on 21 August 1930 at Salisbury Station, Christopher Wood killed himself because he was of unsound mind, as the jury rightly believed. That unsoundness was precipitated by that most unromantic of causes – a 'combination of factors'. He was suffering paranoid delusions, and it is possible that these were the first symptoms of a psychosis, of a schizophrenic breakdown. However, he was older than most young men when such illnesses begin; there was no family history of it; and there are simpler explanations of the symptoms. He had worked too hard, he had seriously abused powerful drugs and he was extremely worried about money. Ben Nicholson wrote to H.S. Ede: 'Perhaps that lack of the money he seemed to need had got out of all hand. I know he wanted to marry Frosca but felt he had not the money and must give her the best of everything.' It was one thing to be a penurious student in an attic studio; in fact it was part of the bohemian life, particularly when the hunger could be assuaged by large meals in Tony Gandarillas's house in the Avenue Montaigne: but to have the woman you loved denied you a second time because you were still too poor, despite being, as he believed, 'the first English artist since Whistler to be shown in Paris' . . . this was bitterly hard to take.

Wood may also have felt what Winifred Nicholson described in his pictures: that there was no way forward, that he had forced his talent to the limit. If he were to progress from the paintings of 1930 he might, like Ben Nicholson, have had to start again.

Within a year, Nicholson had turned to abstract painting. The Seven & Five Society no longer exhibited figurative work, and English art, so slow to catch the tide of Modernism, began to find its way. Wood was not interested in this kind of painting. His vision derived from his apprehension of the real world. There is pathos in the fact that what may have been his last picture, 'Zebra and Parachute', is dominated by the Villa Savoye in all its harsh, abstracted angles. What was human – the man on the parachute – was already dead.

The subject of the delusions provided a further clue: the Guinness family. The Meraud affair humiliated Wood because it made public all his shortcomings: his drugs, his poverty, his homosexual past. He had not wanted these to be the talk of Cannes and Paris, particularly since his homosexual feelings were intimately bound up with his private debt to his mother and the passage of illness in his youth which had formed his creative ambition. He was frightened by the power of his feeling for Meraud, though he was also ashamed of his inconstancy in the year's separation. Mrs Guinness had read his mind too well: she had doubled his humiliation.

The pressures on Christopher Wood at the end were really of his own devising. He had set out to make his art worthy of his mother and by it to repay her for having saved his life. In so doing, he would validate his life and its choices against the judgement of his father, of his father's generation and all the presumptions of Huyton and Edwardian England. By the time he reached a point when his art was worthy of the task he had set it, the factors in the equation were changed and haywire. He himself had developed; he was exhausted, strung out from drugs, poor, unbalanced and with no artistic way forward. He had come up with the answer he had set out to find, but by then the questions had all subtly changed.

Wood's paintings survived as pleasing and independent works of art with little need of literary explication. The much-remarked 'simplicity' of his character and the direct and figurative style both worked to his advantage. In the years since his death his reputation has slowly risen, though exhibitions have not always been able to show his best work because it is so scattered.

Retrospective exhibitions of his work were held at the Wertheim Gallery in 1931 and the Reid Lefèvre galleries in 1932. Opinions on the merit of his painting ran from the ecstatic to the dismissive, but most were favourable. Some newspaper reviewers were unhappy about a 'childish' quality in the painting and about a clumsy line in the drawing. Most of these reservations collapsed, however, in the face of the Tréboul paintings, which were almost universally admired. The debate was then about the scale of the achievement; its existence was not seriously disputed.

Of the 1932 exhibition at the Reid Lefèvre galleries Paul Nash wrote that the paintings 'seem to express, beyond almost any work I can recall, the mood and consciousness of their author'. Cyril Connolly wrote in the *Architectural Review* that Wood 'had something that other English painters have not got and it was only visible in his late pictures; a kind of architectural pleasure, a deeper happiness at getting over to France than the others felt and a stronger palette to express it', which was partly true, but seems to say as much about Connolly's francophilia as about Wood's painting.

John Piper was a sympathetic visitor to the exhibition, and wrote with slightly muddled passion about what he saw. He was quick to stamp on the 'childlike' criticism, though his method of doing so was not conclusive and depended on praising Wood's restraint. Piper's most interesting reaction was his belief, shared with his fellow-painter Winifred Nicholson, that Wood might actually have 'realised himself more or less fully'. It is not completely clear how Piper reached this conclusion, but it was certainly interesting that while most non-painting critics spoke of what might have been and of the tragic loss, Winifred Nicholson and John Piper suspected that there might not, in fact, have been any more to come.

In London, the *Morning Post*, most conservative of daily papers, was deeply impressed. Wood's early work, the art critic wrote, 'was proof of genius in bud, but few of his most ardent admirers could have hoped for the wonder of its opening apparent in the collection on view.' To this reviewer, Wood was 'the most gifted young artist of this century'.. It is impossible not to think of the emotions with which the newspaper was passed across the breakfast table at Reddish House, Broad Chalke.

The *Manchester Guardian* hoped that 'the fact of his early death will not make a peg upon which to hang a sentimental myth. His work was good enough to have no need of it.' The *Spectator* gave and took away: 'Too much must not be made of his actual achievement in spite of the unusual promise that is evident in his last work, but it was good enough to secure him a place at least in the history of contemporary painting.'

A place at least . . . That was what Wood's work had won him, and the nature of that place could later be seen more clearly by critics and public. For Wood's friends and family there was the anguish of thinking that he might have done more; that if he had painted for just another five years he would have established himself unarguably – beyond captious remarks about clumsiness, childishness or bright young things – as the equal, for instance, of Sickert. Against this must be set John Piper and Winifred Nicholson's fear that he had, like the swan, sung his song.

Wood's paintings have consistently increased in value over the last sixty-five years, with the best fetching prices of £50,000 or more. The unsentimental register of the market is one way of judging a painter's worth. Another instructive way of looking again is to focus on the watercolours. Many of these, done while he was travelling with Gandarillas in the Mediterranean, are not subject to the same reservations as the early oils. And, as Geoffrey Grigson pointed out in a subtle review of Wood's watercolours at the Reid-Lefèvre galleries in 1934: 'He could do [his] best in oil; but he could also do it in watercolour; and since watercolour is the most deceptively difficult of media, one's belief in his excellence is refined.'

A final clue to Wood's status can be found in superior criticism, such as that of Geoffrey Grigson, or that of Eric Newton, the art historian and *Sunday Times* critic. Newton wrote more knowledgeably than any of his contemporaries about Wood's painting. He was an enthusiast, and, on the principle of excluding extreme opinions from the consensus, he should perhaps be discounted; but the internal authority of his writing is persuasive.

Reviewing the huge exhibition mounted by the Redfern Gallery at the New Burlington galleries in 1938, Newton wrote:

> In order to realise Christopher Wood's achievement one has to ask oneself how many British painters of our century could fill a gallery of this size with 500 paintings without seeming monotonous or pretentious or trivial. The question is not a rhetorical one. I could think of three painters who could do it, but not more than three.
>
> Throughout his early years . . . he rarely escaped the influence of this painter or that, and yet everything he did took its life from his own vitality and not from the mannerism of the moment. He imitates Van Gogh or Braque or Modigliani in an attempt to discover the secrets of their language, not from a desire to emulate their performance.
>
> But by 1928 he had shaken off this dependence. He not only had discovered his own language but also could turn it to astonishing account. In the paintings of his last two years Christopher Wood can be compared to no one but himself . . . His nearest parallel is perhaps the poetry of Keats. His paintings of Tréboul – the church on the cliff, the white houses among the rocks – have a clarity and a lyrical intensity that take one right back to Piero della Francesca.
>
> Partly this is due to a colour-sense so finely adjusted as to make almost any other contemporary British painting seem by comparison a clumsy hit-or-miss approximation; and partly to a gift for so organising his picture within its frame that everything in it is immovable, inevitable . . .
>
> Those who have secretly arranged their own list of British painters, from Hogarth onwards, in order of merit, will probably rewrite it after seeing this exhibition.

Wood's funeral took place at All Saints Church, Broad Chalke. The officiating clergy were Dr Prideaux and Mr Fuller, the vicar of Broad Chalke. As the coffin entered the church the organ played 'O Rest in the Lord', and as the cortège left for the churchyard it played 'I know that my Redeemer Liveth'. The grave was lined with flowers and the coffin bore the inscription: 'John Christopher Wood. Age 29.' Clare Wood was not listed among the mourners. Perhaps the local paper did not think she was important; perhaps her courage failed her.

As the summer turned to autumn the winds began to blow again on the coast of Brittany, rattling the green shutters of the Hôtel Ty-Mad. The holiday-makers were gone, the beaches were deserted: in the narrow lanes above the Plage St Jean the fishermen climbed up to their whitewashed cottages where their anxious wives were waiting for them. The festivals of saints' days, the burials, the baptisms and the mending of nets went on into the winter. The exotic visitors of the early summer were forgotten. All except one.

Alone in the Ty-Mad was the anguished figure of Max Jacob. On 1 October 1930 he wrote to Frosca Munster:

> Dear Madame, my good friend,
> I didn't dare to write. I still don't. I live with him in my thoughts night and day. He never leaves me. I cannot speak of him; I remain stunned by his disappearance. My God, is it true that we will never see his dear face again, never hear him speak again, so admirably, so well. Oh my dear, dear boy! And he could have carried on with his career as a painter that he'd started so well . . . I would very much like to have some details about how he died. Tony told me it was an accident and not suicide – and anyway why would he kill himself? He was loved by us and he loved us in return and I don't think a problem with money could have depressed him that much. All we had was at his disposal, my God, my poor boy, my poor dearest, dearest boy. I will never stop grieving. You talk about your loss, Madame, but you're still young; I promise you that at my age I can never be alone without the presence of the dead assaulting me and I cry, I am crying as I write to you: weep with me, a poor sick old man who has survived so many young people that I have loved and tried to help. May God have pity on our pain and on our grief. My dear Kit!!!

Frosca had asked various of Kit's friends for recollections or tributes for a book she was hoping to compile. Most of the responses were too solemn, too obviously eulogistic or, in Cocteau's case ('Wood first met me when I . . .'), too self-serving. Only Max Jacob had let her have the full force of his feeling, though this tribute too was, in its way, unusable. A little later, when he had collected himself, Jacob wrote a '*Souvenir sur Christopher Wood en Bretagne*', an abbreviated version of which was published by the Redfern Gallery in their catalogue to the exhibition of the complete works in 1938. This is what he wrote:

The Bretons, Kit used to say, make you believe in Paradise. He understood them well because he was like them. Always a little bit sad, even when joking, quiet until you got to know them – and it was not easy to get to know Kit – but charming in friendship, and oddly childlike . . . I saw the pious, honest girls who waited on us wipe away their tears and I know that they prayed for his soul . . .

Beneath these trees and on these rocks in the corner of the Bay of Douarnenez Kit lived two months, which were alas to be his last. Neither the storms of October nor the awful knowledge of what was to come have chased away their memory. The wind is rattling the door of my room and I dare not go out. I don't want to creep with funereal tread across the landing that used to echo to the sound of our schoolboy laughter . . . or to the confident sound of our work. The fresh canvas is no longer there, not on the wall or the table, not among the pots of house paint or on top of the mirrored wardrobe: no more those great paintings completed in two hours but shot through with indefinable, melancholy doubt. I will never again see from his balcony the larch which hides the sea and the little chapel he loved to paint. 'One can hear the birds singing in your trees,' one of the few poets who knew him commented; and Kit was so modest and so poetic himself that he was less flattered by the compliment than touched by the beauty of the idea.

Today the sea is green and the sky is black. Kit, who always saw Finistère through the eyes of his own country (that of the Brontë sisters) could have painted this autumn in the colours of Courbet. A few days ago, just before dawn, his voice awoke me: having lived in another world he seemed even more real than when on this earth. I went downstairs. He was there, and his characteristics, those of the philosopher-warrior, his openness, his sad and humorous good nature, were shining in his face. He mentioned two names that I cannot repeat, and I felt his protective arm around my shoulder.

May God take care of this man who was a hero, strong and sure, a child whose curiosity touched everything.

Max Jacob was besotted with Wood, but his choice of the word 'hero' was significant. Wood had lived a life of cultural daring: his heroism was in his dedication to a wider world. Or as Winifred Nicholson put it: 'Longing in him was not discontent. Life to him was not a sense of existing but a driving power which set him striving in the endeavour that was high adventure.'

The days grew shorter in the vale round Broad Chalke. Clare Wood had kept all Kit's letters from the day he went to Paris and now she had time to look back through them. From Alphonse Kahn's house he had written: 'I honestly believe I am born under a lucky star.' From Bruges, where he had gone with Tony Gandarillas, he was struck by the sight of people at prayer: 'Some day I shall paint exactly what I saw then.' And he had; at Tréboul in 1930. From Tunisia in April 1922 he wrote: 'Some day I hope to repay you for all your great kindness and love and the care you took of me when I was ill. I never forget.'

From Sicily the same year: 'It is surely not intelligent to worry about the time when one will die. Live for the present, not much for the future, and think you are going to live for ever.'

From Paris in 1924: 'All I want is to succeed, and I shall do it somehow.' From Le Canadel in August 1924: 'I know I can be a great artist because I understand and feel the things I like so much if I can only be left with them.' From Paris in the spring of 1925: 'The time goes terribly quickly. I hope the whole of my life won't pass as fast as this.'

At the start of 1928, after his affair with Meraud, he had written: 'I feel freer, happier and with my face in the wind, which is a real exhilaration and ready to start on the biggest journey one can make. I will get there and I do trust it will be quick.' And from Tréboul in 1930: 'It's extraordinary how I have to hurry, hurry from one thing to another, but it's just the one moment or the chance I have to get on.'

In his last year he had repeated his favourite proverb: '*La vie s'arrange . . .*' 'Life always works out'; but he added '. . . *mais autrement*' – 'not how you expect it'.

Each year in August, on the anniversary of Kit's death, Winifred Reitlinger sent flowers to Mrs Wood. She wrote back one year: 'I have them in my room by Kit's photograph and quite close to a lovely picture. The door of the house is wide open all the time so everyone in the house enjoys them. It means a great deal to me to know you are thinking of him and I love you for doing it. I feel certain he knows everything, especially everything that is being done out of love. It is eleven years now since he left us but he is the same Kit – just as lovable.'

Clare Wood kept in touch with Tony Gandarillas and worried about Frosca. Her letters remained firm and composed until 1942 when she suffered the first of a series of breakdowns. In 1944 she spent eight weeks in a nursing home in Salisbury; her final letter was a trembling pencil scrawl.

It was too much to bear. In the first winter of his death it seemed like failure, when she had only those letters to read. There were the paintings, too, but their wild colours and melancholy doubt were not the kind of things that people understood in Broad Chalke.

Clare Wood was much occupied and much exhausted by the running of a doctor's house, alone with no domestic help. It was to this strain that she attributed her nervous collapse.

When it was dark it would be time to draw the curtains and to shut away, as before, the troublesome events outside; but with them now would also be closed for ever the foreign shining world: the noonday sun on a plate of lemons in Taormina, the glimpsed face of Mussolini in the Roman crowd, the candle-lit gardens of the Comte de Beaumont; the lonely country by the sea with the ships blazing on their final voyage, the mystery of which her son had tried to grasp.

The chandelier in the dining room would draw up the light only of its own reflection in the polished table, as damp England settled down into another autumn.

Richard Hillary

A mile and a half from Broad Chalke in Wiltshire is the small village of Fifield Bavant. In May 1995, fifty years after VE Day, the village held its celebrations. In the tiny Norman church there was a display that included various wartime mementoes – identity card, medals and so on – that had belonged to the pilot and writer Richard Hillary, a branch of whose family lives in the village. A modest crowd of mainly local people came to pay their tributes.

British celebrations of the event split people along a bitter little divide that has run through much of the domestic political discussion of the last quarter of the century. On the one hand were the latter-day Empire Loyalists who tried to suggest that the global war had been won by Britain alone, and that the decisive participation of the great powers, the United States and the Soviet Union, had been little more than a convenience. On the other were the disgruntled internationalists who were unwilling to believe that Britain might ever have performed a useful or morally just role, and that to suggest otherwise was a conspiracy of an undefined 'establishment'.

Somewhere among the bunting and the bitterness there were reasonable accounts of what British forces achieved. What might have struck anyone who had no hard allegiance to either side of the political fault line was not so much the size of the British contribution to the Allied effort as its continuity. From 1939 to 1945, from Holland to Tunisia, from Italy to Burma, from Normandy to the waters of the Atlantic, Britain was continually fighting. Its singular position placed it under certain obligations. The disgruntled internationalists pointed out that Halifax, not Churchill, might easily have been its leader; the nationalist romantics claimed that the 'British character' was immune to such infection. But however it came about, the isolation of 1940 and 1941 was met in a distinctive way. The International Brigades who fought against Franco in Spain were motivated by a self-conscious political idealism, but the infantry at Dunkirk and the fighter pilots in the Battle of Britain had no such crusading passion. Memoirs of the War made it seem as though at times it was almost a matter of taste: the Nazis were so lacking in self-awareness, so crude, so strangely unimpressive in their way, that they must – albeit reluctantly – be taken on and defeated. Their army might be the finest ever to take the field, their air force might conceivably, as its commander claimed, be able to clear the RAF from the sky, then bomb Britain into submission; but the people behind these outstandingly well-drilled services – those men with their goose-step, their bragging and their hysterical rallies – were preposterous.

Although this contempt lasted throughout the War, it lived, in 1940, with fear. The British armies were on the retreat; and while the Navy went about its work unseen, it was the RAF – the smallest service, whose members often fought in single combat – that seemed best to embody Britain's position. The public had been bombed, battered and scared, yet in the scruffy, nonchalant figures of the Spitfire and Hurricane pilots it found men on whom it could fasten its hopes.

Many of the airmen were from Commonwealth countries, many more from Poland or Czechoslovakia. The RAF seemed to have a different social feeling from the other services. Those who cared about such things noted a preponderance of 'minor public school' men; they called them the Brylcreem Boys in semi-affectionate recognition of the fact that no 'gentleman' would use such cheap hair cream. None of this mattered. What was significant was the character of a man who wanted to fly fighter planes. He needed to be competitive and scornful, eager for a chance to prove himself; he needed also a rarer combination of qualities: he had both to be young and alert, yet attach no great importance to his life. This was the requirement that came before patriotism, political belief or even skill in flying. It was not like being in the infantry where, even during the slaughters of the Western Front in 1914–18, you had a better then even chance of surviving. If you flew more than a certain number of missions in

1940–1 you were not likely to come back. This did not mean that all the pilots were reckless, willing to risk their lives for the sake of the chase and kill above the clouds; nor did it mean that they had to be more patriotically motivated. It meant only they had to have, at heart, some indifference to dying. The public were encouraged by Churchill's speeches to believe this indifference was heroic; the pilots themselves did not see it as such. Far from subscribing to the myth, they tried to subvert it. They cultivated understatement in a private slang; they came close to callousness: they claimed to feel nothing.

If the RAF represented Britain in those two years, and if the fighter pilots were its epitome, there was a short time when the most emblematic of them all was Richard Hillary. His book about his experiences, *The Last Enemy*, was published in 1942 and struck some mysterious answering note in the British wartime mood. Christopher Wood's stricken man on a parachute had found his powerful, symbolic hour.

It was fitting that the hero of the moment should be a twenty-one-year-old Australian with an ambivalent feeling about 'English' virtues. Hillary was born on 20 April 1919, in Sydney. His father Michael was a civil servant of Anglo-Irish descent; his mother Edwyna had Scottish and Spanish blood. Michael Hillary had served in India and Mesopotamia during the Great War, had won the DSO and was twice mentioned in dispatches. From 1921 to 1923 he was private secretary to the Australian Prime Minister, Billy Hughes. Then, when Richard was three, Michael Hillary was posted to Australia House in London. Richard lived the rest of his life in England and did not appear to think his Australian beginnings important. He was sent to boarding schools at an early age and adopted the manners they taught. He was too emotionally open to be regarded as typical, but he certainly viewed himself as English.

As a child he was pugnacious and self-assertive. He would hop about in a fury if he was denied, but soon afterwards he could laugh at himself. His nerves and emotions were close to the surface, and he was tiresomely quick-tempered. The loss of a game of tennis or beach cricket would mean a heavy fire of hurled bats and rackets; the thwarting of any whim would mean tears and abuse. It was some compensation to his parents that he was doggedly truthful. When he had behaved badly he never sought to escape the blame; his father could recall no instance in his life in which he had shown less than complete dedication to the truth. Richard respected his father, but did not feel close to him. Michael Hillary was a friendly, hospitable man up to a point; but he had strict views on how things should be done. For warmth of emotional contact, Richard Hillary turned, like Christopher Wood, to his mother. Personal connections were her strong point: as a spiritualist she even believed in communication with the dead. She was a good-looking woman, mild-mannered and devoted, to the point of indulgence, to her hot-headed son. Photographs of Richard as a child show a plump, cheeky-looking boy with the confident look in the eye of one who will jump off the highest wall, take on the biggest bully and persecute those less brave than himself.

Michael Hillary's visit to London preceded a permanent posting as Auditor-General in the Sudan, so the question of boarding schools arose at once. The real separation came in September 1926 when Richard was seven and a half. Shortly before their departure for the Sudan his parents left him in the headmaster's study at his preparatory school. The full implications of his abandonment somehow escaped the child until the moment when his mother leant down to kiss him goodbye. His skin turned crimson, his eyes shone, his jaw clamped tight. He watched his mother leave, but he did not cry. She had taught him to be a 'man'.

He wrote to her in Khartoum, begging her to take him away. Mother and son had developed the rugged intimacy that was necessary in a relationship which had to survive separation for two-thirds of the year. When they were reunited Richard was too happy to worry about school: the last thing he wanted to do in the holidays was to trail round alternative places, to be shown down further brown corridors that smelled of loneliness and chalk and boiled dinners. He finished his time at the school; in the phrase employed in such cases, he 'stuck it out'.

In 1931 he went to Shrewsbury, a public school in Shropshire, where he took part enthusiastically in the traditional activities. At the age of fifteen he was taught English by a Mr McEachran, an inspiring teacher who, Hillary told listeners to an American broadcast in 1942, was the most important influence in his life. Richard told him that he wanted to be a writer when he grew up and that his model would be Steinbeck: McEachran encouraged him, and Richard read widely. He became a handsome and sexually precocious youth; he lost his virginity at the age of sixteen, a feat that was the subject of incredulous schoolboy envy.

In the school holidays he would go off to Europe on his own rather than visit his parents in Khartoum. His mother agreed only reluctantly to this arrangement, but it enabled Richard to learn French and German as well as to enlarge his sexual experience. He took what public school had to offer, but remained cantankerous and provocative. He had few friends at Shrewsbury where most of his contemporaries regarded him as aloof and unreliable; a kind of choric response developed at the mention of his name: 'Oh, that shit Hillary.'

He became tediously argumentative and crudely personal in his comments; he refused to accept such concepts as 'house loyalty', and this made him unpopular. Although he was intellectually more mature than the other boys he was never chosen for any honours or teams. Forced by his parents' absence to develop some self-sufficiency at an early age, he had allowed it to develop into an assumed superiority. His housemaster wrote: 'He seemed to dislike the conventional views of things, often merely because they were conventional . . . He liked shocking people in a mild way.' These were also the characteristics of the adult man: he was inclined to argue and strike attitudes, but he never had the intellectual curiosity or perhaps the capacity to develop coherent alternatives to the conventions he opposed. *The Last Enemy* was at times an angry and rebellious book, but in his deepest beliefs its author did not seriously differ from others of his age and occupation.

Hillary was none the less an inquisitive and intelligent boy, good enough at work to win a place at Trinity College, Oxford, where he went in October 1937. Trinity was a small and friendly college whose spacious garden included a lime walk that dated from the eighteenth century. It was noted less for its scholars than for its sportsmen. Hillary said that the ethos of the college at the time was one of 'alert philistinism', though contemporaries in other colleges questioned the adjective. Trinity was often thought to be rather grander than it really was, perhaps out of confusion with Trinity, Cambridge. Scott Fitzgerald's Jay Gatsby made this assumption when claiming that as an 'Oggsford man' it was at Trinity that he had spent his undergraduate days – 'I always carry a souvenir of my Oxford days. It was taken in Trinity quad – the man on my left is the Earl of Doncaster.'

Hillary's main contribution to the college was as an oarsman. He had grown two inches since school, but his disruptive personality made him a tricky crew member: on one occasion he engaged in a fist fight with the bow man Derek Graham. He stroked the Trinity boat in his first year when it went to the Head of the River (came first in the college summer races). This achievement meant that he was considered for the university eight to row against Cambridge. He would not figure prominently among the twenty-five-year-old colonial postgraduates who make up the team today, but in 1938 a slightly-built natural athlete with a hangover could still do well.

Nearly all the young men at Trinity had been to public schools (Hillary claimed that they came from the 'better' public schools), where they had been well enough taught to be able to drift through three years at Oxford and still gain a respectable second-class degree. Hillary read history under the tutorship of Melville Paterson and Reggie Weaver, of whose teaching it was said that 'Patters can't and Reggie won't'. The public school atmosphere of the college was carried into Oxford life: it was considered unacceptable to be different or unconventional in any way. Displays of learning were as suspect as suede shoes or beards. This sense of cohesiveness or uniformity was enforced by the enormous number of clubs and societies which offered an even tighter bonding and even stricter elimination of the 'peculiar'.

Societies, however, usually have a defensive purpose, and what Hillary and his friends wished to protect themselves against was the bungling and bureaucracy of politics. They knew that a war was coming, but they wanted to fight it on their own terms. It had been made inevitable by the low calibre of the 1930s politicians throughout Europe, who had fudged, postponed and appeased; but when it came to the action, Hillary's generation wanted it to be swift, clear and, as far as possible, undisciplined. There was little sense of idealism in their attitude and none at all of ideology.

A University Air Squadron offered training at the Government's expense: Hillary learned to fly on Tiger Moths at an airfield outside Oxford. Members of the squadron regarded students who did artillery or infantry exercises with the Officers Training Corps as absurdly solemn. Although he stressed how uninterested he was in politics, Hillary was scornful of left-wing undergraduates who had fallen under the influence of the Auden group. Such people, he thought, despised the middle classes from whom they received their education, but could not gain entrance to the world of labour they admired. They were thus useless. Hillary's criticism of them was less a political than a practical one: their beliefs, he reasoned, had rendered them incapable of participating. It seems curious that Hillary was able to overlook so completely the Spanish Civil War, in which many such men had found redeeming action and even death. He must have been aware of the participation of George Orwell and Stephen Spender in Spain, and of the death of others, such as John Cornford. The French writer André Malraux, despite his lack of flying experience, raised a squadron for the Republicans. The Prime Minister Léon Blum was unable to supply planes officially because he needed Britain's continuing support against the Germans, and Britain was fastidiously neutral in Spain on the grounds that the 'Bolshevists' were as bad as the Fascists. However, Blum managed to allow some planes to find their way, unarmed, over the Pyrenees, for the use of Malraux, who lobbed out bombs by hand on to Franco's forces, who were using planes supplied by Hitler.

In *The Last Enemy* Hillary condensed the left-wing position in a pacifist figure called David Rutter. Although the name of Rutter appears on no university lists, he appears to have been a real person whom Hillary wished to protect, by changing his name, from public disapproval. In a dialogue with Rutter Hillary clearly stated his own reasons for fighting in the RAF: 'In the first place I shall get paid and have good food. Secondly, I have none of your sentiments about killing, much as I admire them. In a fighter plane, I believe, we have found a way to return to war as it ought to be, war which is individual combat between two people, in which one either kills or is killed. It's exciting, it's individual and it's disinterested. I shan't be sitting behind a long-range gun working out how to kill people sixty miles away. I shan't get maimed: either I shall get killed or I shall get a few pleasant putty medals and enjoy being stared at in a night club.'

His idea of what war ought *not* to be was based on the Western Front, with its long-range artillery bombardments and mass, anonymous slaughters. War in the air would be 'exciting, individual and disinterested', by the last of which he meant free from ideological or institutionalised motive.

He was right about killing or being killed, wrong about not being maimed.

Hillary had matured considerably since leaving Shrewsbury. Straightforward young Trinity men like Sammy Stockton and Frank Waldron no longer considered him a 'shit' but were in awe of his charm, sophistication and physical daring. On one occasion he climbed out of the window of a second-floor room in Garden Quad and inched his way along a narrow ledge to the amazed protest of friends on the ground. He liked to test his courage because he was aware of his limitations.

On various excursions to London he impressed his friends with his precocious *savoir-vivre*. He favoured a club in Beak Street called the Bag o' Nails, where a bored-looking band played shuffling music while girls smooched up to half-cut customers at dimly lit tables. While Hillary's friends, in varying degrees of embarrassment and virginity, managed only to buy warm, over-priced champagne, Hillary always contrived to leave with the best-looking girl. They suspected that with Hillary she even 'did it' for free. The others left with empty pockets and nothing to take home but the cheery call of Millie, the owner, to 'remember the dear old Bag'.

In Oxford Hillary joined the staff of the university magazine *Isis*. His father was anxious that he should follow him into the colonial service, and as a compromise Hillary modified his declared ambition from 'writer' to 'journalist'. To this end he spent more time on *Isis* and neglected his rowing. He was consequently dropped from the Trinity first eight, though this did not prevent him setting off for Germany in July 1938 to take part in a regatta.

By describing themselves as an Oxford University crew, Hillary and Frank Waldron had persuaded the German and Hungarian governments to pay for ten of them to travel to Bad Ems in Germany and thence to Budapest. They suffered the usual fate of sporting students on an overseas trip; their exuberant drinking was encouraged by hosts anxious to see their own teams do well. The competitive atmosphere was intensified and soured by Nazi pride. A local coach found them an almost watertight boat, though they did no practice. A number of well-muscled Aryan youths sneered at them before the race, and a misunderstanding over starting orders meant that they set off some way behind five German crews. Halfway up the course someone spat on the Oxford boat from a bridge, and this apparently provided the necessary spur to their performance. They stormed up the last part of the course to win the General Goering cup by two-fifths of a second. It was not a popular win.

In Budapest two days later, the team was sabotaged by dastardly Hungarians, who filled them with wine and goulash and made them row three times in the heat of the day. The triumph of Bad Ems could not be repeated: Sammy Stockton, the man who had stroked them to victory in Germany, failed to stay the course. Defeat went down well with their hosts, however, who had a further explanation of why the 'Oxford University Team' had lost: a cartoon in a local paper showed eight men in a boat looking over their shoulder at a naked girl in a skiff.

The delights of Europe drew Hillary back twice before the War, once on a farewell gastronomic tour of Brittany, and once to a regatta in Cannes. In England he had begun an affair with a girl called Anne Mackenzie, whom he had first met in the summer of 1938 after his triumph on the Thames. His letters to her show a capacity for despair that would have surprised Frank Waldron and the other militantly unsentimental members of the Trinity boat. It was camouflaged in some self-conscious banter: 'The spring has had a bad effect on me,' he wrote in May 1939, 'and I have burst into verse – also composed a song about mountains and the moon and you! You must hear it sometime. It will thaw the icy walls of your heart.'

The letters show that Hillary had developed a mental framework and a vocabulary for dealing with such affairs. His approach was conventionally romantic but with a ragged edge of truculence. In July he wrote: 'Sometimes now I wish there would be war – as I feel then that so many things would clarify themselves and you and I could be together again anyhow for a short time and there would be no false values and muddled thinking. Life would have a purpose while it lasted. I'm afraid that I'm becoming very heavy and rather boring. But a young man in love was ever a pitiable object. I wish I could be with you – have you in my arms, but the day when I shall be able to do that again seems very remote.'

There was something false about the feeling Hillary was claiming; and, like most of his relationships with women, his affair with Anne Mackenzie was short-lived. His expressed despair seemed to stem less from the anguish of love thwarted than from a reluctant acceptance that he must fight. On the morning of 3 September 1939 he listened to Neville Chamberlain's broadcast at the house in Beaconsfield that his parents used on their visits to England. When it had finished he said goodbye to them and borrowed his father's car to drive over to the headquarters of the University Air Squadron in Oxford. It was the end of his second year at Oxford, but he had no qualms about leaving his degree until 'later'.

Hillary was initially made a sergeant and put in charge of a platoon of fellow-undergraduates. He found himself too unmilitary to shout at them and therefore gave drill orders only after democratic consultation. Soon afterwards he was commissioned into a different wing and found himself among several old Oxford friends, including Frank Waldron and an Armenian called Noel Agazarian, who combined intelligence, sporting ability and a disrespect for authority in about the same proportions as Hillary and had consequently become a close friend. Agazarian had intended reading for the Bar after having been sent down from Oxford for what Hillary called 'breaking up his college'. Hillary and Agazarian were posted to a flying school at Kinloss, on the north-east coast of Scotland. They drove up with a third Oxford undergraduate called Peter Howes, a scientist who proved helpful on the technical aspects of subsequent flying exams.

At Kinloss they met regular RAF men who treated them with disdain, referring to them as 'weekend pilots' and 'long-haired boys'. Hillary was quite able to withstand the mockery and even became mildly cooperative when the flying began on American trainers called Harvards. He was taught by a Sergeant White, who turned him into a competent, if not a brilliant, pilot. He made mistakes through arrogance and inattention, but in a crisis that was not of his making he showed speed of reaction. The sensation of flying was intoxicating and still untainted by any sense of duty. The war by land had not yet started, so, alone in the air, Hillary and the other long-haired boys could make carefree swoops through soft white canyons, watching the shadow of the plane move down the long pale embankments of cloud.

It was in Scotland that Hillary first heard an aircraft crashing. The pilot was doing a height test and had presumably fainted; little of him was found, so they filled the coffin with sand. It was on the same station that he first flew by night. After two practice circuits with Sgt White, he was allowed to take the plane up on his own. He took off without difficulty and flew for some minutes; all went well as long as he kept his gaze on the instrument panel. Then, unable to resist the temptation, he stared out of the cockpit and found the horizon had vanished. This is a sensation the pilot dreads. With cloud covering up the light of the stars, he has no way of knowing where he is, or how far from the earth. He is aware simultaneously of the vastness of the space around him and of feeling trapped in a constricting and dangerous little box. Hillary looked down for the flare-path of the runway: he saw nothing, but noticed that he was gaining speed. He jerked back the stick to slow down, but could still see nothing. He half stood up in his seat, craning his neck. Suddenly he saw the lights of the flare-path: there was space between him and the earth – he was safe. After a moment of shame, he felt powerful and exhilarated. He experienced the feeling of arrogance, of mastery of himself and his destiny, that was common to airmen when they had regained control of their machines.

Back on the ground he was tersely congratulated by Sgt White. As they smoked a cigarette in the hangar another pilot tried to land. He overshot the runway and disappeared out to sea. They found his body, with his machine half in and half out of the water. In his pocket were ten pounds he had drawn to go on leave the next day. He was the same age as Richard Hillary: twenty.

Hillary and his colleagues were somehow able to dismiss such incidents from their personal assessments of the War, which they continued to discuss only in terms of what selfish pleasure or satisfaction it might offer. The arrival of a Spitfire squadron in Scotland caused particular excitement. These fast, manoeuvrable fighters were what all the training pilots wanted to fly, but casualties in Fighter Command were as yet so light that no further pilots were required. When they completed the course in Scotland most of the young pilots, including Hillary, Noel Agazarian and Peter Howes, were therefore posted to 'Army Cooperation'. This meant training in cumbersome Lysanders at Old Sarum in Wiltshire.

Hillary, slightly to his surprise, enjoyed the further training, which included aerial photography and long-distance reconnaissance. He even warmed to the Lysander after a while. It was more like flying an old single-decker bus than a Spitfire, but it was commendably easy to control and appeared impossible to stall. Hillary tried his best by putting his plane through various loops and rolls; it was only when he realised his observer was not strapped in but had been hurled around in the rear cockpit that he put an end to the aerobatics: he had taken the man's shrieks for boyish enthusiasm. Agazarian meanwhile managed to flip over his Hector while trying to take off. The plane did not catch fire, but Agazarian was not out of danger: many young flyers when overturned in the cockpit undid their straps, fell out and broke their necks. Fortunately the upside-down Agazarian retained some mental equilibrium and escaped with a severe reprimand.

The days of innocence ended with Dunkirk in June 1940. Hillary motored down to Brighton with Agazarian and Peter Howes to see some of the returning soldiers for himself. He found them resentful at the lack of air cover they had received from the RAF, but, in a moment of uncharacteristic self-control, Hillary forbore to point out that if the RAF had not gained supremacy above Flanders there would have been no evacuation at all. They spent the day at Brighton in the traditional way of off-duty servicemen, and on the way back to Old Sarum Peter Howes drove the car off the road. It was almost the last of the undergraduate pranks.

Leave was cancelled and side arms were issued. The Government appealed for calm and volunteers for a Local Defence force, the forerunner of the Home Guard. Up and down the country people began to understand for the first time that there might soon be German tanks in their streets, swastikas on their town hall and a summer sky dark with descending paratroops.

The Air Ministry rushed to strengthen the country's air defences, and this meant drafting in more fighter pilots. Of the twenty young men at Old Sarum, fifteen would be required; the names of the five who would remain in Army Cooperation would be drawn from a hat. Hillary, with a grim little flourish, described the draw as his worst moment of the war. He was lucky in the draw: he was to be a fighter pilot at last.

Their training was completed by instructors of No. 1 Squadron in Gloucestershire. Among Number 1 were the first pilots of the War to be decorated. They were famous throughout the country for their recent exploits in France, and even Hillary treated them with their due respect. The men from Number 1 were impressed by the German machines, the Messerchmitt 109 in particular, and by their pilots' skill; but they showed contempt for the Germans' tactical inflexibility and preference for fighting only when numbers favoured them. Many airmen at the time spoke like this, depicting the Germans in a way that seems almost like national caricature; but for the purpose of building their own morale it was sensible to focus on German weakness, and the subsequent performance of the RAF against the Luftwaffe bore out some of their claims.

At last the moment came when Hillary climbed into a Spitfire. It was not a big plane: a tall man could stand beside it and place his hand on the top of the cockpit. Pilots wore a lightweight flying suit to keep the oil off their uniform, fleece-lined boots (maps stuffed down one, revolver down another, though the gun always flew out when the parachute jerked open), and a Mae West life-jacket, with a thick collar to keep sagging heads above water, and a number of pockets and whistles at the front. The pilots were sceptical about the value of whistling in the vastness of the Channel. The flying helmet had an oxygen mask and a micro-phone built into the mouthpiece with earphones stitched in at the side. The mask had a characteristic smell of old rubber. Some pilots used goggles with tinted lenses when flying into the sun, many kept them on top of their heads; it was agreed that their chief purpose was to protect the eyes from fire. The gloves (silk beneath wash-leather) did the same for the hands.

The parachute was strapped like a bulging nappy beneath the pilot's backside. The tighter the fitting, the less chance of injury when it opened. There was no dignity in the resulting waddle to the plane, and the pilot needed a hand up from the ground crew on to the wing. The seat was no more than a piece of moulded metal, as on a child's pedal car, designed to accommodate the parachute; later in the war it had also to take a one-man dinghy pack.

Once inside, the pilot strapped himself tightly into his seat. Flying upside down with orange tracer grazing your cockpit was made worse if you were also banging around inside the plane. Not that there was that much space: the bigger pilots would touch the canopy with their heads and either side of the cockpit with their shoulders. The hands and feet had only a few inches of movement, but that was all that was needed. The Spitfire was a delicately responsive plane.

Richard Hillary was enthralled by its beauty and simplicity. His first flight ran smoothly; then came an aerobatic flight in which he was told to 'make her talk'; then came oxygen climbs and fighting exercises. It all went well; and if Hillary did not describe flying the Spitfire as a 'piece of cake' he may well have been the first pilot in Britain who did not.

The Spitfire had been designed by a young man called R. J. Mitchell; the Merlin engine with which it was fitted was the work of Sir Henry Royce. Both men died before the plane had been properly tested. Its chief backer in the RAF was Sir Hugh Dowding, who was Air Member for Supply and Research in the years before the War and Commander-in-Chief of Fighter Command to the end of 1940. The Spitfire was a superlative piece of engineering, and in the hands of the young RAF pilots in the Summer of 1940 it was – just – able to prevent the Luftwaffe from realising its declared aim. Enthusiasts therefore argued that the performance of the Spitfire saved Britain and the then free world from conquest. The flying facts were more complicated. The Messerchmitt 109 was the plane responsible for most of the damage inflicted on the RAF, and it was an equally sophisticated machine. It was as fast as the Spitfire, much faster than the Hurricane, and could out-dive or out-climb either. It was also better armed. A cannon fired explosive shells through the propeller hub, in a variation of the syncopated technique that Roland Garros had allegedly developed from watching the electric fan in the apartment of Jean Cocteau's mother. The Me-109 also had four, sometimes six, machine guns, two of which were mounted above the engine cowling. These were much more powerful than the Spitfire's eight Browning machine guns, though the Brownings had a higher rate of fire.

Where the British fighters were superior was in their turning circle. Both Spitfires and Hurricanes could out-turn the Me-109, and in one-to-one fights this manoeuvrability was crucial. The best tactic for a Messerchmitt was a high-speed attack, followed by a sudden dive or climb. Because, however, they were detailed to escort flights of bombers, they were not supposed to stray too far from their formation. Thus they found themselves drawn into fights over a small area, where the more agile Spitfires turned inside them and delivered their lighter fire in quick bursts. The German tactical inflexibility that the No. 1 Squadron instructors had described to Hillary and his colleagues became important when Goering, anxious about the losses inflicted on his bombers, instructed the Messerchmitts to stick even more closely to them, thus limiting further his fighters' potential superiority.

They remained a frightening weapon. Many were painted yellow about the nose and all of them fired tracer bullets; the sight of orange lead issuing from a yellow plane had an unsettling effect on young RAF pilots. Both the Messerchmitt and the Spitfire were improved as the war went on, so that either might edge ahead at any one moment; but in the critical summer of 1940 they were evenly matched. The older Hurricane enjoyed a swan song in the Battle of Britain, and although it was not used in large numbers again after 1940 it remained much loved by the men who flew it.

The drawbacks to the Spitfire were few. Most of the pilots, including Richard Hillary, bought rear-view mirrors from car accessory shops and screwed them to the top of the cockpit windscreen. Flying upside down in a slow roll was unpleasant because pieces of dust and grit fell down into the pilot's eyes as he hung from his straps; but this could happen in any plane. It was only in night flight that the Spitfire showed serious defects. The bulky engine cowling reduced vision on either side of it to an angle of no more than 45 degrees. Blackout precautions meant that the flare-path on which the pilots were supposed to land was in 1940 limited to a single line of 'glim-lamps' which were masked in such a way that they could only be seen on a shallow angle of approach. Night landings in Spitfires were excruciating, even for experienced pilots. Richard Hillary, significantly, seems to have avoided night flying almost completely.

The normal flying formation for Spitfires was an inverted V, with the leader at the apex. When they wanted to attack, they would go into 'line astern' – ie a straight line behind the leader – until the leader called 'Echelon starboard' when the two machines behind him would draw to his right, still remaining close. They would then dive down on to the enemy formation and open fire from behind. When they were only 100 yards away from them, they would kick hard on the rudder and slam the stick forward so that they would tear downwards and away. They would then reform to repeat the attack from the left.

They broke downwards to avoid the fire of the enemy tail gunners; if the enemy planes were Me-109s, which had no rear-gunners, the Spitfires would break upwards. Engagement with fighters often came down to one-to-one combat or 'dog-fights'. Here there were no real rules, except always to try to turn inside your opponent, think fast, shoot when you had the opportunity, and, above all, to break away fast. Aerobatic manoeuvres were of little use, as most of them presented longer and slower targets to the enemy. The exception was a controlled spin – a corkscrew movement vertically downwards – which might make the enemy think you had lost control and were no longer worth following.

The pilots were not able to convey in words the sensations they experienced in the air. The speed, danger and exhilaration were hard enough to describe; but there was a metaphysical element too: an impression of having escaped terrestrial restraints, of being not only in control of your destiny but in some sense beyond it. It was no wonder that when these men returned to the airfields and gathered in the mess they cultivated an ironic understatement, reducing what they had experienced to a few set formulae – 'Money for old rope', 'Piece of duff' and so on. Since they could not communicate to the outside world what it was like, they might as well use an agreed code amongst themselves. When they spoke of someone who had crashed and died as having 'gone for a Burton' (ie gone to the pub for a glass of (Burton's) beer) it neither diminished their sympathy for the dead man nor quelled their own fear of dying.

By this time Hillary had begun to irritate his two Oxford friends, Peter Howes and Noel Agazarian, and they him. They decided to separate. Agazarian, known as 'Aga', appeared like a festive wraith in various other war memoirs. His arrival at an airfield, usually in a borrowed 'Maggie' (a Magister trainer) was always the prelude to a punishing evening. When the training was over Hillary applied for a vacancy in 603 (City of Edinburgh) Squadron with two new friends: Peter Pease and Colin Pinckney. Peter Pease was to have a profound if curious influence on Hillary's life.

Hillary's French publisher assumed that Richard Hillary fell in love with Peter Pease. His description of him in *The Last Enemy* was certainly ardent. He called him 'the best-looking man I have ever seen'. Photographs of Pease, which showed a pleasant-seeming young man with crinkly hair and full lips, were not always just. Hillary was handsome and arrogant enough himself not to be wasteful with his compliments.

If it was love, it was certainly pure, or at any rate not physical. The French enjoy suspecting all English men of homosexuality (not without reason in Christopher Wood's case), but Hillary was proudly heterosexual, and, perhaps surprisingly, good at making friends with women. Pease was shortly to be married and was too conservative a character to have tolerated any homo-erotic feelings in himself. What apparently fascinated Hillary about Peter Pease was his mind, and what he stood for; and in view of Hillary's self-consciously 'rebellious' temperament this is the more perplexing part of it.

Pease was an old Etonian, a member of the Tory squirearchy, whose family came from Richmond in Yorkshire. Peter had been at the beginning of his third year at Cambridge when the War broke out. He was modest, shy and utterly conventional. He believed in his country, his society and his place within it. He was motivated by a sense of *noblesse oblige* and an unshakably rooted belief in the natural virtue of the country for which he was prepared to risk his life. His beliefs were firm and secure; his surface shyness concealed a serene sense of his privileged debt to an ordered world. He had been a gifted schoolboy at Eton, known at first for his beautiful treble voice (he made a record of 'O for the wings of a dove') and later for the way he dragged his tall figure up the High Street on his way to edit the school magazine or consult the history library. His school career had been crowned with both academic and social glories; it was accepted that he had both the mental equipment, the inclination and the self-discipline to command the career of his choice in the Diplomatic Service.

So they motored north, a pushier Charles Ryder and a sober Sebastian Flyte. The gravel of the Pease ancestral home crunched beneath the well-mannered tyres of his two-seater. The dinner was a quiet affair with Pease's parents and brothers; as the port circulated Hillary felt disturbed and confused by the sudden thought of how much Pease's death might mean to him. After dinner Lady Pease told how she had declined to send Peter's younger brother away from Eton to America because it would set a bad example.

Hillary enjoyed trying to provoke Peter Pease out of his Anglican quietism. He accused him of being vulgar in his patriotism, archaic in his religion and sentimental in his notion of public duty. In fact, Hillary was, through Pease, testing out the extent of his own belief in these things. It probably did seem absurd to him that such an intelligent man could be so complacently certain of such conventional values, without any of the anguish and self-examination that people of twenty normally go through: there was possibly real irritation in his questioning. It seems, however, that what Hillary was trying to tease out of Peter Pease was a reason for dying.

Hillary was by no means an intellectual, but he was clever enough to be confused. Peter Pease had something he envied, and that was his certainty: where Richard was bewildered, Peter was calm. Richard did not believe in the old values that Peter represented, but he had no better ones to put in their place; he had only a childish truculence. There was no doubt in his mind as to which of them would be happier at the moment of his death.

Peter Pease, in his quiet way, appears to have understood Richard Hillary quite well. He both liked him and pitied him. He knew that Hillary was floundering, but he also knew that when it came to a crisis he would not waver. As far as the protection of Britain and the defeat of the Nazis were concerned it did not terribly matter to Peter Pease whether each pilot hurtling towards death in his Spitfire did so with a completely settled system of beliefs. It was enough that he should be prepared to fight, and die. Because he is remembered principally through the distorting prism of Richard Hillary's hero-worship, it is hard to take the full measure of what a remarkable young man Pease was. Although Hillary was not snobbish, he was fascinated by some quality of 'Englishness' in Pease that he felt his own Australian beginnings had not provided. Yet other people, as English as Pease himself, were also profoundly impressed by his grace and mental strength. Hillary felt himself being gradually drawn by the certainty of Pease's character to the point of view he represented. Pease tolerated Hillary's excesses and to some extent encouraged them, because he could see that Hillary's brashness and bravado concealed a drastic lack of confidence and a fear of the future.

From Edinburgh Hillary and Pease went to 603 Squadron's base aerodrome at Turnhouse and thence north to Montrose, where they were assigned to 'B' flight. Here Hillary made further friends. Among the men of 'B' flight was a New Zealander called Brian Carbury who had previously worked as a shoe salesman. He had come to Britain on a short service commission and was to become the best flyer in the squadron. Pilot Officer Berry, known as 'Raspberry', was another man from a modest background. He had a strong Hull accent and a short, expressive vocabulary. Other new colleagues were Hugh 'Stapme' Stapleton, a twenty-year-old South African; 'Bubble' Waterston; the nineteen-year-old 'Broody' Benson; the innocent Pip Cardell; and Don MacDonald, who had been in the Cambridge Air Squadron, where he had known Peter Pease and Colin Pinckney. It was a typical fighter squadron: typical in its national and social make-up, in its age, its nicknames, its keenness and its very short life expectancy.

Fighting at this stage consisted of no more than shooting down the odd single plane sent over by the Germans from Norway. Hillary was not yet fully operational, but was flying up the coast one day when he heard a section being ordered to start tracking an enemy bomber. He should have returned to base, but instead decided to have a go on his own. He assumed the bomber would be flying in cloud cover, so made a number of dives and climbs in and out of the cloud. He found nothing, so returned to base where he was told that the enemy bomber had passed just over the aerodrome. Brian Carbury's section landed shortly after-wards and told Hillary that, seeing an aircraft diving in and out of the clouds, they had fallen into line astern behind him and had been on the point of opening fire when Carbury recognised the Spitfire tail.

The next day the Flight Commander made Hillary operational, explaining quietly, 'I think it will be safer for the others.'
On leave from the station at Montrose, Hillary went up to
Invermark where a local landowner, Lord Dalhousie, had turned
over his shooting lodge to the young pilots. He fished on the loch
and shot a stag, though the look in the animal's eyes as it lay dying
made him vow that from then on he would kill only Germans. He
found two other non-hunters in 'Bubble' Waterson and 'Stapme'
Stapleton who, much to Hillary's surprise, spent their leave not
wenching or drinking but playing hide-and-seek with local
children. Hillary joined their games enthusiastically; there was a
perverse pleasure to be had from picnic and rounders in the
heather while they waited for their part in the War. Hillary
excelled as a storyteller and could hold the small audience rapt.
When they tired of stories they could indulge in some rougher
games. On one occasion Hillary floated out into Loch Lee in a
dinghy they had taken from a crashed Heinkel while Stapleton
fired at it with a .22 rifle from the bank.

The wait for war was not long. The squadron was ordered from
Montrose to Turnhouse, near Edinburgh. With the German air
offensive gaining momentum over southern England, Hillary and
his friends knew they were on their way into action. There was
huge excitement among them; 'Broody' Benson in particular (his
nickname was ironic) was panting to be let loose. The relief
squadron was already in sight, shimmering down over the
boundary of the airfield, coming in to land on delicate wheels.
Hillary was assigned to 'B' Flight, clambered into his Spitfire, and
roared down the runway. They dipped their wings in farewell as
they came over, then headed south. In *The Last Enemy* Hillary
wrote that they then flew down the valley where the children
played and that with white boulders in the heather the children
had spelled out the message 'Good Luck'.

He later admitted that this was an invention: the children
could not have known of the Air Ministry's orders. What Hillary
conveyed by this elaboration was his own feeling that an era had
ended. There would be no more conversations with Peter Pease
about the meaning of life and whether Richard was an 'anarchist';
there would be no more rounders and picnics; no more self-

doubt; no second chances when the plane on his tail forbore to fire because he was a friend: from now on there would be only metal and fire.

On 10 August 1940, after a short delay at Turnhouse, the squadron was switched to Hornchurch in Essex, twelve miles east of London on the Thames estuary. By the time they landed they found that many of their colleagues had already been in action. They watched the Spitfires landing with the leading edges of their wings stained with smoke from their own guns. Brian Carbury told the new arrivals, 'You don't have to look for them. You have to look for a way out.' Don MacDonald had already been killed.

At this stage the German strategy was to try to eliminate the British fighter force by drawing it into combat with their own Messerchmitt 109's and 110's. They would then have a clear run for their bombers, and Britain could be pulverised into submission. German attacks began before breakfast and continued until about eight in the evening; the Spitfire squadrons were in the air all day and the pilots took what rest and food they could between flights. Some of the men were close to exhaustion; among them was Peter Howes, who was at Hornchurch with another squadron and was worried because he had not yet shot down an enemy plane.

Hillary was in the air almost at once. When the moment came there was no time for reflection, though he did acknowledge as he faced the instrument panel that he would soon be taking a human life for the first time. It was that way about; he did not think that he himself would shortly die. He believed most pilots had a similar trust in their own invulnerability. It was not an acquired or cultivated thing; it was a faith that sprang from the sense of mastery that the physical action of flying gave to them.

They found the enemy at 18,000 feet: twenty Messerchmitt 109's above their eight Spitfires. The Germans came down to get them and Brian Carbury led his eight planes in line astern, head-on towards them. Carbury went down briefly, then up, leading the others in a climbing turn to the left. He caught the first Messerchmitt as he went and Hillary found the plane come flush into his own sights. He switched the gun-button to 'Fire' and watched the tracer from all eight guns hammering into its target for four seconds. The Messerchmitt hung still for a moment, then spun downwards in a spurt of red flame.

Hillary felt no pity because he knew that none would have been shown to him. The exercise seemed to have some chivalric dignity which robbed it of selfish emotion. Broody Benson, who had been so keen to get at the Germans, was killed in this first engagement.

The losses that followed daily in August and September were greeted calmly at the airfield. The men were not callous, but they were indifferent. They were so wholly engaged in what they were doing, so mentally and physically committed to the fight, on which, after all, their own lives depended, that they felt they had no time to grieve. They were always outnumbered and were therefore rarely able to keep their formation; they would land individually over a period of minutes, sometimes hours, and the fate of each man in the squadron took time to determine. Prolonged absence was not necessarily the prelude to news of another death; a pilot who had parachuted from a stricken plane might take some time to reach a telephone.

They found that what the men of No. 1 Squadron had taught them was true: if the Germans did not have numerical superiority they would not engage but would turn round and head back for the Channel. The sun caused problems for all the pilots. Hillary did not wear his dark-lensed goggles because they interfered with his vision and made him feel shut in; before going into action he would push them up on to his forehead. He also refused to wear gloves because they were too hot and decreased his sensitivity on the controls.

Richard Hillary continued to flout the rules. The War had become exactly what he had hoped: exciting, individual and disinterested. Up in the air the pilots were as selfishly engaged and motivated, as free from discipline, as it was possible for a fighting force to be. They accepted the concomitant risk not so much without qualm as without thought. There was the possibility of fighting in a way that protected your friends but also gave you room for the most extreme form of self-expression. In one of the outstanding sequences of *The Last Enemy* Richard Hillary described such a flight in the language of rapture.

It was early evening in the last week in August. Brian Carbury had received a bullet wound in the foot and Hillary was to take his place in the next 'show'. The day was uncharacteristically quiet; by six o'clock they were still playing cards in the mess. Then came the voice of the controller: 'Six-o-three Squadron take off and patrol base: further instructions in the air.'

They were detailed to intercept twenty enemy fighters at 25,000 feet. Hillary looked through the glass of his cockpit to the plane next to his. He could see Hugh Stapleton's mouth moving. This usually meant he was singing; sometimes he would do this with his radio-transmitter (R/T) switched to 'send', so that the others would receive their instructions from the ground against a background of 'Night and Day'. On this occasion Hillary picked up the Germans on his headset and shouted back as many pieces of invective as he could remember from his schoolboy holidays abroad. Below them, above the pattern of the English fields on a hot August evening, they watched the German planes form a tight defensive circle, a formation which could only be broken up by dangerously exposed individual attacks.

The Spitfires peeled off into an echelon starboard formation and down in a series of power dives. After picking out his machine and discharging his guns into the nose, Hillary had to pull out in a climb so steep he felt his eyes being driven down into his neck. Then as he circled above them he could see that the attack had successfully broken up the defensive circle. It then became a matter of individual dog-fights. He saw Peter Pease making a head-on attack on a Messerchmitt; the two planes were on a collision course, both firing. Then, just before they would have crashed, the German pulled up, and the grateful Pease was able to fire full into his belly.

The sky was alive with the sound of fighter planes, diving, roaring, spinning, and with the sound of their guns, fired sometimes in long-distance optimism, sometimes in desperate self-defence. Hillary found the sweat coursing down his face. Then suddenly the noise was gone. He looked round for the reflection of the evening sun on metal and saw nothing. This instantaneous dispersal and isolation could happen at any time; the obvious thing for Hillary to do was to return to base. About a mile away, however, he spotted a formation of about forty Hurricanes and set off to join them. The only reason for doing this was bravado: he had some ammunition left and was enjoying being up in the sky.

Just as he was coming in behind them, he looked down and saw, roughly 5,000 feet below, another formation of about fifty planes flying in the same direction. He knew that there were not that many Hurricanes available to make such a 'step-up' formation in this part of England: he had made a serious mistake. He looked again at the last plane in the formation he had been about to join and saw that it was carrying a swastika. The Germans seemed unaware that a lone Spitfire was on their tail, with the sun behind him. Hillary kept his nerve in a way that Peter Pease could have admiringly predicted. He closed to within 150 yards, then fired a three-second burst into the tail of the last enemy aircraft. It went over on its back and spun down out of sight. Hillary looked round him for signs of retaliation, but still none of the other planes seemed to have noticed. He considered trying to take out the next plane in the formation in the same way, but decided in a moment of rare discretion to be satisfied with a single kill. He peeled off in a half-roll and headed back to the station, where he found to his irritation that Berry was claiming to have shot down three.

The Battle of Britain had many crises, but there was no more continuous anguish than that suffered in the last week of August and the first of September.

On 13 August Goering had sent his aircraft into battle for what he imagined would be the knock-out blow. He termed it *Adlertag* or Eagle Day. German intelligence reports persuaded him to believe that attacks on the previous two days had made radar defences in the south of England inoperative and that 11 Group, whose twenty-two squadrons covered the south east, was down to its last planes. *Adlertag* consisted of attacks on the north of England as well, but Dowding, despite much advice to the contrary, had long been reluctant to move all his fighters to the south-east, and the German attackers therefore met unexpected resistance over the coast of Yorkshire, Durham and Northumberland. The Luftwaffe lost seventy-six planes in a day, compared to thirty-four British.

They had more in reserve. When the first major attack came on London on 7 September, Air Vice Marshal Park, a New Zealander who was in charge of the critical South East 11 Group, had not only to scramble every fighter he had but to call in five squadrons from the adjacent 12 Group which had been assembled under Douglas Bader at Duxford in Cambridgeshire. When at the height of the battle Churchill asked Park how many fighters he had left, Park answered, 'None, sir'.

By the end of August the slow attrition was working in Germany's favour. Although the Spitfires and Hurricanes were always finishing the day slightly ahead, the British were starting to run out of pilots. Dowding had to take men out of squadrons that were supposed to be resting or re-forming in order to fill the constantly recurring gaps in the squadrons of 11 Group in the south-east.

Jack Wolfenden, the thirty-four-year-old headmaster of Uppingham, a public school in Rutland, was eventually seconded to the Air Ministry to coordinate the recruitment and training of more young pilots. It was a desperate move, whose results were not available until the following year. In September 1940, Dowding and Park faced a crisis of manpower that appeared to have only one outcome, the defeat of the RAF and the conquest of Britain.

At this moment Hitler, impatient at the extraordinary resilience of the RAF, ordered Goering to change his tactics. Instead of clearing the skies of RAF defences, Hitler now wanted to see London burn, and it was to this end that Goering switched his attacks to the capital on 7 September. The error of this change of tactic was not immediately obvious since, as Park's desperate remark to Churchill indicated, it seemed only to precipitate a new crisis, with the further symbolic anguish that the destruction of a capital city involves. Had Hitler known how close to collapse the RAF was coming in that week, he would have allowed Goering to continue with his initial plan.

What was it like to be a Spitfire pilot in these critical few days? Almost all of those involved struggled to find words. They did not contemplate the larger strategic implications of what they were doing. If they read the papers, it was for 'Jane' in the *Daily Mirror*. They did not dwell on the deaths of their colleagues. Towards their own fate they cultivated a cocky indifference. They concentrated on the things of the moment: flying, tracer, drink, sleep, flying.

You would have slept in your uniform, a couple of hours in an armchair because you were too drunk to go to bed. If you were clever, like Hugh Dundas who flew at Douglas Bader's elbow, you'd have remembered to turn your trousers inside out before you started drinking, so the beer stains weren't visible the next day. Then you'd be in a drafty dispersal hut and the phone would ring. It might be the flight sergeant asking for a cup of tea or it might be operations telling you to scramble. Out on the grass the squadron doctor was ladling out his hangover cure from a tin pail. You ran over to the plane and in the grey light before dawn you could hear the soft, low purr of the Merlin engines warming up. The ground crew helped you on to the wing of the little Spitfire and then you were down in the tight cockpit, radio switched on, strapped up tight. The smell of petrol, oil and glycol coolant came in an unmistakable Spitfire cocktail. Once you had cleared the perimeter hedge and were up in the air, a long draught of oxygen would chase away the last traces of the night before.

At 20,000 feet you saw the sun heave up over the horizon, but the unpressurised cockpit was icy and the mud of the airfield had frozen your boots to the rudder bars. Then from the lightening sky you would see the dark flight of enemy bombers, in stepped formation, with fighter escorts. In theory the Hurricanes would take the bombers and the Spitfires would tackle the escorting Messerschmitts. In practice it seldom worked that way; within moments you were alone with only fourteen seconds' worth of ammunition and the enemy wheeling all about you.

The Spitfire's gunsights were synchronised to 200–250 yards, which wasn't really close enough. The better pilots would chase in to 50 yards before firing. The firing button was on the control column; you moved a switch from 'safe' to 'fire' and that was it: all eight guns went off together with the sound of tearing calico. The recommended burst lasted only two seconds, then you were powering down and away to the left, the forces of gravity pressing your organs against your bones.

The sight of English churches, roads and villages beneath your feet as you straightened up lent a protective edge to your concentration. The constantly visible German tracer that arced towards the thin perspex of your cockpit kept the nerves tight. As you climbed for another attack, you might see a German bomber in flames: it would hang for a moment, then drop from the formation, billowing black smoke. Beside it might be a stricken Spitfire, spiralling down, and you would watch as long as you dared for the blossoming of a parachute.

When your ammunition was used, you had to head back to the airfield. If you were short of fuel, it was usually possible to land at a nearer one: on a clear day you might be able to see as many as five. But it was still dark when you landed back at base; you had been airborne for less than an hour. As you staggered back to the dispersal hut you could watch the beginnings of your second sunrise. You thought of the men who had gone up with you who would never see another.

Two, three, four times a day in those crucial weeks the experience would be repeated. When it grew dark the German attacks finally stopped, and the Spitfire pilots went to the pub. In the numerous White Harts and Royal Oaks of southern England they ducked beneath the beams and pressed up to the bar. They chatted to the locals as casually as if they had stepped off the commuter train from Waterloo. Five shillings would keep them in beer until the local police saw them out at closing time. There would be more drink back at one of the comfortable houses where they had been billeted around the airfield, and eventually a few hours' sleep.

Pilots at the bases close to London might have a quick wash after the final sortie and motor up to town, where they liked to shock their more conventional army counterparts by appearing scruffily dressed at London restaurants and night clubs. They knew that there had been a certain snobbery towards them and did nothing to ease the discomfort of those civilians who, having once called them Brylcreem Boys, were now belatedly trying to acknowledge them as heroes.

Hillary enjoyed the puzzlement in the faces of such people as they transparently searched the airmen's faces for the qualities of heroism which had previously eluded them. They could not find what they were looking for; these men still seemed to them raffish and off-hand: how could they be the nation's saviours? Their secret bravery and fragile indifference to death were sealed within the private slang of their mess.

Richard Hillary's war was a short one. The Battle of Britain picked off its pilots with remorseless probability, and Hillary had only two more tales to tell before his own crash. After a flight with his squadron had broken up into dog-fights Hillary found himself once more alone. This time he successfully identified a squadron of Hurricanes and joined them as 'Arse-end Charlie', in which role he was supposed to weave around and protect them from attack in the rear. He was having a pleasant time until he noticed bullets appearing along his port wing. There was a tendency in such circumstances for a pilot to do nothing, but somehow to become mesmerised by what was happening. Hillary was able to react, however, by going down into a spin and trying to call up the Hurricanes to warn them off imminent attack. This was made impossible by the fact that his radio had been shot away. That seemed to be the only damage done, and he began to climb again to rejoin the Hurricanes. Then he noticed black smoke coming out of his engine and a smell of escaping glycol; he decided to go back to the station. When his windscreen became covered with oil he thought he had better put down at the nearer station of Lympne. That too became impossible as the engine began to lose power: the only course of action now was to crash-land in a field.

He selected a corn field and put the Spitfire down on its belly without incident. As he switched off the petrol and climbed out of the cockpit he saw an ambulance entering the field. It was not for him, but for Colin Pinckney, who was in his parachute dangling from a tree. They had come to earth next to an army cocktail party. While Pinckney was taken off by a doctor, Hillary joined the party and was swiftly stoked up with whisky by the admiring officers. He consumed so much that at dinner that night with the Brigadier he dared not speak, but stared silently whenever a question was put to him and hoped that his hosts would assume his vacant expression was caused by shock. The next day he took his helmet and parachute up on the train to London and demanded a car and a driver from the Air Ministry. By the afternoon he was flying again.

Hillary's last pre-crash anecdote concerned a flight that same evening. Hornchurch aerodrome had been the focus of an intense German attack and Hillary found himself above twelve Dornier bombers on their way back to France. He was returning to the airfield when he saw them and should have continued, but found the target too big, too slow and too tempting. He dived down amongst them and switched the button to fire. Nothing happened. He had already used all his ammunition. He wrapped both hands about his head and went straight through the enemy squadron, preparing for the end. The Dorniers' tail-gunners opened fire, but Hillary managed to get through. He landed at Hornchurch with the Spitfire in working order, though a little draughty. Bubble Waterston was killed on this flight.

On 3 September 1940 Edwyna Hillary was on her way to work at the Red Cross when she felt that something had gone wrong. It was a typical day in the Battle of Britain and the Spitfires had been up since dawn; but Mrs Hillary was instinctively convinced that her son had been killed. She told her taxi-driver to take her back to her flat. The rooms were silent and empty. There was no telegram or scribbled message put through the door; just the empty flat which was unaccustomed to her presence at this time of day. She positioned herself for a long vigil, staring at the silent telephone.

Richard emerged on to the airfield at about eight that morning. It was foggy and overcast; he was worried because he had a new hood on his cockpit and it was reluctant to slide back and forth along the groove. He worked with a corporal fitter to file and lubricate the hood until, by ten o'clock, they had managed to get it to slide halfway. That was all there was time for; the order came to take off and patrol base. As Hillary started the engine, the corporal stepped away from the plane, giving a sinister fingers-crossed sign.

Hillary was flying with Brian Carbury and Hugh Stapleton. They went through the clouds at about 12,000 feet and into a dazzling sun. Almost at once they flew straight into a large formation of Messerchmitts; they had no time to group themselves before the sky was filled with individual fights. As Hillary fought to gain height he saw a single Messerchmitt climbing away from the sun and he closed in behind it. He fired from about 200 yards and saw smoke coming from the plane's engine and splinters of metal tearing off its wing. It did not go down, however, and Hillary, instead of breaking away, decided to go for the kill. Perhaps it was the RAF's insistence that 'aircraft must be seen to descend with flames issuing. It is not sufficient if only smoke is seen' that was responsible for his exposing himself to danger. At any rate, as soon as he had hit the Messerchmitt a second time, and seen it spiralling downwards, he felt an explosion knock the stick out of his hand and found his own cockpit filled with flames. He reached up to open the hood, but it would not move.

He tore off his straps and tried again. This time he managed to move it halfway. He dropped back into the seat and reached for the stick so that he could turn the plane over and allow himself to drop out. His oxygen cylinder was on fire and there were flames inside his mask. The heat was so strong that he fainted. The pilotless plane went into a spin and, by some chance of gravity, chucked him out of the half-open hood.

When he regained consciousness he found himself falling through space. He was able to pull the rip-cord of his parachute, which jerked open and checked the rate of his fall. As he looked down he saw the grey mass of the North Sea beneath him. He could not release himself from his parachute before flopping into the water with the silk billowing about him.

Once in the sea, he tried again to undo the harness, but his hands were too badly burned. As usual he had not been wearing gloves, and the skin was shredded and white back to the wrists. There was a nauseating smell of burned flesh. Nor had he worn his goggles; and the pain of the September sun in his face made him suspect that he had paid a price for that too.

His life jacket supported him efficiently in the sea, and the water itself was not too cold, but he could see that he was a long way from land. After half an hour his teeth began to chatter. The sun went in but his face still burned. He tried to look again at his hands, but could not see them. He believed he was blind and about to die. He unscrewed the valve of his life jacket to hasten the end. The air rushed out and his head sank beneath the waves. After swallowing some water, he came back to the surface: he was so entangled in his parachute that it was keeping him afloat. He tried once more to release the harness, tearing at it with his raw hands. There was nothing he could do, so he lay back exhausted and thought of those who would miss him. He thought of his mother; and she, crouched in the dark flat, was thinking of him.

Then there were voices and there were hands lifting him. There was the metal spout of a brandy flask between his flayed lips. The Margate lifeboat had been searching for three hours and was 15 miles east of its station when the crew finally sighted him. In the boat he began to feel the pain of his injuries properly for the first time. The crew rigged up a shade to keep off the rays of the reappearing sun. After an agonising journey, they docked at Margate, where Hillary was transferred by ambulance to the local hospital. There at last he felt the welcome invasion of a needle in his veins.

Towards evening in Edwyna Hillary's flat the bakelite telephone thundered on the table. Squadron Leader Fraser asked to speak to Michael Hillary; denied this possibility, he went into such a long preamble about Richard's popularity and achievements that Edwyna assumed her son was dead. She had to interrupt Fraser to force him to the point. No, he said, Richard was not dead; but he had gone down in flames and was missing. Fraser told her the chances of his being picked up were good, but his words of official optimism were not reassuring.

A long three hours followed before the telephone rang again.

From the Squadron Leader's friendly bluster, Edwyna Hillary extracted directions to the hospital in Margate. The next morning she and her husband set off.

Throughout the years of separation, Richard Hillary's mother had remained single-mindedly devoted to him and she felt the full force of a mother's anguished tenderness when the nurse opened the door into Richard's darkened room. She and Michael Hillary could make out no more than a shape on a bed, until the blinds were thrown up and the lights turned on with a theatrical flourish. His body hung on straps, just clear of the mattress. The legs and arms were wrapped in bandages, and the clawed hands were propped in front of his face. His eyes had been painted with gentian violet, while the rest of his face and his hands were coated with black tannic acid. To conceal the horror of the burns they had covered his face with white gauze, in which was cut a narrow slit for the lips. The handsome boy with his big eyes, his thick hair and his mocking, slightly cruel smile now looked like a corpse awaiting burial.

'Cocky', 'argumentative' and 'arrogant' were the adjectives his contemporaries had most often used to describe Richard Hillary at school and university. He had other qualities, too: a genuine sensitivity towards himself, and to others when he chose to indulge it; and a largeness of spirit that was manifest in his curiosity and openness to experience. His challenging manner, allied to his striking facial beauty, made timorous people fear and distrust him. None of these qualities, the bad or the good, made it any easier for him to adapt himself to his new circumstances. Even those who did not like him found something poignant in the sight of a man so physically proud rendered so dependent and vulnerable, without even a skin to protect him.

Edwyna and Michael Hillary talked to their son, while his awareness of them flowed and ebbed. The lifetime of partings and enforced self-control had to some extent prepared them all. When it was time for his dressings to be changed, they quietly stole away, just as they had on his first day at school.

On the fifth day he was put in an ambulance to be moved up to the Royal Masonic Hospital in London. He was driven by two anxious ATS women and accompanied by his nurse. The journey went without incident until they came to London, where they lost their way. By the time they arrived in Ravenscourt Park Hillary was exhausted and in pain. There were tears from both of them when his Margate nurse came to say goodbye. The house surgeon gave him an anaesthetic and removed the tannic acid from his left hand. In theory tannic acid formed a hard protective layer beneath which the skin could heal at its own pace, leaving the acid to be chipped away gradually. In fact most pilots treated in this way developed septicaemia beneath the crust, and Hillary was among the first to have the treatment reversed. His fingers had already clawed and curled down into his palms, partly as a result of the stiff tannic coating. They operated on only one hand because the risk of shock was too great for them to do both.

While under the anaesthetic Hillary, who prided himself on being almost without any access to mystical or synthetic thought, had a vision. He saw Peter Pease flying in his Spitfire, calm and level. Then he saw a Messerchmitt closing on his tail. He tried to shout and warn Pease, who was oblivious to the danger. His Spitfire was hit, turned slowly on its back, and plummeted to the earth. Hillary woke up to find himself being restrained by nurses: he had been screaming in his sleep. Two days later he received a letter from Colin Pinckney asking after him, giving him news of the squadron and telling him that Pease was dead.

Hillary made slow progress in the Royal Masonic Hospital. It was run more informally than official RAF hospitals, and he was looked after by dedicated and slightly flirtatious nurses. His dressings needed to be changed every two hours and the performance itself took an hour, so they were with him most of the time. Once they had stopped passing out at the sight of his wounds, they developed a happy relationship and connived at keeping him in Ravenscourt Park when officialdom muttered about a transfer. After a few weeks he was allowed to walk about and to take a bath, though as his hands were useless everything had to be done for him.

Edwyna Hillary came and sat with him every day. She would read to him with the rapt pleasure of a mother who has somehow recaptured her son. In *The Last Enemy* Hillary claimed that his

(144)

mother said to him at this time: 'You should be glad this has to happen to you. Too many people told you how attractive you were and you believed them. You were well on your way to becoming something of a cad. Now you'll find out who your real friends are.' It is not just the unnatural speech rhythms that make this passage look invented; it too conveniently opens the way for what is to be the main literary theme of the book: Richard's conversion from selfish arrogance to an altruistic concern for 'humanity'.

It was not Edwyna Hillary, in any case, who tapped the gentler reserves of Hillary's character, but an unexpected visitor who came several days later. Richard was at an emotional nadir. He had learned that Pip Cardell was dead and that Berry and Brian Carbury had been awarded the DFC, with Carbury already down for a bar to his. His friends were either dying or fighting, and either would have been preferable to his pain and immobility.

The Matron knocked at the door and announced 'Someone to see you.' It was Denise Maxwell-Woosnam, Peter Pease's fiancée. Richard Hillary wrote about her in the terms he reserved for passages of flying or for Peter himself. She was 'the most beautiful person I have ever seen'. It was an awkward meeting, according to Denise. Richard was in severe pain, and she was not sure if she should have visited him. Once she began to talk about Peter, however, she felt an intense sympathy radiate from him. He said, 'Don't tell me how he died. Let me tell you.' He recounted his premonitory dream at some length. He would not let her speak until he had finished. He was correct in every detail.

Denise was deeply moved. She found herself forgetting that Richard was suffering, because his identification with her own wound seemed so complete. He asked her to visit again, and she did.

She indulged herself with talk about Peter and felt encouraged by the completeness of Richard's sympathy. When she had talked as much as she could, she felt Richard turn the conversation to the future, and to the plays and books they would write together. In due course Richard used her rather as he had used Peter: as a template against which to measure his beliefs and convictions. He believed that she and Peter were very similar people; certainly they had faith in the same institutions and believed fiercely in the War as a moral crusade to rid the world of the Nazi evil.

Quite what emotions Denise roused in Hillary is hard to say. It may be that there was no more than either of them admitted; that it was a case of altruistic friendship and mutual support. Hillary's stress on her physical appearance, however, and his powerful feelings for her fiancé complicate this premise. To fall in love with the woman you are comforting, the woman who is mourning the death of a man you also loved, and who is depending on you for disinterested support . . . the possibility had at the very least a kind of literary appeal.

That autumn Hillary certainly had time for romantic intro-spection. He was allowed out of the hospital during the day, and would roam around London. The city was crouched beneath incessant bombing and Hillary admired the way the people had responded. He liked the nonchalance, the frantic gaiety, and the busy, uncomplaining way in which rich women who did not normally emerge before cocktails at noon would be at the desk of some voluntary organisation by nine. Some people recoiled at the sight of his injuries, but others, from nervousness or understand-ing, looked kindly on him. He found the smiles of women soothing. He was only twenty-one and he was proud of the sexual rewards his exceptional good looks had brought him. His attractiveness to women was an integral and important part of his idea of himself; if it had been burned away, then he would not merely miss the physical consolations of sex, he would have to revise his whole sense of who he was. It posed a test for him as complete as that posed by polio for Christopher Wood when, at the onset of puberty, it changed him from an athlete to a bedridden artist.

Hillary spent many evenings at Denise's house in Eaton Place, where they talked about Peter. A Christian faith made Denise believe that she and Peter would be reunited or even that they had not, in some way, been truly parted. Richard tried to tease her out of this belief because he thought she was using it as a pretext for prolonging her mourning and delaying her inevitable treaty with the hard world that remained. It was during one such

1. Christopher Wood,
c. 1920

2. Richard Hillary, 1937

3. Jeremy Wolfenden

4. La Foire de Neuilly (1923)

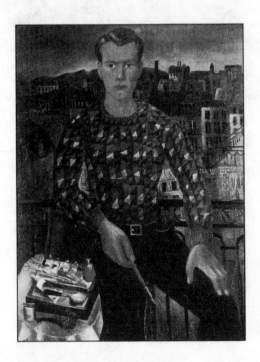

5. Self Portrait,
Paris (1927)

6. Dieppe (1929)

7. Building the Boat, Tréboul (1930)

8. Little House by Night (1930)

9. The Yellow Man (1930)

10. Sleeping Fisherman, Ploaré (1930)

11. Zebra and Parachute (1930)

12. Frosca Munster, 1925

13. Christopher Wood on a
Cornish beach, 1928

14. 54 Operational Training Unit, RAF Charter Hall, December 1942.
Richard Hillary fourth from left, and inset.

15. Loch Lee, 1940: the dinghy from the crashed Heinkel. Under fire from Hugh Stapleton.

16. Eric Kennington's copy of his original portrait of Hillary, commissioned after Richard's death by his father.

17. Funeral of Guy Burgess, Moscow, September 1963.
Left to right: John Miller, George Hanna, Jeremy Wolfenden, Nigel Burgess and Donald Maclean.

18. Jeremy Wolfenden: a summer's day at Magdalen College.

19. The little-known rôle of the Bartender in the Russian Course production of *Measure for Measure*, 1953.

PROPOSAL TO RELAX LAW ON HOMOSEXUALITY

REPORT URGES NO PENALTY FOR CONSENTING ADULTS

STRONGER ACTION AGAINST STREET PROSTITUTION

From Our Political Correspondent

The report of the Departmental Committee on Homosexual Offences and Prostitution, published yesterday, recommends that homosexual behaviour between consenting adults in private should no longer be a criminal offence. This is one of the principal—and most controversial—recommendations made by the committee after a thorough inquiry which has occupied nearly three years.

Under the existing law the maximum penalties for various homosexual offences and crimes range from a fine of £5 to life imprisonment. The chairman of the departmental committee was Sir John Wolfenden, Vice-Chancellor of Reading University, and the members included two judges of the High Court, three women, two M.P.'s, doctors, lawyers, and ministers of religion.

20. *The Times*, Thursday 5 September, 1957.

21. Lord Wolfenden at his desk.

evening that he claimed, not quite credibly, that he 'became aware with a shock of never before having thought of her as a woman, a creature of flesh and blood'. Much though Denise liked Richard, there was no question of any sort of affair. She was, and remained for some time yet, emotionally frozen by her grief.

At the Royal Masonic Hospital Hillary met the plastic surgeon A.H. McIndoe, and it was one of the crucial encounters of his life. McIndoe came with a mixed reputation. He was a thick-set New Zealander with stubby fingers, colonial vowels and horn-rimmed bifocal glasses. He was ambitious, bullying and crafty. He had charm, but he used it only when his natural aggression had not won him his way. He had compassion, vision and generosity of heart, but they were not qualities he found it necessary to keep on display. He had one further ability: he could give his patients hope. They came to believe that, whatever his shortcomings, he was a great man.

McIndoe was of Scottish Presbyterian stock and was brought up in Dunedin, a dead-end town that had been enriched by a goldstrike in 1862. McIndoe's father was a printer and his mother an amateur painter. The young Archibald trained as a doctor at the University of Minnesota. In 1929 he went to England to work with his cousin Sir Harold Gillies. He switched from abdominal surgery, which he had practised in the United States, to plastic surgery at his cousin's suggestion.

Plastic surgery at this time was considered by many surgeons to be the domain of quacks and make-up artists. Its practitioners were accused of having turned the operating theatre into a 'beauty shop'. Even before McIndoe's work made the craft respectable, this judgement was unfair. Plastic surgery became vital, whatever its detractors said, in the treatment of bullet wounds during the Great War. Gillies had trained at Aldershot at a unit set up to treat facial casualties from the Somme in 1916. Machine-gun bullets left tearing damage on both entry and exit; they had a habit of spinning on the bone, which increased their destructive torque and compounded it by firing the splinters of the bone itself at high velocity. There are photographs of living soldiers whose faces have been almost completely slashed away by bullets.

Gillies learned from the Somme casualties and made discoveries of his own. The most important was that of the 'tubed pedicle'. The ordinary pedicle attached skin from adjacent parts of the body; by his tube, Gillies was able to graft skin from quite widely separated parts of the body, sometimes by stages. The principle behind it was that if the new flesh were wrapped on to itself in tubes it would be more 'portable' and less prone to infection.

McIndoe began as his apprentice and bag-carrier but soon became a partner. Gillies was thought by other surgeons to be more of an originator, but McIndoe was technically his superior. He held the scalpel between thumb and forefinger with his little finger cocked. His thick fingers, encased in size eight gloves, were capable of astonishing dexterity, and he was scornful of surgeons with delicate hands: 'The man with ladies' fingers is no surgeon,' he was heard to say.

McIndoe always worked with the same team. His anaesthetist was a burly bald-headed man called John Hunter, who took pride in making the most po-faced ward sisters smile at his saloon-bar jokes. He was indefatigably good with children and waggish with patients as they went under. 'Hello, I'm John Hunter, better known as the Gasworks,' he would tell his prone patient. 'Do you know the one about the girl called Virginia? Just a little prick, if you'll pardon the expression' and so on. Despite his blustering geniality, he was a sensitive doctor, admirably precise with needle and gas. McIndoe's other indispensable colleague was a theatre sister called Jill Mullins. Although she was repelled by surgery, she was attracted by McIndoe. He liked her dexterity, her reliability and her elegant presence: she was said by her admirers to resemble Gertrude Lawrence.

In the years just before the war, Gillies was invited to Germany to lecture and took the opportunity, like Richard Hillary's crew in the General Goering cup, to mock his Nazi hosts. He told them of a nose job he had perfected which left the patient with a choice of different bridges. 'It is perfectly possible,' he told his solemn audience, 'for a patient to pocket several different-sized bridges and change his racial and facial characteristics by sleight of hand.'

By 1939 McIndoe had become Consultant in Plastic Surgery to the RAF and was assigned to the Queen Victoria Hospital at East Grinstead. He descended on Sussex like a stumpy whirlwind. Flanked by John Hunter and Jill Mullins, he strode through the grounds and buildings of the hospital. There were only twenty-four adult and six children's beds. 'Bit of a shack,' said McIndoe. 'Still, we can probably tart it up.' It was well placed for London and there was space in the grounds for further development. Members of the hospital staff panted along behind him as he made a rapid inspection through his thick bifocals. He liked what he saw.

To begin with there was not enough to do. The staff stood idly about the wards, cleaning and recleaning the floors, checking that the equipment was in place and the beds correctly aligned. Then, as the sunshine of the summer of 1940 lingered on into autumn, the staff of the hospital were able to stand outside on the parched brown lawns and watch the twisting, intricate manoeuvres of twinkling fighter planes above them. They could hear the whine and complaint of the single engines some time after the slick of their vapour trails had crossed or parted. To all of them there was a sense of something distant, barely real. It was more chivalrous, more individual then they had imagined war to be; but it was also more cruel.

McIndoe had been driving round the hospitals of southern England in his Vauxhall, finding out what kind of cases he could expect. In the Royal Masonic Hospital at Ravenscourt Park he was told of a young man who had been shot down and badly burned on his hands and face. McIndoe was conducted into the ward and brought not quite face to face – because the other man's features were concealed by gauze – with Richard Hillary.

McIndoe and Hillary were bound to irritate each other. Hillary's innate self-regard and hectoring manner had been intensified by the pain and humiliation of his injuries. He was not in the mood to be loved or healed; and McIndoe himself provided sufficient reasons for any young man to be wary. What he had to offer Hillary at first was quite simple. He could see that the gentian violet on his eyes was doing him no good, and ordered it to be stripped off. He also saw that Hillary was in danger of losing the sight in his lidless eyes and ordered them to be covered at once. Lukewarm brine was prescribed for the burns while McIndoe found Hillary a place at a Red Cross convalescent home two miles from East Grinstead. This was Dutton Homestall, the home of John and Kathleen Dewar. McIndoe housed his patients there while they were waiting for operations at East Grinstead; with the Dewars' cooperation, they were allowed to live as normally as their injuries permitted.

When McIndoe took the dressings off Hillary's hands, he tapped something white on the knuckle of his right forefinger. 'Bone,' he said. This was the kind of brevity that Hillary could respect. What came next was less welcome. Hillary asked when he might fly again. 'Next war for you,' said McIndoe.

When Hillary was eventually moved from the Royal Masonic Hospital to Dutton Homestall he met two men of a kind that appealed to him. Tony Tollemache was a casualty from a Blenheim bomber. The plane had somersaulted on landing and thrown Tollemache clear. He, however, believing his gunner was still inside, went back into the flaming aircraft to look for him. He took his time searching. The gunner was lying dead beside the plane; but by the time he saw this, Tollemache was burned all over.

Hillary's other new friend was Colin Hodgkinson, who had been injured when the Albatross he was flying had been in collision with a Hurricane. He had fallen 500 feet and ended up trapped beneath the instrument panel. It was not until after dinner on the first day at the Dewars', when Hodgkinson walked away from the table, that Hillary noticed he had tin legs.

He retired to bed feeling pleased with his new home. He enjoyed the soft linen and the prospect of breakfast in bed. The next day, however, he was told that he would be going straight into the Queen Victoria for an operation. Although his eyes were still infected, it had been decided that if they waited any longer he would lose his sight. McIndoe was to give him some eyelids. Until this time Hillary had been pampered. He had not been in a condition to appreciate it, but the conditions in which he had lived in London were, by hospital standards, luxurious.

The Queen Victoria Hospital was different. Hillary and Tollemache went into the main building in a daze of whisky. John Dewar was of the distilling family and made supplies available to the men McIndoe had told him to treat like house guests. After some banter with the Irish nurses, they were persuaded into bed, where McIndoe visited them that night. He prescribed a stomach pump for both of them and peered into Hillary's eyes. 'They're still pretty mucky,' he said, 'but I think you'll find it a relief to have some eyelids on them.'

In the morning Hillary was prepared for the operation. The skin for his new eyelids was to come from the soft inside of his left arm. The whole of the arm and the armpit was closely shaved, then sterilised. His first injection did not make him feel sleepy, so he asked for a cigarette and lay behind the screen puffing with provocative insouciance. Tony Tollemache was wheeled back into the ward after his operation, breathing ether, and Hillary was taken out in his place. In the theatre he was welcomed by the ever-genial John Hunter with his tubes and cylinders. McIndoe lowered over him in skull-cap and multi-coloured gown; Hunter slid the needle softly into the vein, contenting himself with nothing more rib-tickling than a friendly, 'Well, goodbye.'

Hillary felt no particular pain when he came round, but was completely incapacitated. Effectively blind for five days, he had to be bathed and fed where he lay. He could not read, but what he could do was talk. He and Tollemache competed in the careless devilry of their conversation. Needing a focus for their energies, they criticised the hospital and its staff. Hillary could not see whether any of the sisters were in the room and relied on Tollemache to give him the all-clear for his ribaldry. To a determined joker like Tollemache the possibilities were irresistible; he provoked Hillary into his most vulgar abuse when the ward sister was present. As a result the two men were separated, with Hillary being moved into a glassed-in extension off the main ward.

Here McIndoe came to take off the dressings and let his patient see. The new eyelids were grotesquely too large. The only way

Hillary could look ahead of him was by turning his face towards the ceiling. McIndoe was unconcerned; and within a few days the skin shrank into position, so that Hillary could move the new lids up or down. McIndoe next provided him with a pair of lower lids. This time when the dressings were taken off Hillary thought he looked like an orang-utan: the flesh beneath his eyes had been built outwards to make ledges from which the new lids would contract. For the first time since the accident, however, he could close his eyes: until then he had had to roll up his eyes when he wanted to sleep, leaving the whites exposed in a picture of frozen horror.

Hillary was not required to have further operations until January 1941. He spent the intervening time either at the Dewars' convalescent home or up in London with Tony Tollemache. After dinner they would go to a night club and watch the young people on the dance floor. They were like old men, still capable of going out for a pleasant evening with a good cigar to finish, but no longer able to participate in the vital exchanges that they watched. Neither admitted to any feeling of frustration; they pretended to be relieved that they were now excused from the hot imperatives of youth.

When Hillary returned to East Grinstead for a new upper lip the only available bed was in Ward Three – a long, low hut about fifty yards from the main hospital that took the most serious cases. Hillary's burns, though agonising, were not as extensive or as deep as those suffered by many of the inmates of Ward Three.

It was a place in which even Hillary's perverse bravado was tested. The men lay in strange postures, some with their faces attached by grafts to their shoulders, some with their hands on their stomachs and some with their inner forearms flush against their foreheads with the wrist bent over their skulls like creatures from a medieval depiction of torment. Patients with burned hands lay in soft cocoons of cotton; some with smashed faces had their heads held up on pulleys by delicately balanced weights. Warm air was thought to give grafts a better chance to take: the paraffin heaters were kept burning even in summer and the windows were never opened.

The atmosphere, while fetid, was also curiously informal.

Richard Hillary

Those who were dressed wore civilian clothes; beneath the beds were crates of Worthington and Double Diamond. The men behaved as though there were nothing wrong or even particularly unusual in their circumstances. When one of them could not contain his pain, another would simply turn up the volume on the wireless that played all day long, so that the groans rang no more than a descant on the songs of Vera Lynn. Some of them saved their own painkillers to give to a man in torment from his spine.

Near the door was the saline bath in which McIndoe prepared his patients for their operations. At first it had been an ordinary bath with salt added by hand; later the taps were removed to prevent the patients injuring themselves and brine was pumped from a tank through pipes on the ceiling of the ward. The water was kept circulating at just above blood temperature. McIndoe claimed to have discovered the uses of brine, though a version of his bath had been used to treat mustard gas casualties in the Great War.

Next to the bath, in a curtained-off section of her own, was a girl of fifteen who had been terribly burned by boiling sugar in a factory. She was in with the men because she could not be moved too far from the saline bath, but however gently the nurses handled her, she always screamed. A degree of tension affected the others every evening as her bath-time approached.

Most of the men in Ward Three were the age of students. They had helped to win the Battle of Britain, but were now so mentally and physically damaged that they found it difficult to believe they had any life worth living. Among them moved the strange figure of McIndoe in his threadbare sports jacket and baggy flannels, and they came to idolise him. His insistence on civilian clothes and laxity of manner was a relief after the rigours of the service; his brusqueness was as close to sympathy as they could bear. They were facing the prospect of ten, twenty, or in some cases as many as forty, further operations, each one excruciating in its way. McIndoe was forty-one at this time, old enough to be the father of most of what he called his 'guinea-pigs'. They called him Archie, and he didn't seem to mind; he himself spoke in exactly the same way to visiting dignitaries as to the junior

(153)

porters. He shuttled between the beds on his short legs with Jill Mullins at his elbow taking notes. A little way behind would be John Hunter, who usually had a number of complicated bets to settle with patients. The idea was that he would buy them a drink if they had felt sick after his anaesthetic, but these wagers were more a matter of honour since he always bought the drinks anyway.

However fast he moved, McIndoe took time to explain the full course of intended treatment to each patient. He made no promises and did not underplay the degree of permanent disfigurement they could expect, but merely to hear someone offering them an organised and practical route back to normal life seemed miraculous to many of the men who believed they would pass the rest of their lives as freaks. The sweaty camaraderie of Ward Three was partly an accident. Officers and men were at first segregated, but McIndoe discovered that the officers in isolation made a slower recovery than the men who mucked in together. The officers dwelled too much on their traumas and tended to lose their appetites; in the hothouse of Ward Three they had to compete with the clamorous stoicism of the men. In any case, segregation became impossible when the numbers increased: there were not enough staff, and there was only one saline bath. The writ of the new democracy ran outside the wooden walls of the hut. Residents of East Grinstead grew used to seeing officers pushing ordinary airmen in wheelchairs to a pub in town. Sometimes McIndoe, Hunter and Mullins would go with them. McIndoe would whack out a few chords on the piano while Hunter waved a ten-shilling note at the barman.

McIndoe became a powerful figure in town and was invited to dinner by most of the socially conscious families. He did not resent this; on the contrary, with Jill Mullins at his side, he enjoyed the gush of their admiration and, when he had drunk of it long and deep, he asked them for donations.

In the course of the war 4,500 allied airmen suffered serious burns, or as McIndoe put it, 'had their bark knocked off'. For the public's benefit he developed a straightforward explanation of the process: 'A pilot is hurled like a blazing torch from his plane and sustains burns of the exposed parts of his body, or his plane crashes and he is enveloped in flame, lying unconscious against red-hot material. He sustains deep burns of the exposed part of the body, together with a greater or lesser extent of burning of the covered parts, depending on the efficiency of the protective material.' The injuries were made worse by the habit of many pilots, including Hillary, of flying without goggles or gloves. More than 200 of the cases that passed through East Grinstead were men whose faces had been burned away.

McIndoe found Hillary a difficult patient. His supercilious manner and provocative conversation at first made him unpopular on the ward. Gradually, however, people came to respect his integrity and to see that in a loud-mouthed way he was a brave man, with his own peculiar battles to fight. Geoffrey Page, a Hurricane pilot with injuries similar to Hillary's, found him a 'basically pleasant young man hiding behind a barrier of cynicism, a defence mechanism perhaps evolved from an over-doting maternal influence.' When Page first arrived another guinea-pig, Roy Lane, told him Hillary was a 'conceited young man with an inferiority complex'. Lane too believed Edwyna Hillary was responsible: 'For years he's been told by his mother what a wonderful boy he is, but in the service he's had his backside kicked. Not surprising he's a bit mixed up.' Page took several weeks to overcome his awe at Hillary. In the mean time he joined the other patients in attacking him verbally, telling him to shut up, or even hurling their rationed eggs at him.

Hillary mentioned none of the antagonism in *The Last Enemy*, though his dismissive attitude and obvious impatience with hospitals and fellow-sufferers make it easy enough to imagine. His new upper lip was to be made from skin on his left arm, next to the site of his new eyelids. Hillary's reasoning was that if he went for the inner arm rather than the leg, which was the other possibility, he wouldn't have to shave. When the dressings were taken off, Hillary saw that his right eyebrow had been lifted higher to bring it into line with the left. There were stitches beneath both eyes where McIndoe had trimmed back the ledges left by the earlier graft of the lower eyelids. When he visited Hillary that evening McIndoe looked with some anxiety at the scar under the right eye, which appeared swollen and blue. He said nothing, but moved on; and for once his anti-bedside manner was not effective. Hillary was left feeling forlorn.

The next day he and seven others were moved into isolation in a ward in the main part of the hospital. An infection was flourishing in the jungly atmosphere of Ward Three. The others in with him began to succumb. A man called Neft started to suppurate about the face; a Squadron Leader Gleave became infected in the nose; the bandage on Hillary's upper lip smelled so powerfully that he had to pour eau-de-Cologne on to it. Their heads were shorn and rubbed with powder; all had swabs sent for analysis. The results said that six of the eight were infected, but the nurses would not tell them which two were safe. Hillary was not one of them. He developed mastoiditis, an acute infection of the bone behind the ear, the treatment for which (a drug called Prontosil) made him feel sick.

Eight days after his operation the dressings were taken off. Hillary's relief at ridding himself of the suppurating gauze was tempered by the dismay at the new upper lip that McIndoe had given him. It had no central ridge, it was completely white and it was narrower than his previous one. He went to ease the bandages from the donor site on his arm. When he had completed this delicate process, the sister removed the stitches. The wound, however, immediately peeled back like a burst sausage. His body's reserves, depleted by the infection, had not been sufficient to fuse the two sides of the cut.

Hillary now faced another unwanted trial of his resolution. The pain in his ear, and the nausea caused by the Prontosil, made sleep impossible. He walked about the ward in his distress, but in the gloomy light could make out only people in equally dire circumstances: charred, fearful, feverish. The next day he had an operation to treat the mastoiditis, but the infection had also taken root in his lip. The pain was worse than anything he had endured since the crash. The thundering pressure in his head was matched in horror by the sound of footsteps in the corridor when they came to pierce the hole behind his ear with a steel probe to drain the pus.

For much of this time he was either delirious or unconscious from morphia. He was moved to the glassed-in extension where he had first been sent as a punishment. It was from here that he had heard a large bomb whistling down through the night. The impact of its landing was such that it took Hillary some time to work out that the bomb had not actually exploded. He was so disappointed, so powerless and frustrated, that he began to sob. He had wanted to die.

The next day he argued with a doctor who planned to move him back to Ward Three, where he would be safer if the bomb exploded. His humiliation, his pain and his disappointment that the bomb had not gone off slopped over into petulant abuse. No power on earth, he said, would take him back to that place of human refuse; if anyone touched him, he would get up and walk back to London. Sister Hall, who had nursed him throughout the infection, offered to convert a consulting room into a bedroom for Hillary, and the young doctor, relieved to be rid of his difficult patient, swiftly agreed.

That night McIndoe came to see him. He tried to explain to Hillary the difficulties of running the hospital, and how, although Hillary had had an unlucky time, he must try to keep going. Hillary noticed that McIndoe was still in his operating robes and felt slightly chastened when he noticed McIndoe's tense, exhausted expression.

The next day he was visited by Denise and his mother, who had motored down together from London. The delirious sweating had caused him to lose almost three stone in the course of a week and the Prontosil had made his face grey. His mother, who had borne up stubbornly thus far, looked crushed. She believed her son was going to die. She sat with Denise at the end of the bed, within the narrow field of his vision, and tried to find words to comfort him.

He did not die. Slowly the infection retreated; the grafts took; he began to put on weight. When he was eventually moved back to the main ward, he found he had a new neighbour. This was a 26-year-old South African called Edmonds, who was the worst burned pilot in the RAF to survive. He had crashed at night while still training. His plane caught a wing as he was taking off, flipped over and burst into flames: Edmonds was trapped inside. When he arrived he was barely recognisable as a human being. McIndoe performed two emergency operations but then had to leave him to lie in his own suppuration. After nine months, McIndoe sent him away to build up his strength for the ordeal of surgery. On his return to the bed next to Hillary's, Edmonds was facing several years under the knife. He never once complained; and his manner affected Hillary. Edmonds's first operation went wrong: the infection got under his right eyelid and it had to be taken off and thrown away. It was McIndoe's first failure with an eyelid. Through the insensitive crash talk of his neighbours, the well-meaning questions of visitors, Edmonds remained even-tempered and polite. When a visitor twittered about how well he looked, Hillary turned his face to the wall, expecting some explosion. But Edmonds merely replied, 'Yes, and I'm feeling much better, too.'

Hillary could not understand where Edmonds found the courage to confront his future. He wondered whether he derived strength from having been very close to death, but McIndoe, who had seen almost 200 men die, told Hillary they were never aware of how close they were to the end. Hillary could find no answer to the problem other than to think the will to live must be 'instinctive'. Even at the time he was aware that this solution was improbable.

The following day the ear surgeon said Hillary was fit enough to move, and, since McIndoe was planning no operations for the time being, he went back to the Dewars' convalescent home. It was here that his mother brought him the news that Noel Agazarian had been killed. That meant Richard Hillary was the last surviving member of the group of friends from the University Air Squadron who had originally gone north to Kinloss; he was in his own words 'the last of the long-haired boys'.

He was a changed man. The alteration was clearest in his face. Almost all the skin on it was new, and although McIndoe had done as well as any surgeon at the time could have done, the results looked hasty and peculiar. The eyes had no lashes, and their habitual half-smile had been replaced by an involuntary glare. His lips were thin and straight; the fetching bow and curve of the upper one had been replaced by a featureless strip from his inner arm. The stitching that joined the different flaps of skin was plainly visible, and, in areas where it was stretched over the bone, the skin was thin and shiny. The face, however, was a triumph of normality compared to the hands. The severity of the burning and the early tannic acid treatment had drawn the fingers down into the palms, like a bird's claws. Although McIndoe hoped to work further on them, for the time being the fingers on each hand were strapped to a device like a miniature tennis racket, which was supposed to straighten them. Hillary was no more patient about wearing these than he had been about wearing gloves in the cockpit, and took them off when they irritated him.

At Dutton Homestall Hillary became friendly with the Dewars' daughter Barbara. Their intimacy displeased Kathleen Dewar, who was jealous of her daughter and was herself attracted to Hillary. Her jealousy took the form of bitter verbal exchanges in which she questioned Hillary's character and motives. Despite his outward bravado he had always been morbidly sensitive and was particularly so at this low point in his life. He tried to be philosophical about Kathleen Dewar's remarks, but they wounded him at the time and later came back to trouble him profoundly.

McIndoe encouraged his patients to go into town for a few hours each day to remind themselves of what normal life was like. The next stop was to go up to London, a day at a time to begin with, then for longer periods. The residents of East Grinstead were used to seeing badly burned men, but the reaction of Londoners was a trial. Some of the pilots were contemptuous of people who recoiled from them: clearly they didn't understand that a war could not be fought without cost. This contempt was a protection for them. Others found it harder to reconcile themselves to having become repulsive.

Hillary relied on Denise's beauty to draw the eyes of strangers from his face; and when once a good-looking woman smiled at him he felt a return of self-esteem that went beyond simple vanity. Denise had knitted him some gloves and wore an identical pair herself so that he should not feel they had been made specially for him. In the winter of 1941–2 Hillary frequently spent the night at Denise's flat in Eaton Place. She shared it with her sister Penny, who worked at the Admiralty. Denise was in the ATS, and the house was full of young men and women in various uniforms. When they had all gone home, Richard and Denise continued their long conversations against the sound of bombs falling on the docks and on the residential streets nearby.

Richard was beginning to reach the end of what he could take from Denise. Her attitude to Peter's death and to her own situation was too resolutely mystical for him. Although he had himself had a vision of Peter's death, he was not prepared to infer from it the existence of any spiritual world. He seemed to see his premonition as no more than an extreme example of male comradeship: when your mind and body were so fully stretched in the taking and saving of life at hundreds of miles per hour 25,000 feet above the earth, when you depended for your existence on the bark and crackle of the R/T system, it was only natural that you should see, beneath the green fog of anaesthetic, an Me-109 closing on your best friend's tail.

In April Hillary returned to a guest night at Hornchurch, but found it difficult to racapture the careless indifference with which he and his fellow-pilots had viewed their flying lives. So many of them were dead. He invited twenty old friends to a party at his mother's flat in London, but after an hour he could bear it no longer and walked off into the night.

In *The Last Enemy* Hillary wrote that when he heard of Noel Agazarian's death he 'felt no emotion at all'. If this is true, and it seems improbable, it can only be that the emotion that the news provoked was too complicated to be registered at once. He felt lucky and he felt guilty. There seemed to be no purpose in his survival. Yet he shied away from the rhetoric of sacrifice; he refused to be part of the way that politicians talked of the War. At this stage in his life he tried to recultivate the arrogance and selfishness that others had critically described in him. He wanted to feel the same contempt for the politicians, the enemy, and the unthinking people of his own country that had enabled him to take to the sky as though it were some superior joust between the best knights of either side. He could not recapture his old state of mind, however; the death of so many friends had bound him both to them and to some sort of common cause that he could as yet neither understand nor describe. He very much disliked this new sensation of fraternity; he recoiled from it for reasons of intellect, taste and snobbery.

In *The Last Enemy* he dramatised this change of heart in an invented piece of narrative. A chapter called 'I See They Got You Too' tells first of all how he went to Norfolk to see his old Oxford pacifist friend David Rutter – a man who at one stage held all the anti-war 'progressive' views. Rutter has undergone a terrible transformation; he has seen that his socialist objections are false, that the war has become a crusade, and that personal conscience is an indulgence at a time when the battle is for civilisation itself.

Back in Liverpool Street Hillary takes a taxi west, but has not gone far before the intensity of the bombing forces the cab to stop. Hillary goes into a pub called The George and Dragon, on which a bomb falls. The house next door takes most of the blast and Hillary helps an ARP warden to dig out a woman who is trapped. They first remove her dead child. When he looks down into the woman's 'tired, blood-streaked, work-worn face' Hillary has 'a sense of complete unreality'. He gives her some brandy; as she takes the flask from his clawed hand and looks up at his face, she says, 'I see they got you too.' Hillary leaves the scene in a fit of incoherent fear and anger. The prose becomes hysterical as he tries to explain what effect the woman's words have on him. He dramatises it as a sudden and complete self-knowledge: 'With awful clarity I saw myself suddenly as I was. Great God, that I could have been so arrogant!'

The enlightened man then vows to put his new self-knowledge to good use. He will write a book, and his subject will be the men he has known. The story will be addressed to 'Humanity', the amorphous and previously despised mass of people of whom he now feels himself to be a part.

Hillary admitted later that the incident was invented. He did change, but the process was slow. The theme of personal growth in the book is at best unclear and at worst factitious and embarrassing. Without a belief that some kind of transformation had taken place, however, Hillary would not have attempted the descriptions of flying, of life on the station and of plastic surgery – all that is most valuable in *The Last Enemy*.

Back in the convalescent home at Dutton Homestall he began the painful task of writing. To begin a book is almost always an act of perverse and unattractive self-assertion; to do it when you have not written one before and when you have to grip the pen in a clawed hand requires a particular stubbornness. Hillary at once emitted signals of distress: the words wouldn't come, he was useless, what was the point? His natural author's feelings of presumption and unworthiness were intensified by the personal doubts and re-evaluations that his experiences had precipitated.

But what he wrote was good. He had begun with a description of his blazing descent into the North Sea. At Dutton Homestall there was a volunteer nurse called Patricia Hollander with whom Hillary had become friendly. She knew Rache Lovat Dickson, an editor at the publishing house of Macmillan, and late one afternoon she took Hillary to see him in London. Despite the warning he had been given, Lovat Dickson was shocked by Hillary's appearance. The March wind had flayed his skin and made his lidless eyes water. Pat Hollander explained that Hillary would like to read out the first chapter of his book.

Lovat Dickson was horrified by the idea. A publisher did not work in this way. There should have been lunch at the Garrick first, then lunch with Hillary's agent. The manuscript should have been completed, typed up, then delivered over another lunch, perhaps at an Italian restaurant in Soho. There then should have followed a few telephone calls from Hillary's agent wondering whether Rache had yet had time to have a look at . . .

Hillary just fixed him with his sore-eyed glare and read. Lovat Dickson was too fascinated by the skeletal hands that gripped the pages to be able to take in the words. When he did manage to concentrate he noticed that Hillary did not read well. A strange shyness made him flush, and this caused the weals of his burns to stand out. Somehow, beneath his horror both at Hillary's appearance and at his series of publishing *faux pas*, Lovat Dickson managed to recognise that what he was listening to was 'first-class reporting'. He told Hillary that many people could write, but that few had the perseverance to finish their books. If Hillary could write another half dozen chapters as good as the first, then they might do business. With such words had Lovat

Dickson seen the last of many would-be writers in the past.
Would Hillary be different?

The condition of his hands made it difficult for him to write for
long periods, so he tried dictating instead. The results seemed far
from what he had set out to say. Faced with this impasse, he
decided to do something else. He wanted to go to the United
States and talk to the workers in aircraft factories that were
supplying the RAF with planes. He thought it would be a good
idea if he could 'try to make something living out of the job of
putting nuts and bolts into an airframe'. With the same directness
with which he had approached Lovat Dickson, he this time
presented himself to Duff Cooper and Sir Walter Monckton at
the Ministry of Information. They decided to send him to
America, subject to Air Ministry approval. He was officially
attached to the Air Mission, so that his visit would not look like
propaganda, and duly arrived on his mission to encourage the
workers.

The British Embassy in Washington, however, took one look at
him and shuddered. Sir Gerald Campbell, the minister in charge
of such matters, thought a speaking tour of women's clubs of the
Mid-West by such a badly mutilated man would prevent the
United States from ever joining the Allied cause. He suggested
that Hillary give some talks on the radio and perhaps publish
them as a pamphlet. Hillary was upset by the thought that the
face that had once lured young women to his bed would now
determine the mothers of America against committing their sons
to battle. He had come, in any case, not to address ladies'
luncheons but to speak to the factory workers; and surely, he
argued with Sir Gerald, he could still manage that without
frightening anyone. The chiefs of various aircraft companies in
New York said they could smuggle him in and out of the factories
with no publicity and no photographs. Hillary lobbied hard
among British and American diplomats; with their support, he
presented his case to the British Ambassador, Lord Halifax.
Unfortunately Halifax had already been briefed by Sir Gerald
Campbell and had himself commissioned a briefing of President
Roosevelt, who replied that the whole enterprise was clearly a

'psychological error'. Halifax told Hillary that he himself, of course, still had an open mind.

Various official doors swung soundlessly shut. Hillary was flown to Boston with a view to having plastic surgery from a man called Quesanazian who unwisely told Hillary he had orders to keep him there. Hillary at once flew back to New York to try to prolong the debate. Eventually he was barred – apparently by both governments and their diplomatic representatives – from writing or broadcasting anything at all under his own name. He was allowed to write anonymous agency copy for the British Press Service for distribution to American newspapers, who were largely uninterested. Although the question of America's involvement in the War was a matter of global importance and the subject of extremely delicate negotiation, the insensitivity with which Hillary was treated was by any standards remarkable.

In these circumstances, with the pen clutched in his charred hand, he settled down again to write *The Last Enemy*. He was lent a room in which to work by the banker Edward Warburg and patiently scratched out his recollections of Oxford and his summer travels. He was writing a memoir, but he felt able to embellish, omit and invent. He later referred to the book as a 'novel', which it certainly was not. It was autobiography, shaped by a fair literary sense of what to include, what to dwell on and what to pass over. Its falsities were minor, its fidelity to the wider truth of his experience in the War was almost total.

In July and August Hillary was allowed by the British and American governments to make four anonymous broadcasts. These were essentially readings from drafts of what was to become *The Last Enemy*. Hillary spoke with the accent of public school and Oxford, though not exaggeratedly so by the standards of the time; he still said 'parachute', for instance, rather than 'perachute'. His voice was mournful and deep. What was shocking about it was that it could under no circumstances be identified as the voice of a man of twenty-two. The timbre, the inflection and the sheer weariness of it, preserved on tape, would make most listeners put its owner at nearer fifty. He performed well. His melancholy tone and his slightly soft 'r' somehow helped to make the flying adventures sound more credible.

Richard Hillary

In New York Hillary also met Antoine de Saint-Exupéry, the French author-pilot who was at this stage wondering how best to help the Free French. Saint-Exupéry was a shambling, clumsy man whose flying life had been marked by frequent crashes. He had gained popularity by his accounts of long-distance flight in the service of the French mail. His books combined lucid narrative with philosophical musing; and although the cause of the French colonial mail was scarcely as pressing as the defence of European freedom there was something genuinely heroic in this burly cavalier with his long nose and mournful, doglike eyes. Saint-Exupéry had just delivered a book called *Pilote de Guerre*, an account of his time in the French airforce during the fall of France, a subject that called for the philosophical resources of a Pascal. It was to be published in America under the rather plodding title *Flight to Arras*.

Hilary was introduced to Saint-Exupéry by his translator, Lewis Galantière, who invited them to lunch together. Hillary appeared to think that the older man would patronise him, but Saint-Exupéry disarmed him with champagne and an offer to write a preface to his book. Galantière explained that in America there was no tradition of established writers introducing young talent in this way, and that the gesture might be misinterpreted, particularly since he was hoping that Hillary would be published by the same house as Saint-Exupéry.

Michael Hillary believed Richard's meeting with Saint-Exupéry was decisive in making his son decide to return to flying. There were certainly some highly suggestive passages in *Flight to Arras*: 'What do I accomplish by risking my life in this mountain avalanche [ie the eponymous flight]? I have no notion. Time and again people would say to me, "I can arrange to have you transferred here or there. That is where you belong. You will be more useful there than in a squadron. Pilots! We can train pilots by the thousand! Whereas you –" No question but that they were right. My mind agreed with them, but my instinct always prevailed over my mind.'

Or even more plainly: 'I accept death. It is not danger that I accept. It is not combat that I accept. It is death. I have learnt a great truth. War is not the acceptance of danger. It is not the acceptance of combat. For the combatant it is at certain moments the pure and simple acceptance of death.'

There were also many passages that exalted the nobility and danger of flying in comparison to the 'barbarous dilapidation' of life on earth. 'Up here at any rate death is clean. A death of flame and ice! Of sun and sky and flame and ice. But below! That digestion stewing in slime . . .'

In *The Last Enemy* Hillary was meanwhile writing: 'The fighter pilot's emotions are those of the duellist – cool, precise, impersonal. He is privileged to kill well. For if one must either kill or be killed, as now we must, it should, I feel, be done with dignity. Death should be given the setting it deserves; it should never be a pettiness; and for the fighter pilot it never can be.' A death of flame and ice . . .

Other of Saint-Exupéry's reflections took time to work their influence on Hillary. Meanwhile, he received a visit from Eugene Reynal, the senior partner of the publishers Reynal and Hitchcock, who, on the strength of the passage Hillary had read out loud to Lovat Dickson, offered him a contract. This early commitment proved vitally encouraging. Through the summer of 1941, the book grew beneath his hands. Both Reynal and Lewis Galantière, who had considerably helped Saint-Exupéry, gave him encouragement and advice.

He was clawing something back from the flames.

Meanwhile, Hillary's attractiveness to women began to return. He lacked his old beauty, but not the old manner. If there was an element of pity or concern in their attentions, that made no difference to the way in which it was expressed. At a party given by his publisher he was introduced to Merle Oberon, then at the considerable height of her fame as an actress following her role as Cathy in Alexander Korda's film of *Wuthering Heights*. She was an emotionally volatile woman whose two-year-old marriage to Korda had done nothing to stabilise her. She had herself been disfigured in a car crash, though had regained her looks almost completely; when she first saw Richard Hillary she felt a passionate bond with him. Her publicity agent Tessa Michaels reportedly said that Hillary excited a protective feeling in Merle

Oberon: she believed she could reignite his passive sexual self-confidence. Just how dormant that side of him had been is open to question: he had mentioned in passing that he sometimes feared women only wanted to sleep with him for the perverse pleasure of feeling his clawed hands. This argues that, for whatever reason, he had already had lovers since his crash. In any event, the affair with Merle Oberon was relatively light-hearted; it took his mind off his humiliation by the British Embassy and gave him relief from the rigours of writing.

Merle Oberon was of Eurasian origin, though she became engaged, with Alexander Korda and various studio publicity hacks, in elaborate attempts to conceal her beginnings. They pretended she was originally Tasmanian, and this led to farcical and unhappy scenes when she was required to open a Merle Oberon memorial theatre in her 'native' island. She had shuttled from one lover to another in the belief that the latest would provide her with the love and rootedness she lacked. She was hopelessly fickle and studiously indecisive, but she was a very beautiful and charming woman and there is no reason to think that her affair with Richard Hillary brought him anything other than pleasure. It was certainly better than being stuck in the soupy air of Ward Three.

It came to a natural end when Hillary returned to London in October 1941. In his briefcase were the proofs of what the American publishers called *Falling Through Space*. He went to see Rache Lovat Dickson at Macmillan's one evening, just as the office was closing. Lovat Dickson was again shocked by Hillary's failure to understand how things were 'done'. He made excuses about shutting up the office and getting off home while Hillary sat hunched up in his greatcoat, watching him with an ironic smile.

'You told me to come back when I'd finished the book,' he said eventually. 'I've done it. Here it is.'

Lovat Dickson was astounded. To have written the book so quickly and to have found an American publisher . . . this was not at all what was supposed to happen. English writers should be published in London first, and their English publishers might help them to find an American publisher in due course, but that should take time, and usually never happened at all.

'Saint-Exupéry read it in America and liked it', said Hillary. 'I hope you like it too. Telephone me when you've read it.'

He waved Lovat Dickson goodbye and sauntered off into the dark evening.

Lovat Dickson liked it all right. Although he told the story against himself of how Hillary had twice confounded him, he was a perfectly competent publisher. When he read the bundle of dog-eared galley proofs he believed that he was holding a book that not only contained outstanding accounts of action but also in some way captured the feelings of a generation.

He was proved right. *The Last Enemy* rapidly acquired the peculiar aura of a book that says something vital, whose importance goes beyond what it literally describes. In the years since Hillary's death its reputation has remained high. Though minor compared to the great prose memoirs of the First World War, it has succeeded in holding its own as a book whose passionate reporting no internal shortcomings and no change of fashion can devalue. It became, and has remained, a 'classic' in the sense that, whatever its failings, it has something to say about flying, about the War and about people's attitudes to the War, that will always need to be read as long as interest in the subjects themselves continues.

So what did Richard Hillary put into *The Last Enemy*? He began with an account of the events of 3 September 1940, the day of his crash. Quaintly titled 'Proem', this flashback was the part he read to Lovat Dickson at their first meeting. It is arguably the best sequence in the book. It reveals at once Hillary's strengths as a writer: the ability to describe action in a clear, laconic, but not affectedly laconic, style; an ease and charm in first person narrative that is unusual in a writer of any age; and a modest reticence about his own sufferings which neither obscures them nor descends to a merely dismissive stoicism.

He leaves himself unconscious in Margate hospital and begins the narrative proper with his arrival at Oxford. He describes the 'alert philistinism' of Trinity and gives a very rapid sketch of the left-wing and anti-war positions. It is not presented as an argument but as a first person memoir; his purpose is merely to describe what he and his friends felt – which turns out to be not much: 'We were disillusioned and spoiled.' Hillary welcomed the fact that the War would solve his problems over choosing a career; as a fighter pilot he would find 'a concentration of amusement, fear, and exaltation which it would be impossible to experience in any other form of existence.' The War itself would give to him and his friends a chance to prove that their 'effete veneer was not as deep as our dislike of interference . . . that, undisciplined though we might be, we were a match for Hitler's dogma-fed youth.' Although he wrote about himself, Hillary stressed that he believed he 'differed little in essentials from the majority of young men with a similar education.'

The second chapter describes training in Scotland and the third the move to Old Sarum. Hillary devotes a good deal of space to his various friends and their out-of-hours exploits. Though trivial in themselves, they have a poignancy lent by the knowledge that the War is about to begin in earnest. From the moment he climbs into a Spitfire, Hillary's writing recaptures the verve and tautness of the opening 'Proem'. He is much better when describing flying than when recreating late-night conversations.

Chapter Four is called 'The World of Peter Pease' and indulges the less interesting aspect of Hillary's writing. His feelings for Pease are hard for the reader to share when the descriptions that Hillary offers to justify them make Pease out to have been no more than a kind and thoughtful man. Hillary's passion for him is puzzling, unless you believe either that he was in love with him or that he is at this stage withholding – consciously or otherwise – many of his own doubts and worries from the narrative. His long recreated conversations with Pease are laboured and unconvincing: the intellectual content is not sufficient to justify their inclusion at such length. Where Hillary does much better is in his descriptions of life on the station at Montrose, and in his brief accounts of his fellow-pilots, such as Brian Carbury, Hugh Stapleton and Pilot Officer Berry (he gives Berry no Christian name). Hillary is pleased that he is able to mix with what he calls 'the Carburys and Berrys' – men, in other words, of an inferior social class; and his appreciation of them, which becomes more marked as the book progresses, is touched with an unconsciously comic snobbery. This is one of those tricks that hindsight plays; all writers suffer from the changed orthodoxies of later generations: the bomber pilot Guy Gibson, for instance, meant no harm by calling his black Labrador 'Nigger'. Hillary's terse affection for his fellow-pilots would not have seemed patronising in 1941 and remains, in context, one of the most touching qualities of his book.

Chapter Five sees Hillary at Hornchurch during the Battle of Britain and contains the best passages of writing about flying. In Chapter Six he rejoins himself where he had finished in the 'Proem'. The second part of the book tells of his time in hospital and gradual recovery up to the episode with the attempted rescue of the woman from the bombed house.

In his hospital chapters Hillary exhibits the same attitude towards his own injuries that he had successfully used in the opening. It is not much more than a tone of voice, but it successfully enables him to give detailed descriptions of the surgical processes as well as following his own reactions to it. He is frequently in pain, sometimes in despair, and does not mind admitting it. His occasional weakness effectively highlights his habitual resilience. His sympathy for other victims is done without sentimentality; the truculent, questioning side of his own character is helpful to him in viewing these other wounded men: his continual puzzling over why and how they manage is more affecting than straightforward pity. The arrival of Denise Maxwell-Woosnan at his bedside has great dramatic force, though less for what Hillary says than for what the reader (rightly or wrongly) infers – that under the guise of comforting her he is falling in love with his best friend's fiancée. The conversations with Denise that Hillary actually recreates or invents, have the same rhetorical, dead quality as those with Peter Pease.

The next two chapters, 'The Beauty Shop' and 'The Last of the Long-Haired Boys', became deservedly famous. They deal with McIndoe's work in the hospital and with Hillary's own progress through operations, mastoid infection and the continuing news of other squadron deaths. He remains complaining, awkward, sometimes bitter, and this attitude continually saves the book from becoming an example of the 'Our Island Fortress' propaganda he deplored. Yet the agony suffered by Hillary and the other patients, particularly during the mastoid episode, is movingly evoked. Hillary's prose is essentially one of action; it is not much suited to the mimetic falsities of 'realistic' dialogue and becomes incoherent when faced with abstractions. However, in the East Grinstead chapters his writing proves more flexible than one might have expected, and he successfully integrates his own psychological development into the action.

The last chapter is 'I See They Got You Too'. Here Hillary's technique fails him, and the book ends with a series of rhetorical declarations which lack the authenticity of the descriptive chapters. The problem comes with the moment of enlightenment, when he believes that the scales of self-delusion have fallen from his eyes. 'With awful clarity I saw myself suddenly as I was. Great God, that I could have been so arrogant!'

It is almost always embarrassing when a writer invites you to join in such epiphanies. While you may accept his criticism of his earlier self, the concomitant invitation – to believe that he is now remade, enlightened and beyond criticism – is less easy to take. In Hillary's case, it is hard to believe in his version of either side of the volte-face. Although he has certainly been arrogant and selfish, he has also shown admirable qualities of stoicism and, like all the pilots, a dazzling indifference to his own fate. If he has grumbled a little in hospital, that has endearingly reduced him to a human scale with which we can more easily identify. It seems quite wrong for him to reject so floridly all he has been. Worse than this, we suspect that he is himself not sincere in his repudiation.

The change that took place in Richard Hillary does not seem to have been a sudden revelation, experienced in the psychological and, at times, almost spiritual terms he describes. On the contrary, the change was gradual. And, although his grief at his own disfigurement and the deaths of his friends may have provided the emotional triggers, the change was ultimately an intellectual one. It was a change of conviction: he came to believe that the War was not only worth fighting but was an historic emergency with universal moral implications.

Hillary himself put it clearly in a letter: 'I got so sick of the stuff about our Island Fortress and the Knights of the Air that I determined to write it anyway in the hope that the last generation might realise that while stupid, we were not that stupid, that we could remember only too well that all this had been seen in the last war but that in spite of that and not because of it, we still thought this one worth fighting.'

In the last paragraph of *The Last Enemy*, he put the point more floridly and added a note of personal emotion. Beneath this, however, it is recognisably the same point: 'If I could do this thing, just tell a little of the lives of these men, I would have justified, at least in some measure, my right to fellowship with my dead, and to the friendship of those with courage and steadfastness who were still living and who would go on fighting until the ideals for which their comrades had died were stamped for ever on the future of civilisation.'

The odd word in that sentence is 'my', in the phrase 'my dead'. Much speculation has swirled about the last year of Richard Hillary's life, and it hangs heavy over his insistence on returning, against medical advice, to flying operations. But if one bears in mind the words that Hillary had written and published, and in particular the phrase 'my dead', then his motivation is not so very puzzling after all.

Hillary's own view of his book is preserved in a letter he wrote to Rache Lovat Dickson on 24 December 1941, accepting the invitation to write the jacket notes or 'blurb'. Publishers commonly ask authors to do this: it saves them time and the possible embarrassment of making clear, if they write the blurb themselves, how completely they have misunderstood the author's intentions.

Dear Lovat Dickson,
    Taking you at your word and casting shame to the winds, I enclose the following blurb which you can cut and minimise to your heart's content.
    'RH is a young man at Oxford at the outbreak of war. He had hoped eventually to become a foreign correspondent, an ambition

which everybody reading this book will have no doubt that he will achieve. This is his first book and with it he has set himself a high standard, but one which he will doubtless maintain. Here is a writer who happened to be a pilot, not a pilot who happened to write a book. It is no mere record of fighting experience; it tells not only how but why the youth of this country went to war, tracing with an ease and clarity of style that is admirable the transition from a left-wing Oxford egocentricity to a spirit which from August to October last year drove the enemy from these shores.

'Starting at Oxford before the war the author takes us through the Battle of Britain and his months in hospital to the final dramatic climax of a blitz on London.

'By turns humorous and tragic, it is an essentially human document and the book which everyone knew must come out of the Royal Air Force.'

It is not a very good example of the form, but that is not surprising. Hillary fairly selects 'ease' and 'clarity' as the outstanding facets of his style. What is most striking about the blurb is his description of himself at Oxford as 'left-wing'. His intolerance of state or corporate interference in individual affairs was such that he could barely grant the RAF the right to put its 'duellists' into numbered squadrons. His position at Oxford might playfully have been described as anarchistic with a very small 'a', but his remarks in the book itself about the 'Auden group', as well as his consistent distrust of the state place him a long way from any recognisable Left position.

Wartime printing restrictions meant that it would take Macmillan even longer than it usually took a publisher to produce a book. *Falling Through Space* was due out in February 1942 in the United States, but meanwhile Hillary had nothing to do. He applied to be a reporter with the RAF in the Middle East, but was refused on medical grounds. When the United States entered the war on 8 December 1941, he volunteered to train American pilots, but this application was also unsuccessful.

Merle Oberon had given him a letter of introduction to a friend of hers called Mary Booker, and one damp evening in December Hillary called at her flat on the Bayswater Road. The housekeeper let him in and told him Mrs Booker would be back soon.

While he was waiting for his hostess, Hillary fell asleep in an armchair.

Mary Booker was a 44-year-old divorcee, elegant, mondaine and famously beautiful. Her dark hair had gone white in her twenties and rose from her forehead in two shimmering curves. She had deep brown eyes, a small nose, and a magnolia-coloured skin that had remained almost unlined. An early marriage to an insurance broker had produced two daughters who by this time were almost grown-up. Although she had been photographed and fêted as a 'society beauty' in her youth, she had shown an elegant indifference to such attention. Her beauty and charm were intensified by her nonchalance and the simplicity of her style. Her father was a merchant called Charles Walter, whose business was principally in South America, and her mother was Ada Yeats, first cousin of the poet. After her divorce in the early Thirties, Mary tried to support her children by working in films. Despite the patronage of Alexander Korda, she was not successful. She became an adviser on interior decoration and made some money in partnership with two friends. What she was doing at the time she met Richard Hillary is not known; even her second husband Michael Burn was not able to discover, though some people believed that one of her numerous friends in the Foreign Office had secured her job working in 'something secret', probably in Naval Intelligence.

She had lovers, but did not become the kind of divorced Thirties beauty who lived only for men. She had many female friends, to whom her kindness rendered her beyond jealousy. They remarked on her sympathy, her capacity for listening, and her serenity. She was an unusual mixture: smart and conventional, yet not fussy about money or fashion; gentle and understanding of other people, yet troubled in her own life and, for all her worldly experience, unsuccessful at organising her own affairs.

Not everyone was charmed by Mary Booker. There were some who found her fey, some who believed that her apparent indifference to material things masked a manipulative nature, and some who found her unembarrassed references to 'love' and 'the spirit' to be – in the brutal adjective of the period – 'common'.

As she crossed Hyde Park on that damp December evening Mary Booker noticed that the blackout was not fully drawn in the sitting-room window of her third-floor flat. When she went upstairs she was able to take a long, slow look at the figure sprawled in her armchair before he finally awoke. In the first hour that they spent together Mary Booker saw at once that while Hillary was brash, he was also sensitive. Although he spoke with what she described as 'a pose of nonchalance, and a slightly aggressive attitude to life', she had no doubt that he had also 'a sensitivity which must have caused him a degree of mental suffering far beyond the physical torment of those months after his rescue from the sea.'

Mary Booker had arrived, by a different route, at an attitude towards the War that was curiously like Hillary's own. She had become aware of what she called a 'blind selfishness' in her previous attitude to life, and saw the War, and the necessary victory, as a way of morally redefining herself.

Their affair did not begin at once. Hillary remained officially on leave until 1 January 1942 when he left London to go on a course at the RAF Staff College at Gerrards Cross. He found it physically exhausting, but that did not prevent him from beginning to plan his return to active duty. He wrote to Edward Warburg in New York: 'After this Staff course I may come out on the Staff in Washington if Bill Thornton [the Air Attaché] will have me. If not, I'm going back to hospital to get medically fit again. I shall fly again. This I think will be possible. I have no intention of taking an office job at the Air Ministry.'

This decision to fly again was thus already taken when his affair with Mary Booker began at the end of January; the implications of it hung over their relationship throughout its brief but intense duration. There were one or two scruples over Merle Oberon to be cleared away before Richard and Mary could be quite relaxed about their new intimacy. Merle Oberon, after all, had provided the introduction on the grounds that Mary would look after Richard, not that they should fall in love. Richard was impatient with all this: he would have met Mary anyway, through other friends in common; and, as he wrote to Mary Booker, 'I love you, and do not, nor ever have loved Merle . . . My dominant emotion on arriving back [from America] was one of relief.'

He stayed at Gerrards Cross until his course finished at the end of March. He was due for another operation at East Grinstead on 10 April, but he was still feeling weak and was prone to fainting. Macmillan, meanwhile, had managed to schedule publication of *The Last Enemy* for the end of April, which was a considerable achievement in the circumstances and reflected Lovat Dickson's belief in the book's urgent topicality. They might have got it out even sooner had they not had to print a further 10,000 copies for the Book of the Month Club.

On 29 February Hillary heard that Colin Pinckney had been killed in Singapore. He was now not only the last of the long-haired boys, he was the last of the triangle of friendship with Pease and Pinckney that he had described in *The Last Enemy*. The continuing presence of death seems to have intensified his feelings for Mary as well as raising in his mind, 'yet again the question which I have put in the book, and have attempted to answer, of what is the responsibility of the man who is left.' In early April he spent a holiday with Mary in the cottage she had renovated in Llanfrothen in North Wales. Each spoke rapturously of the time, yet the intensity of their happiness seemed to underline how troubled each one was at heart.

The course at Gerrards Cross showed that Hillary was not well enough organised to be a staff officer. The Commandant recommended he join Combined Operations. The idea was that he would accompany commando operations in France and on his return write about them for the newspapers. Before anything could happen, however, he had to return to East Grinstead for more surgery on his hands. It was while he was there in April that, in conversation with another 'guinea-pig', Geoffrey Page, Hillary developed the idea of flying night-fighters. He accepted that the injuries to his hands would limit his speed of response by day, but he believed that at night, 'you can creep up behind your target and shoot the bastard down.' McIndoe told Hillary and Page that they had 'not a chance in hell of getting back. Not only do I disapprove, but the Air Ministry would not allow it.' In fact

McIndoe simply believed that they had done enough: Page had had fifteen operations in the course of his two years in hospital. But they kept nagging at McIndoe until finally he told them, 'If you're determined to kill yourselves, go ahead. Only don't blame me.' He wrote out the necessary medical certificates. Three months later Page was made operational and flew till the end of the war, collecting the DSO and DFC with bar. The Medical Board was at this stage prepared to pass Hillary fit for light aircraft only, and in daylight.

In the Queen Victoria Hospital he had operations on his eyelid and on his hand. The latter procedure produced pain that Geoffrey Page, not a complaining man, compared to having nails driven through the hand and withdrawn with clumsy pincers. Hillary described his fingers as 'a bit of a bore'. His eyebrow became infected with one of the many streptococci that had bred since his last visit to East Grinstead; the graft on his upper eyelid was successful, but he believed McIndoe had done the wrong one, as it was his lower lid that was troubling him. He vented his frustration in fierce arguments with the hospital staff. He behaved like the pre-'enlightenment' boy who had first arrived there, but no one who understood the pain he endured was blaming him for that. No one, that is, except the embittered Kathleen Dewar, who took the opportunity to call him a coward. Hillary was not in a robust enough state to treat the jibe with the contempt it needed, and was wounded by it.

In May he was moved to the RAF Officers' Hospital at Torquay to recover his strength. He found no relaxation or peace of mind there. All aspects of his life were troubling him. He wanted to fly again and was not sure what, if anything, an attachment to Combined Operations would entail. He was agitated by the strength of his feeling for Mary Booker and the strong sexual appetites that were frustrated by their separation. While he had a large envelope of favourable reviews from the United States, he was still in the anxious weeks before British publication, which had been slightly delayed, and *The Last Enemy* was a vulnerably personal first book. Even if it went well, he was aware of his limitations as a writer and had no new idea on which to work. Pain, infection and continuing disfigurement did nothing to comfort him.

Meanwhile, Richard and Mary wrote each other letters. Mary's second husband Michael Burn found a well-preserved packet of them and published a selection in 1988. Their intense and self-regarding quality made them uncomfortable to read. Mary writes at this time of the 'extraordinary contrasting and many-sided quality of our love' and 'the seriousness of our love'; 'We are,' she tells Hillary, 'the most extraordinary couple that ever loved.' It is more than seriousness that is conveyed by their letters, it is a self-conscious solemnity. Perhaps the circumstances made it inevitable. Richard was thinking of a return to flying and was aware of the dangers it would entail. It was far from clear at this stage that Britain would win the victory that they believed would have such profound personal implications for them both. It was a strange and risky thing for each to do, to embark on an affair so all-involving at such a precarious time.

The Last Enemy was published on Friday 19 June and fulfilled all its publisher's ambitions. Although Churchill had ensured that the whole population was aware of the importance of what the fighter pilots had done in the Battle of Britain, few people were aware of quite how it was achieved, or at what cost. The hospital at East Grinstead began to receive hundreds of donations from readers of the book. Desmond MacCarthy, Storm Jameson and Elizabeth Bowen were among its reviewers. They were impressed by Hillary's story, though V.S. Pritchett, among others, was unconvinced by his climactic conversion: 'Mr Hillary conveys the impression that he likes the spectacle of himself believing, and not that he believes . . . he remains egocentric, busily self-conscious in defiance and remorse.'

The tersest verdict came from Geoffrey Page, who read it in hospital. 'I think it's beautifully written, Richard. In fact I'm surprised a supercilious bastard like you could produce something like this . . . However, there's one thing I don't quite understand . . . You write of being an irresponsible undergraduate before the war, then, as a result, you change, and, presto, here you are, a different person . . . In my opinion, you're still as bloody conceited as ever.'

On 1 July Hillary returned to East Grinstead for a final operation on his eyes. Despite a seizure as he was coming round from the anaesthetic, the operation was deemed a success, and a week later he was posted to Fighter Command HQ at Bentley Priory near Stanmore with orders to rewrite the Pilot's Order Book. This was a wise way for the RAF to capitalise on the talent of a man who had just published an acclaimed literary memoir, though as a job it lacked excitement. 'The Pilot's Order Book,' Hillary explained, 'is the thing every pilot has to sign as understanding the rules and regulations that apply locally . . . This entails reading through some 4,000 orders, deciding what is obsolete and what is relevant – retype the whole bloody lot' – or at least instruct a typist on which bits to delete.

At the same time his application to join Combined Operations was turned down on the bureaucratic grounds that if he had passed through RAF Staff College he ought to remain at the RAF's disposal. Hillary regretted not only the missed posting, but also the London flat that should have gone with it. Meetings between him and Mary were difficult to arrange without such a base, and Mary's sense of discretion would not allow him to stay in the flat she shared. The Blitz had made property extremely scarce, and the lack of somewhere private to meet was a major irritant in their affair.

Hillary's commander in chief at Bentley Priory was Sir Sholto Douglas, who later became Marshal of the Royal Air Force. In his memoirs some years later he gave a detailed picture of him:

Richard Hillary was typical of the intellectual who becomes a fighter pilot. That in itself sounds formidable enough, because the qualities of both must produce in a man obsessively strong traits of individuality. By the time he arrived at Bentley the whole force and expression of his character had become excessively individualistic. It was known that he was exceptionally talented and highly-strung. That was clear enough from a reading of his remarkable book . . . There was some devil goading him on which none of us could understand. He never spoke about it, but the result of that goading was to be seen in his manner. From the moment he arrived at my Headquarters he started nagging at everybody about being allowed to return to operational flying. He had been through a hard and trying time, and many people went out of their way to help him; but Hillary simply could not reconcile himself to having to stay on the ground. He spoke to me several times about getting back to flying, and each time I told him that I simply could not recommend it. But he kept pestering me, and in the end I gave in with a rather foolish suggestion.

'If you can get the doctors to pass you,' I told him, 'you can go back on ops.'

I said that because I felt certain that the doctors would never pass him fit for any sort of operational flying. But I had not counted on Hillary's pertinacity and persuasiveness.

So, in order to rid himself of Hillary's attentions, Douglas passed the decision on to someone else. It was similar to the way in which McIndoe had finally yielded. Other people who talked to Hillary at the time also tried to dissuade him from flying again, but in the end they tended to give way both to the force of Hillary's personality and to a feeling that a man should, after all the arguments have been put to him, be allowed to decide the shape of his own destiny.

Eric Linklater, a writer whom Hillary had met through Lovat Dickson, described the process: 'I was one who tried to make him change his mind. I was alternately rough and plausible. I wanted to keep him out of the sky and make him earthbound. And then, one evening, I was frightened that I might succeed; and said no more . . . I remember very clearly the night when I discovered that I could try no more to dislodge him from his resolution for fear that happened. In his character – in his mind, his spirit, his personality – there was a quality like something with a sharpened edge and a fine surface, and I was suddenly frightened that my argument would dull the edge or tarnish the surface. And that is the sober truth of it.'

This sophisticated, almost existential, argument seems, curiously enough, to have been accepted by most of Hillary's friends. Their regard for him extended to allowing him into danger.

On 21 July 1942 Richard Hillary was back in the air. He flew a light aircraft – all that he was permitted – on a mission to collect material for the Order book, and in the course of it came across his old friend Raspbérry – now Squadron Leader Berry. Within a week or so he was flying Spitfires again, though he was aware that he would not be able to handle the plane in battle. He flew sixty hours in single-engined fighters, some with the tacit connivance of his superiors and some without. In the late summer he was in touch with Max Aitken, whom he had met in 1939, and who had become one of the toughest and most successful fighter pilots in the RAF. Aitken told Hillary that if he could pass his medical and complete the necessary training, he was prepared to accept him into his night-fighter squadron.

As Hillary built up his strength and his defences for his next encounter with the Medical Board, there were a number of literary activities to occupy him. He wrote a script for a propaganda film about the work of the Margate lifeboat and did a radio broadcast for the BBC, which was chiefly a reworking of passages from *The Last Enemy*. He was a good publicist for his own book, and spoke stirringly at a Foyle's lunch about the nature of fascism. Lovat Dickson commented that 'Everything which he touched seemed suddenly to reflect the light of publicity on him, when what he wanted was the quietness and security of the shadows.' Lovat Dickson was working closely with him at this time, but his view does not coincide with Eric Linklater's opinion that Hillary was 'fertile of stratagem and device to make [the book] more widely known and numerously read'. And while part of Hillary was certainly looking for quietness and security, his confused search seldom took him close to the 'shadows'.

Where it did take him was to the painter Eric Kennington, to whom he was introduced by Eric Linklater. Hillary was ecstatic about his new friend. He wrote to Mary Booker: 'I have quite lost my heart to Kennington. He has the most extraordinary personal magnetism of anyone I have met – a great man I think. Certainly his sculpture of Lawrence is a masterpiece. His farm is so restful, that I feel the life in me stirring and the writing is beginning to come.

'I return tomorrow until Thursday to sit for him. He is no longer with the RAF, so it must be a private arrangement . . .

Now I really shall have something to leave you. As soon as it is done, I will make my will and set my family's mind at rest.'

Hillary's letter crossed with one from Mary terminating their affair. She felt he had become too remote and too self-interested; the strain of being continually separated from someone who in any case seemed more concerned for himself than for her had become too much to bear. She marked the date in her engagement diary: 'Dismissal R.H.' and asked if they could still be friends.

Hillary accepted that she was right. 'I must give all of myself or nothing,' he wrote. The circumstances of their separation and his own increasingly desperate quest to understand what he should do next meant that he could not give all of himself; it had therefore to be nothing. Some of Hillary's friends had remarked that Mary Booker was not only old enough to be his mother, she was almost exactly the same age as Edwyna Hillary. Whatever the peculiar needs of each party, both behaved with dignity at the end of the affair.

The emotional void in Hillary's life was largely filled by his friendship with Eric Kennington and by his reading of T.E. Lawrence. Kennington had been one of Lawrence's closest friends and had done an admired portrait of him. He had illustrated *Seven Pillars of Wisdom* and shared much of Lawrence's outlook on life, particularly his ideas about heroism. Kennington allowed Hillary to read a privately circulated copy of Lawrence's book *The Mint*, which was, on Lawrence's instructions, not to be published before 1950, when the people who might be offended by his uncompromising portraits would presumably be dead. The book tells of Lawrence's flight from fame in 1922 and his enlistment in the ranks of the RAF at Uxbridge. He felt that the wealth and glory that had come to him from his Arabian adventures had in some way corrupted him and set him apart from 'humanity'; in a confused but passionate gesture of fraternity he tried an 'inclination towards ground level' in an attempt to 'make myself more human'. Among the Ordinary Aircraftmen Second Class, or 'erks' as they called themselves, of RAF Uxbridge Lawrence purged his soul. Richard Hillary, who had less far to descend, but who felt a similar confusion about the 'responsibilities of the man who is left' and had seen it compounded by a vague feeling of guilt at the success of *The Last Enemy*, responded wholeheartedly to Lawrence's extraordinary book.

The Mint was written in note form in the barracks at night and Lawrence never gave it a gloss of fluency. The result, with its largely Anglo-Saxon vocabulary, occasional alliteration and frequent absence of articles, sometimes sounds like a Middle English poem crossed with the Henry Green of *Living*. The effective plainness of style is complicated by murmurs of homosexual masochism. Lawrence's attitude to his colleagues is inconsistent, as was Hillary's. In one striking sequence Lawrence weeps in the back of a lorry that is taking him and a squad of twelve on a fatigue to a neighbouring aerodrome. 'I was trying to think, if I was happy, why I was happy, and what was this overwhelming sense upon me of having got home, at last, after an interminable journey . . . word-dandling and looking inward, instead of swaying upright in the lorry with my pals, and yelling Rah Rah at all we met, in excess of life. With my fellows, yes; and *among* my fellows: but a fellow myself? Only when in concert we obeyed some physical movement, whose pattern could momently absorb my mind.'

So the key to fellowship was physical action. The most important difference between Hillary and Lawrence was that Lawrence's *nostalgie de la boue* involved no more danger than the chance of lice or sore heels, but Hillary's reimmersion of himself in the active world of male comradeship was likely to cost him his life.

To Kennington Hillary wrote: '*The Mint* helped to clear up something that had been worrying me for months. To fly again or not. I had got to the stage when I could rationalise no longer, but relied on instinct to tell me when the time came . . . I have despised these men I have lived with in messes – pilots too – despised them above all drunk, and have felt a longing to get away from them and think. But Lawrence is right. Companionship such as this must depend largely on trivialities (the wrong word), ordinary things is perhaps better.'

It is one of the tender paradoxes of Richard Hillary's life that a man rightly described by his senior commander as 'excessively individualistic' should yet have chosen to sacrifice his life to some vague idea of comradeship.

Mary Booker wrote to him: 'I am glad, darling, that you are nearly out of the tunnel concerning your decision [to return to flying], yet I find myself *with* Linklater. We on the outside could not help finding ourselves on the same side. True justice should not have put the decision on you at all.'

She dined with him on 22 October, the day of his speech at the Foyle's literary lunch. Any bitterness there may have been seems to have been forgiven; there may even have been a final re-consummation of their feelings. A week later on 30 October, Mary wrote in her diary: 'Dine Richard. Miracle.' It was the last word she wrote about him.

Hillary's life had until this point played in a resoundingly major key. There had been comedy and pain, despair and excitement, but there had not been much ambivalence or mystery. From the day the Medical Board passed him fit for flying in November 1942, the whole tenor of his life shifted. It became cloudy, frightening, and harder to understand.

The Board essentially left the decision to him; and when he had declared himself fit he returned to compel Sir Sholto Douglas to keep his promise, which, against his better judgement, he did. Douglas sent him to an Operational Training Unit in Berwick-shire with a view to becoming a night-fighter pilot. He later commented: 'I should never have made him that promise.'

Rosie Kerr, Hillary's friend and a former patient at East Grinstead, was outraged at the RAF's 'Boys' Own' attitude, not only to Hillary's life, but, if he was to be in night-fighters, to the life of his navigator/radio operator: 'Incomprehensible. He was not fit. They only had to say, once and for all, that they could not afford to lose more planes, let alone two lives, and reject him. After a few weeks he would have accepted it, and found something else.'

But the RAF, for all its talk of 'wizard prangs', was a peculiarly – perhaps irresponsibly – sophisticated service. They allowed their men to fight alone, with as little pressure from the institution as possible. They may have even taken the view that it was healthier for the service as a whole for men to risk their lives than to infect others with their frustrations.

Richard Hillary then had the dreadful task of breaking the news to his mother. He wrote to her: 'I just want to thank you for always having faith, for not questioning my decision, for never betraying that you feel unhappy and, above all, for your unfailing sense of humour . . . Finally one must listen to one's own instinct, and the time will come when I shall know that my instinct was right and my reason wrong. You must try not to worry about me and to have the same faith I have that I shall be all right, for I know it . . . There are few things to which one can cling in this comic war. To see straight and know where one is heading is perhaps the most important of all. God bless you always. Richard.'

He wrote the letter on the evening of 19 November at the Oxford and Cambridge University Club. When he had finished it he wrote out his will.

It was an odd little document, but very eloquent of its author. It included these clauses:

> To Tony Tollemache I leave my gold watch.
> To Merle Oberon (Lady Korda), I leave my gold aeroplane clip.
> To my mother I leave my everlasting love and gratitude . . .
> I want no one to go into mourning for me.
> As to whether I am buried or cremated – it is immaterial to me, but as the flames have had one try I suggest they might get their man in the end.
> I want no one to feel sorry for me. In an age where no one can make a decision that is not dictated from above, it was left to me to make the most important decision of all. I am eternally grateful to the stupidity of those who left me that decision. In my life I had a few friends. I learned a little wisdom and a little patience. What more could a man ask for?

The words 'the stupidity of those who left me that decision' are particularly characteristic. They refer not to Eric Linklater, Lovat Dickson and others who had tried to dissuade him, yet had finally let him go; they are a half-affectionate reference to the men of the Medical Board. Hillary implies that he knew he was not really fit;

but the RAF had allowed him to fight the War in the way he had first desired when at Oxford: exciting, individual and disinterested.

It was almost midnight by the time he had finished writing both the will and the letter to his mother. He left the club and walked through the cold, blacked-out streets to his parents' flat in Knightsbridge. He went and sat on his mother's bed, as he had done when he was a child, and told her of everything he had done during the day.

He did not tell her of the content of the letter that was in the post, nor did he tell her of the third letter he had written: to his new commanding officer, asking him that in the event of his death they should first inform Mary Booker, then allow four hours before officially contacting his mother.

'You will be all right,' he told Mary. 'You can take it.' They dined together on 23 November, and the following day Hillary's father Michael took him to the train at King's Cross. The station was filled with servicemen, the majority of them RAF men bound for Grantham in Lincolnshire from where the bomber squadrons flew at night to pound the German cities. The Berwick train was filled almost as soon as it had drawn into the station; the corridors were packed with men sitting on their kit bags. Here were the reluctant, unbelieving men that Hillary had backed against 'Hitler's dogma-fed youth'.

Hillary, his hands hidden in his greatcoat pocket and with a porter carrying the bag he could not manage himself, was unable to find a seat. His father saw him into a carriage and attempted to say goodbye from the platform as Richard leaned out through the window with his habitually sardonic smile. It was another boarding school goodbye, but it threw the others into bitter relief. Michael Hillary, as usual, could find no gesture of physical affection, nor even gentle words. He made an awkward goodbye and walked away. As he was leaving the station he was overcome with remorse and foreboding. He stopped. He bought a packet of cigarettes, went back to the train, and thrust them stiffly through the window.

Hillary arrived at Berwick at six in the evening and changed on to a chain for Reston. There were two young men fresh from training school in his compartment, but when he examined them Hillary did not feel the bond of comradeship that had made him so anxious to return. They seemed to him callow and less worth dying for than Colin Pinckney and Peter Pease. At Reston he moved into a compartment of his own and felt the weight of a great loneliness. There was a final change of trains and then half an hour in a van to RAF Charter Hall.

It was the end of the world. Freezing winds swept across the tarmac from the North Sea; the sleeping huts had damp walls and no fires; someone had stolen all the plugs from the baths. Hillary wept into his pillow. The next day he was given an armament lecture which turned out to be an exact repeat of the one he had described at Kinloss in *The Last Enemy*. He raised his head from the desk and half expected to see Noel Agazarian and the ghosts of the long-haired boys, but there was only a pinched-looking lad who picked his nose.

Every day at Charter Hall was a new abandonment; the atmosphere was like a boarding school Sunday, only colder and more sinister. Hillary's depression was intensified by a book he found in the small library. It was T.E. Lawrence's letters; and what struck him was a passage in which the editor, David Garnett, wrote of Lawrence's return to the ranks at Uxbridge: 'One wonders whether his will had not become greater than his intelligence . . . The courage of the boy too proud to make a fuss is something we admire; in an educated man it is ridiculous and a sign of abnormality.' Hillary was starting to believe that his own decision had been 'ridiculous'. What was he trying to prove?

Many of the other pilots on the station looked up to Hillary as a Battle of Britain 'hero'. They could not extend to him the fraternity he craved because they were in awe of him. Some showed their feelings by apparent disdain. They queried his lack of experience at flying by night; they pointed out coldly that it was not just his own life he was risking, but that of his navigator/radio operator.

Hillary questioned his own feelings and motives in much the same way. He felt fear in a way that he had never acknowledged before. He wondered whether it was flying at night that scared him, or whether it was some more fatal awareness that his life was coming to a close. 'This is a queer place,' he wrote, 'for journey's end.'

In December he managed to get leave to go to a wedding in London. Here he saw his friends Rosie Kerr and Archie McIndoe. It was clear to them that something had gone badly wrong. McIndoe was alarmed at Hillary's mental condition. He had had to deal with Hillary's aggression and resentment in hospital, but at least they had been emotions that derived from a hunger for life and anxiety about its healthy continuation. The sight of a meekly compliant Richard Hillary was frightening, and McIndoe eventually wrote a letter to the Medical Officer at Charter Hall, strongly warning him that he thought Hillary unfit for duty.

On his return to Charter Hall after the wedding, Hillary made a last, great effort to lift his spirits. 'Much better today,' he wrote to Mary Booker, 'for I have finally flown; with no particular distinction and only dual, nevertheless I have flown. My greatest difficulty is taxi-ing these heavy brutes. I find that I have not the strength in my right thumb to work the brakes, so I am to have an extension fitted to the brake lever.'

Once Hillary was up in the air again, the truth became quite clear: he was not fit to fly. Not only was his mental attitude wrong, but his hands were too weak to work the cumbersome levers of the heavy night-fighters. His eyes were insufficiently protected by their new lids, and he suffered persistent and acute headaches.

Through the pain rang the word 'coward', uttered by Kathleen Dewar. He did not believe he was going to survive; his old fighter-pilot's instinct lent him some absurd hope while he was up in the air, but his reason told him otherwise. Yet while he glared across the frozen airfield waiting for his death, he found at last some of the old comradeship and mutual loyalty he thought had been lost to 'the one who is left'.

The other pilots began to lose their awe of him and to treat him as one of their own. He responded with desperate relief: 'I feel a new-old warmth begin to course through me; the potion is already at work. I pick up the newspaper – Beveridge Report. Oh, the fellow is thinking about after the War: we'll probably all be dead anyway. Let's find out what Jane's doing in the *Daily Mirror*.

We turn the page; we comment on her legs, and I look more closely at the faces around me, and what I see pleases me. I am happy.'

His battle now was with the machines. Gales howled across the runway; clouds sank down to only 600 feet; the brake lever ripped the soft skin from his hands, and still he couldn't hold the heavy plane on landing but bogged it into the soft mud beside the outer track. Hour after hour he ploughed through the grey Scottish cold with no landmark to guide him, flying on his instruments alone; and like all Spitfire pilots he was used to seeing rivers, fields and churches beneath the twitching rudder bars: to trust a needle in a glass dial was against all his fighter instincts.

He felt the eyes of Pease and Pinckney on him; he felt the expectation of all young men who had died, as he fought to justify 'my right to fellowship with my dead'. If in some celestial dispersal hut they might have watched him they would have laughed and told him to get the hell out of it and back to London; but the need to prove himself worthy of them closed his mind to reason. Although he did not seek death, he did, in some incoherent way, long for its release.

His performance in the air made it likely that his wish would shortly be fulfilled. His instructor, Wing Commander James Benson, DSO, DFC wrote: 'I sent him solo and it was terrible. I gave him further instruction and then he challenged me to stand behind him whilst he flew and tell him what he did wrong. I did. He nearly killed us both. But somehow we eventually got it sorted out and he got the hang of it. He thought a lot of me for that.'

Hillary was moved from Bisleys to Blenheims, which were even more awkward to fly. Another Blenheim pilot wrote: 'I have a strong hunch that the designer of the cockpit had a perverted sense of humour as . . . the airscrew pitch and petrol controls were behind the pilot's back where he groped in the dark, tearing fingers and thumbs on every sharp piece of metal that could be cunningly concealed to catch the unwary.' Where the Bisley had a switch to shut the gills, the Blenheim had a wheel behind the pilot's head that needed to be turned about fifty times; where the

Bisley had a simple lever to raise the undercarriage, the Blenheim had a catch that needed to be released with the thumb. Even able-bodied pilots frequently found their fingers immovably trapped by this catch when they most needed a free hand elsewhere in the cockpit. Hillary's thumb was clawed too deep into his palm to be able to work the lever at all, and on his first Blenheim flight he received a radio message telling him his undercarriage was still down. Unable to do anything about it, he was forced to land again straight away. Even then the RAF did not deny him the chance to fly; they merely sent someone with him to operate the undercarriage.

Night flying began at five o'clock each evening, though frequently the weather was so bad that pilots would be hauled out of their planes and sent back to the dispersal hut to wait either until the gale had dropped or the snow had lifted. Hillary strained his watering eyes to see through the muddy, unwashed perspex of the canopy, but could see neither the fitter, nor his torch, nor anything at all but the deep darkness of the night.

From his hut he wrote letters in which he described Charter Hall as 'the forgotten man's last stop'. He formed a close friendship with a navigator/radio operator, Wilfrid Fison, a man whose job was onerous enough in such conditions without the added burden of an incapacitated pilot. Fison had, however, been specially chosen to accompany Hillary, because, according to the Station Medical Officer, he was, 'an old Cambridge Blue, of a temperament just calculated to suit Hillary, and the prospects were that they would make a good pair.' However, Fison was thirty-seven, had no combat experience, and had joined the RAF Volunteer Reserve only a year before. He was known as a kind and selfless man, and there is no evidence that he was frightened of flying with Hillary. However, since Hillary made it clear that he was aware of Fison's shortcomings as a navigator it is inconceivable that Fison could not have seen how far short Hillary fell of the standard required to fly a Blenheim safely. Perhaps the Medical Officer hoped the crippled pilot and ageing navigator could console one another with talk of sporting events at the ancient universities.

On 17 December McIndoe wrote to the Medical Officer at

Charter Hall. He pointed out that Hillary's left eye was not standing up to the strain of night flying. He believed that if he continued to fly it 'can only end one way'. Since there was more work to be done on the eyelid, McIndoe asked if Hillary could be sent to East Grinstead 'at an early date'. 'In the meantime,' he wrote, 'I do feel that if you could restrain him from further flying, it might save him from a very serious accident. After I have dealt with his eye, I can reopen the matter with the Central Medical Establishment, and a more satisfactory disposal could be made for him.

'Would you be so good as to treat this letter as private and confidential to yourself. The feelings of these young men are very apt to be hurt in relation to this vexed question of operative work following an injury. I feel however there is a strong case for intervention.'

The Medical Officer, however, was away on leave and McIndoe's letter remained unopened on his desk.

Charter Hall was known to the men who were sent there as Slaughter All. The Blenheims were old, shaky, and skimpily serviced by a sullen groundstaff. The Flight Commander told Hillary: 'I wouldn't fly one of these Blenheims at night for any price – tried once – shook me to the tits. Can't even see the instruments and fuck all outside . . . Tomorrow you'll have all that and your engine'll cut out too just for full measure, and if you prang they'll say it was your fault.'

The airfield was laid out in accordance with the lessons learned from air raids about the need for dispersal. It was a German bomber raid on Hornchurch that had caused the damage to Hillary's Spitfire canopy which prevented his escape above the Thames estuary. At Charter Hall there were therefore icy miles to cross between mess and billets with further long walks to the flights. The permanent staff were indolent and malicious; while the trainees had all known the rigours and comedy of service discipline, they found the attitude of these superiors curiously dispiriting. 'They are machines, not men,' wrote Hillary. The instructors themselves were of a higher calibre, but they were only on six-month postings as rest from operational duties and many of them resented being there. The pupils, too, were transient and were unable to make any impact on the morale or safety of the airfield.

The mechanics worked mostly in the open. It was not surprising that the only enthusiasm they showed was for getting indoors as quickly as possible and huddling round a brazier with tea and cigarettes. There was nothing of the rapport between pilots and ground crew that had helped win the Battle of Britain. The best electricians and mechanics had been taken by Bomber Harris for his nightly missions over Germany; the mechanics at Charter Hall and similar airfields were merely filling in time. Consequently the ageing planes showed a full range of defects in the difficult weather conditions. Sometimes the pilots were irritated by small things: the oxygen bottles were not refilled, brakes leaked, pitch levers failed to respond. Sometimes it was more serious: the engines would seize or ignite. When one of the Blenheims had landed safely with its starboard engine on fire the navigator initiated a subsequently much-imitated practice by bending down and kissing the runway.

Hillary came down to London again for his Christmas leave and stayed with his parents. He went to visit Denise Maxwell-Woosnam and stayed for dinner with Denise and her brother. He seemed remote, almost stunned. He told Denise several times in the course of the evening that he had finally found the answers to the problems that had been troubling him; that he had finally got things 'sorted out'. She begged him to stop talking in such a way as she felt it indicated that he had given up hope. About midnight he asked her to change out of her uniform and into her prettiest dress. When Denise had done this, he looked at her for some time, sadly. Then he thanked her and left.

Michael Hillary saw his son the next day.

'We were impressed,' he later wrote, 'by the fundamental change in him. Beneath his usual gay manner he was quieter and seemed suddenly to have grown from boyhood into a man . . . It was evident he was in a disturbed state of mind on his last leave. He and I sat in the sitting-room for about half an hour without saying a word to each other, by which time the strain had become almost unbearable. I was aching to say "There was a time when you brought all your troubles to me, old man. Can you not do so now?" Whether from a natural reluctance to intrude upon his privacy or for some other reason I do not know, but the words did not come from me. At that time I did not know that his crippled hands were making it almost impossible for him to fly bombers. If I had spoken he might have told me, and it is possible that I could have done something about it. On the other hand, he might have resented the interference. Whatever the outcome might have been it will be my eternal regret that I did not invite him to confide in me.'

Richard wanted to see no one this time except those to whom he felt particularly close: his parents, Denise, Mary Booker, and Tony Tollemache. It seemed as though he was gathering his friends around him and binding them to him. On 27 December he returned to Charter Hall.

On New Year's Eve there was a dance and 'gramophone recital' in the Radio Transmission hut. The radio speech officer, an elderly ex-choirmaster, played some Rossini to the assembled airmen and a few WAAFs. It was a long way from louche evenings in the Café de Paris after a summer's day in Spitfires.

On 3 January Hillary wrote to his mother. 'Time is very short and there are a great many people in the world. Therefore of these people I shall try to know only half a dozen. But them I shall love and never deceive.'

On the same day Hillary undertook a night flight with Wilfrid Fison. They went in a Bisley because Hillary was 'scared stiff of the old Blenheims at night – you can't even see your instruments – and also as I was to do a height test the cold would have been too much for me – quite apart from fighting with the undercarriage.' Fison sat up front with Hillary and, somewhat to their surprise, they became airborne with no problem. Soon afterwards the heavy plane started plunging to starboard, but they could see no obvious reason. At 10,000 feet the pitch control of the port engine jammed, and at 19,000 feet the radio stopped being able to transmit to the ground.

Hillary pushed down the nose and told Fison to get a 'homing' from the airfield. The radio gave out various homing vectors and

Fison repeated them solemnly, slowly, and wrong. Then the radio packed up altogether. Hillary pressed down slowly through the cloud until he saw the flare-path of the runway. He flashed his navigation lights at 1,000 feet, but there was no answer. Then he rechecked the dial: 11,000 feet. He descended and circled the airfield, put down the wheels, throttled back and waited to land. Then he stalled. He was not at 100 feet, but at 1,000 feet, and spinning.

Finally he got the plane to 800 feet and received an affirmative flash from the green lamp on the airfield. Above the runway the unmasked lights flooded the bottom of the plane and made him turn away his vulnerable eyes. With Fison on his knees, holding his hand across the glare, Hillary found the plane being buffeted by a heavy cross-wind. He fought the stick with his weak hands and landed like a crab, the sweat pouring down inside his icy flying suit.

Twice in the air he promised himself that if he landed safely he would tell the Wing Commander that he could not go on; but back on the ground the thought of quitting merely amused him. He was hungry; he wanted to get into the crew room, have a cigarette and talk flying. The ambulance that had been waiting for them, watching their jagged descent, was dismissed. Hillary went off to find some supper, and on the way went past four men, drunk, carrying a barrel of beer. He could hear a piano playing. Somewhere there was a party. Somewhere, miles away across this dispersed, unhomely airfield, McIndoe's letter was still waiting.

Then on 7 January the Medical Officer opened it. 'I agree with you that intervention is suitable in such a case,' he replied to McIndoe, 'but I am also sure that Hillary's self-respect is an enormous obstacle.' The Medical Officer made Hillary promise that he would visit McIndoe when he next went to London. He did not intervene himself because he found Hillary 'difficult to deal with' and thought that any suggestion on his part that Hillary's health was not good would lead him to conceal his true feelings.

While the letter was in the post to McIndoe, Hillary was

required to fly. In the evening a Polish pilot noticed Hillary looking 'tired, strained and very red about the eye'. He and Fison went up before midnight. There was intermittent sleet with a strong wind occasionally breaking up the cloud. The flight passed without incident, and the two men went back to the hut for a cup of tea and a cigarette before their second flight.

Shortly after take-off Hillary was told by radio to circle a flashing beacon. This was a normal procedure, in which the pilot would gently orbit the airfield while keeping the beacon on his port wing. The weather varied locally between little cloud with starlight to periods of 10/10ths cloud at 2,000 feet. The R/T asked him: 'Are you happy?' This was the standard operational word. Hillary replied: 'Moderately.' There was not necessarily cause for alarm in his choice of word. A former Spitfire pilot, bestselling author and reformed Oxford rake could not honourably answer 'yes' when he was flying a heavy, unreliable old hulk through cloud above a place he had described as the end of the world.

'Moderately,' he said. 'I am continuing to orbit.' The official report of the flight recorded that when R/T called him again there was no answer. An officer on the ground noticed that he was losing height. The report said that he lost control while circling in cloud. Wing Commander Benson wrote: 'I must have overestimated him because I liked him and admired him for what he'd been through. He wasn't happy so we recalled him. I was watching his navigation lights, and he spiralled straight in from a thousand feet.'

If, however, he was in cloud, it is difficult to see how an officer on the ground could make out his navigation lights and thus see that he was losing height. In any case, navigation lights were not generally used in night flying at Charter Hall. If anyone had perceived that the plane was falling, he ought to have contacted Hillary to warn him. It looks as though radio contact, as so often, had been lost. What may have happened is that Benson did not see, but heard the plane coming down.

The noise was loud enough. A shepherd in a nearby village heard the great machine lumbering and screaming overhead, causing his children to wake up in alarm and plaster to tumble from the ceiling of his cottage. The plane buried itself in the ground with a shattering impact that was heard for miles around in the freezing night. The explosion, in Benson's words, 'lit up the entire countryside'.

It was impossible to rescue anything from the flames. Hillary and Fison were annihilated. Hillary was identified by his wristwatch.

In London on the morning of 8 January Mary Booker received the telegram. 'Deeply regret to inform you Flt/Lt Richard Hope Hillary No.74677 killed in flying accident today.' She went at once to break the news to Edwyna Hillary, who was working for the Red Cross at St James's Palace. She looked up as Mary entered the room. 'Is it Richard?' she asked. Mary took her home and spent the day with her and Michael Hillary.

At Charter Hall the story went round that Richard Hillary's was a coffin they had to fill with sand.

The flames, as Hillary had anticipated, had their man in the end. On 12 January 1943, at 10.30 am, he was cremated at Golders Green. But before the ashes were scattered, before his parents had emerged from their shock, strange things started happening to the memory of him. It was as though, despite the finality of his end, the elements that had made up his existence remained unstable.

Richard Hillary's brilliant and short ascent to fame, the disfigurement of his handsome features and his violent death in a broken-down trainer made him the fit subject for a myth that the writing of the previous decade had been preparing. When Hillary himself spoke of 'the pilot' and the mysterious role the figure played in society he was aware of the literary associations he was invoking. In his poem 'An Irish Airman Foresees his Death' Yeats understood and helped articulate something of the sense of mastery, of escape and of fatal indifference that airmen commonly experienced.

> A lonely impulse of delight
> Drove to this tumult in the clouds;
> I balanced all, brought all to mind,

Richard Hillary

> The years to come seemed waste of breath,
> A waste of breath the years behind
> In balance with this life, this death.

Hillary's attempt to express his version of the same thing in *The Last Enemy* was, by comparison, almost incoherent:

> The pilot is of a race of men who since time immemorial have been inarticulate; who, through their daily contact with death, have realised, often enough unconsciously, certain fundamental things. It is only in the air that the pilot can grasp that feeling, that flash of knowledge, of insight, that matures him beyond his years; only in the air that he knows suddenly that he is a man in a world of men. 'Coming back to earth' has for him a double significance. He finds it difficult to orientate himself in a world that is so worldly, amongst a people whose conversation seems to him brilliant, minds agile and knowledge complete – yet a people somehow blind. It is very strange.

It is not surprising that Hillary wrote less well than Yeats. What is significant is that he recognised, in a literary way, the mythic potential of what he was writing.

Throughout the previous decade, when Hillary had been studying literature at school and university, English writers had puzzled over the role of the man of action. Many of them confessed to feeling themselves in some way unmanned by the fact that they had not faced the trial of the Great War. The influence of Wilfred Owen was important, not only in the way he wrote, but because as well as being a poet he had been a soldier who conquered shell shock, returned to the front, and won the MC. The writers Hillary referred to dismissively as the 'Auden group' were aware as early as 1931 and 1932 that they were *entre deux guerres*, and their work was sometimes a contemplation of the next war before it was an accommodation of the last.

The literature of the 1930s was concerned with what to do next. The figure of the pilot kept recurring. In October 1931 an Italian anti-fascist poet called Lauro de Bosis flew in a light plane from Marseille to Rome to drop political leaflets. He never returned, and his flight took on some poignant significance.

When the poet John Cornford, one of the most celebrated English volunteers, was killed in Spain in 1936, his obituarist wrote: 'I could not but think, when I heard of his death, of Lauro de Bosis – the young Italian who went to Rome in his lonely aeroplane, delivered his testimony, and died.'

A man was to make his point, alone, then die. His action should preferably be politically motivated, but there was the possibility that action itself could redeem. In 1932 Auden published *The Orators*, the longest part of which, Book II, is 'The Journal of an Airman'. The character is weak and troubled; the mission he flies is a political one against a class enemy. Auden was helping to create the idea that there was something symbolic in the figure of the pilot: that he above all other people epitomised the private man forced by calamitous events into a public role.

Day Lewis referred to Auden himself as a pilot in a poem in *New Country*: 'Wystan, lone flyer, birdman, my bully boy!' One aspect of the reflexiveness and self-reference of English writing in the 1930s is the irritating, clubby way the poets refer to one another in their poems. However, the self-consciousness and awareness of 'action' and of political developments in Europe also meant that public events were quickly scrutinised, turned over, and transformed into verse. By the time Richard Hillary died in 1943 there was an established technique in overnight myth-making.

In 1934 Day Lewis included in his poem 'A Time to Dance' a narrative section based on a flight from England to Australia made by two Australian war veterans called Parer and McIntosh. They flew in a condemned and ill-serviced DH-9, its condition something like that of the wretched Blenheims at Charter Hall. The poem is remarkable among contemporary works in that it seems to have no political content at all. Day Lewis was at this time a Communist, but the poem is about the thrill of flying. The following year another Communist, Christopher Caudwell, edited a book called *Great Flights*. He worked under the pen-name C. St John Sprigg, while as Caudwell he wrote a Marxist study of poetry called *Illusion and Reality*. His interest in flight was uncoloured by his political beliefs. Flying was seen as a feasible form of heroism and individual self-assertion that

survived the degradation of the infantry slaughters of the
Western Front. It was already depicted by these writers as what
Richard Hillary later called it: exciting, individual, disinterested.

Auden had anticipated Hillary's interest in T.E. Lawrence; in
fact it was Lawrence who was the inspiration for Auden's Airman
in *The Orators*. The year before Lawrence's death in 1935 Auden
wrote: 'To me Lawrence's life is an allegory of the transformation
of the Truly Weak Man into the Truly Strong Man, an answer to
the question "How shall the self-conscious man be saved?" '
Auden returned to Lawrence as the basis of Michael Ransom, the
main character in *The Ascent of F6* the following year. Auden saw
in Lawrence's life the dilemma that Hillary saw: the problem of
heroism and of what a self-aware man should do. The complication is that only decisive action itself appears capable of revealing
such a man's true motives. In *The Ascent of F6* Auden complicated matters further by introducing a Freudian element.
Ransom acts heroically to please his mother, but is then
destroyed by her. Edwyna Hillary, far from being destructive,
tried hard to protect her son, though it is possible that in his
emotional reliance on her rather than on his father, Hillary
developed unconsciously a desire to please and impress her,
comparable with Christopher Wood's drive to honour and
vindicate his mother's love. The pity is that both should have
finished by producing the last consequence that either mother
wished to see.

By the time he came to write *The Last Enemy*, Hillary had put
the writers of the Auden group at arm's length. He had by then
undergone his change of conviction about the War and wished to
distance himself from people who had been pacifist or non-
combatant. Auden and Isherwood had gone to America, Stephen
Spender was in the London Fire Service: these men were not
fighting and dying. Hillary's life and writing, however, fit
comfortably into the cultural setting the writers of the 1930s had
helped to define. He may not have been aware of it, but he shared
many of their assumptions, and in his writing about 'the pilot' he
acknowledged that literary background. His attitude to the
outbreak of war was not very different from theirs. They believed
that war would bring Western civilisation to an end and that the

only fate worse than that would be to live in a fascist state. They felt themselves to be a generation without ancestry, because the Great War had killed ten million men and irrevocably cut them off from the past. A new war, they believed, would eliminate also the possibility of a future. Hillary came to share this belief, though with the important qualification that victory by the Allied forces against the Nazis would 'stamp for ever on the future of civilisation' the values for which his comrades had died.

Under Mr McEachran at Shrewsbury and later at Oxford Hillary had read widely. His cultivation of an 'alert philistinism' did not prevent him from invoking Pound, Eliot and Auden in *The Last Enemy*. Since the whole enterprise of English literature in the 1930s had been devoted to the question of the private faces in public places, to the dilemma of what action a person should take in troubled times, and since a talent as great as Auden's had been involved, it is hardly surprising that Hillary was both influenced by it and remembered in the terms that it had defined.

If Hillary's life fitted the high cultural patterns these writers had created, his death appealed to a more popular taste: the mystery story.

Three months after Hillary died Arthur Koestler published an article about him in *Horizon* under the title 'The Birth of a Myth'. Koestler had known Hillary quite well in London in his brief period of literary fame and they had corresponded. Koestler had an image for the growth of a myth. He compared it to the formation of crystal. The public and artistic backgrounds – books, newspapers, the word on the street – were like molecules trying to find a coherent pattern; the individual was the core about which they crystallised. Koestler had seen some, but not all of Hillary's letters to Mary Booker from Charter Hall and he quoted selectively to show Hillary's submission to a death he believed had become inevitable. Koestler made much of Hillary's distinction between his 'instinct', which told him he would survive, and his 'reason', which told him he must die. What Koestler was trying to do was to suggest a degree of volition. Perhaps he had not read Saint-Exupéry, who used the same word, 'instinct', about his desire to fly as a fighter pilot. Koestler suggested that

Hillary was a more or less willing victim of the forces of myth. He rightly identified the sceptical, reluctant way in which such men as Hillary fought at first and fairly showed from his letters to Mary how difficult he was finding it to fly the machines at Charter Hall.

'But why then, in God's name, did he go back?' Koestler asked. He looked at the influence of T.E. Lawrence, about which Hillary had written to him personally. He was scornful of the idea that Hillary could have returned only for the hope of comradeship, and quoted Hillary himself: 'I ponder Koestler's theory that *l'espoir de la fraternité* is always a wild goose chase unless one is tight or physically exhausted in a crowd – as after long marches.'

Koestler came to no simple conclusion about Hillary's motivation, preferring 'a pattern composed of all the threads we have picked up, and followed for a short while and dropped again. For the pattern is more than the sum of the threads; it has its own symbolic design of which the threads know nothing.' This was the nub of what Koestler was suggesting: that while Hillary's motives were mixed, he was affected by the pressure of public expectation into making some kind of exemplary death.

Koestler again quoted Hillary quoting him, about the distinction between the two planes on which people live: 'Usually we live and move on the plane of the *vie triviale*, but occasionally in moments of elation, danger, etc we find ourselves transferred to the plane of the *vie tragique*, with its uncommon-sense cosmic perspective. One of the miseries of the human condition is that we can neither live permanently on the one nor on the other plane, but oscillate between the two.' Thus the casual, downbeat slang of the mess was the only way the pilots could deal with their experiences in the air. Artists, Koestler argued, have to move constantly between the two planes. He analysed *The Last Enemy* in the light of how well Hillary succeeded in viewing the trivial from the perspective of the eternal and was generous in his estimate of Hillary's success. He compared him with, among others, Hemingway, Malraux, Saint-Exupéry and Raymond Radiguet. To Thomas Mann's opinion that to survive a writer must leave bulk as well as brilliance Koestler had the elegant rejoinder: 'This slim volume of Hillary's seems to have a specific weight which makes it sink into the depth of one's memory, while tons of printed bulk drift as flotsam on its surface.'

Koestler's essay ended, like Hillary's book, rhetorically. He could not answer the question he had set himself: 'What makes this young author-pilot's life into a symbol?' His last, approximate answer is that it is something to do with causes: 'a man's longing for the Holy Grail may become so strong that he flies like a moth into the flame; and having burned his wings crawls back into it again.' He suggested that Hillary was lost for something in which to believe – a redeeming emotion and an unembarrassing faith. This is not how Hillary himself presented his state of mind. Out of literary distaste at its rhetoric, Koestler seemed to ignore the meaning of the final paragraph of *The Last Enemy*.

Koestler's essay, if occasionally self-indulgent, is often shrewd and appears to have been written in good faith. The following year John Middleton Murry published an essay entitled 'Richard Hillary' in his magazine *Adelphi* in which he accused Hillary of 'faking the record'. Murry was not concerned so much with material inaccuracies as with what he believed to be the falsehood of Hillary's conclusions. He could not accept that Hillary really believed the War had become a moral crusade. Murry presented Hillary as a figure from tragedy who was pursued by the fates for his 'dishonesty' and forced to pay the ultimate price. Murry's essay was too self-admiring to state anything so plain as a thesis, but what he appeared to believe was that any glory there might have been in the Battle of Britain was gone by late 1942 when the bombing of German cities had begun. Because, according to Murry, he had lied about his feelings, Hillary was condemned to tread the world in a 'phoney literary role' from which his only escape was through a willing death. Since Wilfrid Fison went down with Hillary, what Murry was suggesting was more than a sensational literary gesture. Murry was himself a pacifist and reprinted the essay in his own imprint in the hope of influencing the conduct of the War. However reasonable an aim that may have been, it seems now as though it was Murry not Hillary who 'faked the record'. 'In Hillary', he concluded, 'the deep urge of contemporary society towards death is made visible.' He judged Hillary's 'self-inflicted' death to be a fitting expiation for the sin of seeing war against the Nazis – or any war – as justified, and recruited him, cleansed by his ultimate act of literary self-criticism, to his own side. There was a rattle of tambourines in his evangelical climax: 'What Hillary foreknew as an individual, Britain will discover as a nation.'

Murry's essay had little influence except to give further currency to the idea that Hillary had killed himself: 'It was no crusade on which he was flying. He was seeking death.' If Hillary had wished to kill himself he could have done so in the early part of his course when he was flying solo. There is also the matter of Fison. Hillary could certainly be obnoxious ('that shit Hill-ary . . .'), but he was not a murderer; indeed by January 1943 he had become obsessed by notions of fellowship. His letters from Charter Hall are frightening because they show a very young man contemplating his imminent and unheroic death. In some unconscious way he may have accepted this fate, or at least feared to go back on his decision; but that is not the same thing as seeking to die.

Middleton Murry was right to draw attention to one thing, however, and that was the effect on Hillary of being the author of a successful book. He took his success modestly, laughing incredulously at the queues of people at the bookshops. The popularity of it, however, had a perverse consequence. He had written the book to honour the memory of men such as Peter Pease and Colin Pinckney and to celebrate the efforts of the 'Carburys and Berrys', the men 'who have come up the hard way'. He missed their company after his crash, and more than anything he wanted their approval: he craved 'my right to fellowship with my dead'. Yet not only did he feel himself less of a human being than Peter Pease and less of an airman than Brian Carbury, he had, by telling their story, by breaking ranks and becoming famous, put himself beyond the circle of their downbeat comradeship. It was almost as though he were guilty of 'shooting a line'. Although the book was modest enough about his own flying, to write a memoir was a showy, individual thing to do. He had lost the natural right to talk shop in the mess and read the *Daily Mirror*; now he was condemned to dinner at the

Garrick with Koestler, Linklater and Rebecca West. Peter Pease's family was outraged at the portrait of their son, which they took to be an invasion of their privacy. Hillary had sought the love of his fellow pilots but had ended up in exile from them.

Hillary gave Denise Maxwell-Woosnam a copy of Wilfred Owen's poems, explaining that Owen was a poet he much admired, and Owen's life helps illuminate the dilemma at the end of Hillary's. When war broke out in 1914 Owen was working as a tutor near Bordeaux and made no hurry to enlist. A passive, gentle man with a soft, velvety voice, Owen did not respond to patriotic calls. Eventually, however, he did join up and spent the bitter winter of 1916–17 on the Somme. His battalion had been involved in prolonged fighting and had operated from shellholes for twelve days. One night Owen was taking cover against a railway embankment when he was blown into the air by a German shell. He lay for several days in a hole by the cutting, with the dismembered body of a fellow officer all about him.

Two weeks later, his colonel noticed that Owen was confused: his hands were shaking and his memory was unreliable. The Medical Officer diagnosed 'neurasthenia'. Owen wrote to his mother: 'Do not suppose that I have had a "breakdown". I am simply avoiding one.'

He was sent to Craiglockhart, a hospital for officers near Edinburgh that had been converted from a hydropathic spa. Here he met Siegfried Sassoon, and the meeting had a powerful effect on Owen's poetry. When he arrived he was writing sub-Decadent whimsy, full of gloomy gardens and fake archaisms. By the time he left he had written '*Dulce et Decorum Est*' and a draft of 'Anthem for Doomed Youth'. Sassoon had helped him find his subject – war, and the pity of war – and Owen was on the way to becoming one of the most substantial British poets of the twentieth century.

Owen's compassion for other men was not a gentle feeling, but a fierce and positive emotion. His determined apprenticeship as a poet meant that he had most of the technical means to control and express it. His life changed and became fulfilled. His voice was the most glorious and the most celebrated of those raised against the inhuman slaughters of the Western Front; he was the only writer who could justifiably call one of his greatest poems an 'anthem'.

Yet he went back. Willingly, almost eagerly, he chose to rejoin the men of his battalion. He felt that he belonged with them; that while such terrible things continued he had no right to hold himself apart. To stay in England was simply to beg the question.

This finally was what Hillary felt too. Of course there were differences: Owen was a front-rank creative writer and Hillary was not; Owen had become an officer and felt a fatherly duty to protect the young men under his command; his sexual feelings were also for men, and this may have complicated the issue in a subtle way. But the main reason for Owen's return was that he felt, like Saint-Exupéry in 1942, that he could not be a spectator – '*Je ne peux plus rester témoin.*'

In the Great War many men joined up from a sense of patriotic duty and were then disillusioned. Their motivation after that point was sometimes no more than a will to survive, but in many cases the lost cause of patriotism was replaced by a desire to honour their dead friends: only by seeing it through to the end, only by enduring, could they make some sense of the sacrifice that had been made by so many.

This feeling was less common in the Second World War because in 1939–45 most men felt they had a proper moral cause to fight for; they therefore had less need of the subtler claims of the dead. Hillary, however, made it quite clear that this '14–18 feeling was a powerful if not primary motivation for him.

On his return to the Western Front, Owen participated more eagerly than before. His war records are lost somewhere in the Ministry of Defence, but reading what one can between the lines of his letters to his mother (he was another mother-dominated boy) it appears that he almost ran amok. After leading one assault beyond the call of duty he was awarded the MC and was killed crossing the Sambre Canal under heavy machine gun fire in November 1918.

Owen had been forced by circumstances into an unbearable position, from which only physical action offered some redemptive escape. He felt that in moral or existential terms he had no alternative. So it was with Hillary – not because he had in Murry's sinister phrase 'faked the record', but because he had filled it in. He had set down what he and his fellow-pilots had done and their reasons for doing so. He had no choice but to 'finish the job' that Peter Pease and Colin Pinckney had started.

Denise Maxwell-Woosnam was among those who agreed with him, and encouraged him to return to action. Admittedly she and his other friends did not realise how heavy the planes would be, how badly serviced, and how lethally dangerous; but in the general matter of the question of whether to fly or not to fly, they were not, like Arthur Koestler, perplexed. Mary Booker did not try to prevent him. Eric Linklater shied away at the moment he thought he might dissuade him.

At the end of *The Mint* Lawrence gave a lyrical evocation of the joys of service life. It takes away the anguish of individual responsibility; it removes the doubts and questions that can plague a man:

> Service life in this way teaches a man to live largely on little. We belong to a big thing, which will exist for ever and ever in unnumbered generations of standard airmen, like ourselves. Our outward sameness of dress and type remind us of that . . . As we gain attachment, so we strip ourselves of personality.

Lawrence talks of a lazy afternoon in the sun, in the mouth of an open hangar and concludes:

> Such moments of absorption resolve the mail and plate of our personality back into the carbo-hydrate elements of being. They come to service men very often, because of our light surrender to the good or evil of the moment.
>
> Airmen have few possessions, few ties, little daily care. For me, duty now orders only the brightness of the five buttons down my front . . . In the summer we are easily the sun's. In winter we struggle undefended along the roadway, and the rain and wind chivy us, till soon we are wind and rain. We race over in the first dawn to the College's translucent swimming pool, and dive into the elastic water which fits our bodies closely as a skin – and we belong to that too. Everywhere a relationship: no loneliness any more.

No loneliness any more. In some ways going back was easier for Richard Hillary than staying out.

Michael and Edwyna Hillary formed a trust, based at Trinity College Oxford, to keep the memory of their only child alive. They became close to Mary Booker, who sent flowers each year on the anniversary of Richard's death, as Winifred Reitlinger remembered Kit Wood to his mother. Michael Hillary refused to appear in a radio programme about Richard because Arthur Koestler had also been invited and he believed Koestler was responsible for having started the suicide/murder theory. Mary Booker eventually married Michael Burn, a writer and journalist. She died in 1974, and in 1988 Burn published a selection of her letters to Hillary and his to her, which he found in a leather-bound album with a brass lock in the boxroom of their house. Mary had written out some lines from Swinburne as a preface:

> They gave him light in his eyes
> And love, and a space for delight,
> And beauty, and length of days,
> And night, and sleep in the night.

Richard Hillary is remembered by those of his friends who are still living. They feel uneasy with the literary process that tried to make a symbolic figure of him in the years after his death. As time has passed the mythic encrustations have largely fallen away, and people are left with a memory of someone very individual, very forceful and very young. *The Last Enemy* is out of print, but it has survived in the culture because it has, in Koestler's brilliant phrase, 'specific weight'.

Denise Maxwell-Woosnam overcame her grief at the death of Peter Pease and married happily. She is well, untroubled in her faith, and still lives in England. She remembers Richard Hillary and his kindness to her.

Brian Carbury became one of the greatest fighter-pilots of the Battle of Britain, recording fifteen and a half kills between July and October 1940, including five Me-109's in a single day.

Archie McIndoe was knighted for his services to plastic surgery. In 1950 he declared that he would divorce his wife and marry Jill Mullins, but changed his mind at the last moment. The second Lady McIndoe turned out to be a widow he met while waiting for the divorce to come through. Jill Mullins's long wait was disappointed.

Shortly after VE Day two German doctors went to visit the hospital at East Grinstead. They had heard of McIndoe from German prisoners who had been treated by Red Cross doctors using his techniques.

The German doctors were allowed into the surgery one morning when McIndoe was about to operate on a particularly mutilated Czech pilot called Frankie Truhlar. McIndoe spent slightly longer than usual washing up, then went into the theatre where Truhlar, already anaesthetised, lay covered in green towels.

Instead of picking up the scalpel, McIndoe ripped back the towels that covered Truhlar's ravaged face and legs. 'This,' he said, rounding on the German doctors, 'is what your war has done.' The two men left in silence.

Compared to Truhlar or Edmonds, Richard Hillary was not so very badly burned; but he was only twenty-three when he died, and he spoke like an old man.

Jeremy Wolfenden

In 1965 A.J.P. Taylor completed Volume XV of *The Oxford History of England*, which was later published separately as *English History 1914–1945*. It was a caustic, sometimes mocking account of the little men who had mismanaged a small island and a large empire. Yet it ended on a note that was all the more curious for the fact that is so clearly took Taylor himself by surprise:

> In the Second World War the British people came of age. This was a people's war. Not only were their needs considered. They themselves wanted to win. Future historians may see the war as a last struggle for the European balance of power or for the maintenance of Empire. [They did.] This was not how it appeared to those who lived through it. The British people had set out at all costs to destroy Hitler and National Socialism – 'Victory at all costs'. They succeeded. No English soldier who rode with the tanks into liberated Belgium or saw the German murder camps at Dachau or Buchenwald could doubt that the war had been a noble crusade. The British were the only people who went through both world wars from beginning to end. Yet they remained a peaceful and civilized people, tolerant, patient, and generous. Traditional values lost much of their force. Other values took their place. Imperial greatness was on the way out; the welfare state was on the way in. The British empire declined; the condition of the people improved. Few now sang 'Land of Hope and Glory'. Few even sang 'England Arise'. England had arisen all the same.

The surprise was caused by the fact that nothing in Taylor's narrative to 1939 had supposed England capable of acting in such a way and nothing he had seen since had led him to believe it capable of continuing.

Taylor was a fellow of Magdalen College, Oxford, and it was

behind its fancy white crenellations that the peculiar story of
Jeremy Wolfenden was fomented and begun. It started in
provincial pride and glory and ended with suspicious death, far
from home, and an ill-tempered visit to the college by the
gentlemen of the Secret Intelligence Service.

In the 1930s Magdalen had set its course to the Left and
determined to lose its reputation as a finishing school for
aristocrats and to compete with the most intellectually accomplished colleges. Its star fellows were Taylor and Bruce McFarlane in history, Peter Medawar in science, the philosopher J.L.
Austin and, in English, C.S. Lewis. A significant recruit to the
cause was a young man called Jack Wolfenden.

Born in 1906, he was the son of an education official at the
County Hall in Wakefield, Yorkshire. He was a brilliant product
of Chapel and grammar school, a walking vindication of the uses
of literacy. He had Yorkshire roots, a trace of Southern swank
after a childhood stay in Swindon, and a hard, competitive
character. Greek and Latin were the only subjects that counted
for scholarship boys, and in due course Jack Wolfenden was
entered for the awards offered by Queen's College, Oxford. On a
wet and windy night Alfred John Spilsbury, the headmaster of
Wakefield Grammar School, tramped to the Wolfendens' modest house to tell them their Jack had won a scholarship.

'My parents,' he recalled, 'did not say much, that night or ever.
We were, after all, taciturn Yorkshire folk, not given to facile
expression of our feelings. In fact, the deeper the feelings, the less
they were spoken. There might be a momentary trembling of a
lip, or a sudden start of tears to the eye, or a quick pressure of the
hand; but there were very few words, either in joy or in sorrow.'

Jack Wolfenden read classics, or 'Greats', as they were called at
Oxford. In his third year he started to have tutorials in
philosophy from T.D. Weldon in Magdalen. Weldon, known as
'Harry' after a music-hall comedian, was a defensive, hard-
shelled, lonely man, afraid of betraying anything that might be
construed as 'weakness', or even feeling. He was also terrified of
women. Under Weldon's tutelage at Oxford, Jack Wolfenden
listened to Wagner, read widely and worked hard. He believed
that, since he had taken a catastrophic second in Mods, the first

part of his degree, he was destined for a life of schoolmastering. Then Weldon made him a surprising offer. In 1928 Oxford was starting a new course called Modern Greats, or PPE (Politics, Philosophy and Economics). Such was the demand for it that Weldon believed Magdalen would need another philosophy don in addition to himself. He offered the job to Jack Wolfenden on condition that he got a First in Greats. The First, after immense toil, was achieved, and, following a year in Princeton, Jack Wolfenden became a don at Magdalen in 1929. In 1932 he married Eileen, second daughter of A.J. Spilsbury of Wakefield GS, who had made the rainy trip with news of his Oxford scholarship. When their boy Jeremy was born in 1934, Harry Weldon became his godfather.

Jeremy Wolfenden was born seven weeks early, on his father's birthday, 26 June. Haruspicators after the event could delight in both these facts: the precociousness and the father's shadow. Jack had left Magdalen to become headmaster of Uppingham at the amazing age of twenty-eight. Jeremy was the first baby born in School House for fifty years. Masters and boys who had thought it indelicate even to notice Eileen Wolfenden's pregnancy could now happily pay court to the little boy. He was everything the earnestly over-achieving Jack Wolfenden might have wanted: a boy, a charming boy, an instantly and prodigiously clever boy.

At two years old he could pick out the letters of the alphabet; at three he could do the same in Greek; at four he could read fluently. In the summer of 1939, aged five, he would get up early to make a start on the Child's Encyclopaedia. Strange words appeared in his conversation, which turned out to be the phonetically-pronounced trophies of his reading. He didn't like it when his parents laughed affectionately; he considered that to be *annoying*. His cousin Sally Hinchliff was evacuated from Dover, where her father was a doctor, and came to stay at Uppingham. Her mother Clytie was Eileen Wolfenden's sister, and Sally was a child almost as prodigious as her cousin Jeremy. Each developed a fantasy world with a secret language; but then, unusually, they fused them into one. During the War they would lie in bed giving

The Fatal Englishman

imaginary wireless reports, from Jupiter, in Jeremy's case, from the Middle of Nothing Land in Sally's. They could talk to one another in such a way that no one else could understand. They might have been twins.

Jeremy was a difficult child to bring up and was more advanced in some ways than others. The constant presence of a nanny protected him from some of the practical demands of life; he would never, for instance, answer the telephone. Every day after tea he came down from the nursery to play with his parents. They were old-fashioned provincial Yorkshire people. Jack Wolfenden remained an ascetic, unsophisticated man: he had a good mechanical brain, but little imaginative flair; the outstanding periods of his distinguished public life were as a quasi-civil servant when he became head of the University Grants Committee and of the British Museum. As a teacher he tended to the Gradgrindian: 'Look it up,' was his favourite advice to children and pupils. He was morbidly frightened of emotion, a failing that his friends put down to shyness. He was too busy to be personally involved with his children's upbringing; his wife believed he was more like an uncle than a father, making friendly but irregular excursions from the smoky atmosphere of his study. Photographs show him looking lean and active: on a hiking holiday he is wearing British Empire shorts and long socks, peering eagerly at the map, mouth clenched round a bough of briar. Even as he sits reading in a deckchair, his spectacles give off an air of twinkling urgency.

Eileen Wolfenden was equally old-fashioned, though in the manner thought more appropriate to a mother. She was content for the nanny to look after her children by day, but was keen to direct Jeremy's reading. She introduced him to books of the Greek legends and amused him by drawing the heroes from the stories. She was a warm and imaginative mother when she had charge of her children; she was good at finding ways to keep Jeremy occupied.

When the boy was four, the trustees of Uppingham came to visit the headmaster. Jeremy was brought down from the nursery and amazed them by naming the countries of the world from a *Times Atlas*. Although he would perform for his father, he did not enjoy being the focus of attention. He was not sociable; throughout his childhood he preferred to be left to his own reading and his own games. The birth of his younger sister Priscilla caused a welcome diversion of interest. In the family photograph albums Jeremy is a fugitive presence: Priscilla dresses up and dances; a later pair of siblings, Daniel and Deborah, cavort upon the sands, have parties, and shoot the garden hose on sunny days. But Jeremy makes only the odd appearance: an unconvincing Robin Hood, a reluctant horse on all fours to be mounted by the baby Deborah, or clasping a book and a newspaper, a picture of concentration and knobbly knees. He didn't like the games that other children liked; when a party was threatened he would lock himself in his room, from where, on one occasion, he had to be extracted by a gardener on a ladder. Much though his mother adored him, even she had to admit that he could be an extremely difficult child.

In School House Jeremy had a governess, and at the age of six he went to a little local school where all the other pupils, except Sally Hinchliff, were the children of Uppingham staff. Sally was the only child who could stand the pace he set; the rest were always at least two textbooks behind. He picked things up so quickly that he barely had to work, and school therefore held no drudgery. His father was ambitious for him, but Jeremy was self-motivated; no one needed to push him. His parents did not consider him ready for boarding school until he was nine, when he was sent to Maidwell Hall in Northamptonshire. Within a year he was in the top form and two years after that he was bored. He was in a hurry to leave. The headmaster, Oliver Wyatt, worried that he was simply too clever; they could not find enough to teach him or enough ways of keeping him occupied. Jeremy complained that he found it difficult to reconcile his life at school with his life at home. He liked games and was reasonably good at them, but a problem with his eyesight which began at about the time he left Maidwell limited his success on the playing field.

It was decided that he should sit the scholarship for Eton. He was awkward and shy, but well prepared. When it comes to the English essay, his father advised him, don't do 'What I did on my holidays' or something like that; pick the one-word title, like

'Rivers', then you can write about anything you like. And don't forget, his mother added, how bored they will be after reading all these essays; why not try writing something funny?

The Eton scholarship concentrated on Latin and Greek. The rewards for the 100 or so entrants were great, and the invigilating masters took it as seriously as the boys involved. One of the Latin questions in Jeremy Wolfenden's year, 1947, invited the boys to parse English words as though they were Latin – *potato*, for instance.

The boys were trained little winners who had been learning Latin since the age of seven. They usually came from one of the preparatory schools that specialised in the Eton scholarship, and it was thought to be to Wolfenden's credit that Maidwell was not one of these classics 'factories'. Wolfenden's entrance papers were unusual in being the source of gossip for some time afterwards among the staff. What had impressed the examiners particularly was his English essay on the subject of 'Dreams'. He had taken his parents' advice with spectacular results. 'I have been in this sort of examining for more than forty years,' wrote G.B. Smith, late headmaster of Sedbergh at the bottom of the essay, 'but I can say without hesitation that it is the most attractive piece of writing I have ever read from anyone of his age under exam conditions.' He won the top scholarship.

The scholars arrived at Eton feeling pleased with themselves. They had come through a fiery competitive test and had paid for their own education for the next five years. They lived in College, a separate entity, apart from the rest of the boys (Oppidans), who lived in houses round the town. The scholars, also known as Collegers or Tugs (from the gowns they had to wear – Latin, *toga*), were accommodated in little stalls in Chamber, a dismal, oak-lined passage on the first floor of a medieval College building. The walls that divided the cubicles reached only halfway to the high ceiling; curtains, not doors, provided meagre privacy from the corridor itself. After three weeks, before they had even grown used to bow ties, collar studs, tails and gowns, the scholars were placed on a mantlepiece and asked a number of impossibly detailed questions about Eton lore. As they answered, they were

pelted with bits of bread by the previous year's intake or
'election', one of whom was nominated Captain of Chamber. All
the Tugs failed the test, which meant they could be 'siphoned' –
beaten with a rubber tube – by the Captain of Chamber, Stephen
Egerton, who subsequently became the British ambassador to
Iraq.

Although they were taught with some of the brighter Oppidans, the scholars' life in College was self-contained, and the rest
of the school looked on them with a kind of awed pity. They ate
in their own dining-hall and played in their own junior common
room. College Library was distinct from the School Library
across the road; it sat on top of a distinguished cloister behind
School Yard that gave the whole place the air of a slightly
impoverished Oxford college.

Midway through the first term all the scholars were thrashed
for being too full of themselves. It made no difference if they
were servile or timid; the beating was a ritual. A fag's pattering
footsteps were heard in Chamber Passage, his unbroken voice
chanting: 'Wolfenden you're wanted in the Sixth Form Room,
Layard you're wanted, Howard go down to the Sixth Form
Room . . .' The big day had come, and down they went to find
various prefects lounging in armchairs looking unconcerned.
Four strokes of the cane, delivered over Wolfenden's eloquent
protests, were considered sufficient to reduce the Tugs to a
tolerable level of humility. Wolfenden was the personal 'fag' to a
grave boy called Douglas Hurd, who became Captain of School.
Recollections among Wolfenden's contemporaries differ as to
whether Hurd ever physically punished Wolfenden; if so, it left
no animosity between them, and Hurd was able to include a visit
to Wolfenden in his itinerary when he went to the United States
as a diplomat in 1964. By then Wolfenden was nearing the end of
his short career as a journalist; Hurd had not yet begun his
political ascent to the position of Foreign Secretary.

After he had settled down, Wolfenden worked reasonably
hard, but he was not the best classicist of his election. He was
outstandingly good at mathematics and by some way the best of
his year at abstract thought, but these didn't count as heavily as
Latin and Greek in the grading of scholars. He was happy to settle

for third place and bore no resentment to those who had nominally overtaken him. It was agreed by everyone that he was the cleverest of them all, and thus, by a natural sequence of Etonian logic, the cleverest boy in England.

But he was always in trouble. He had a way of dragging himself up the High Street; his walk exuded disrespect. He didn't approve of the social side of Eton life, the snobbery and the exclusive little clubs within the school. One day he banged his fist on the desk of the headmaster, Robert Birley, and demanded to know – à propos some small injustice – 'Is this or is this not an institution that respects free will?' Eton didn't want to lose him, however; the school thought he would bring glory in due course and so allowed him more latitude than it would have given to one less gifted.

He was blackballed from the most self-serving of the élite clubs – 'Pop', a group of prefects who elected themselves and wore fancy waistcoats – but was a member of Sixth Form Select, a second prefectorial body appointed by the masters. As a member of this group he had to dress up in breeches and buckled shoes to give a speech. The school records report: 'Wolfenden looked down his nose at his audience with his usual lofty contempt. Whether or not he felt thus for his speech as well as his audience ... he delivered it in his usual impressive tones. He is a competent and forceful speaker who successfully holds his hearers. He carefully concealed from them his own views (if any) ... perhaps this was a good thing.'

At Eton Wolfenden also became precociously and openly homosexual. A tea-time conversation with him might include news of his latest discovery in literature (he was keen on *Goodbye to Berlin* by Christopher Isherwood); it was likely to touch on work, games and school gossip; but it was sure to dwell on the eternally interesting question of which of the juniors was the most beautiful. Because so many of his contemporaries spoke lasciviously of the small boys, Wolfenden's predilection, which was to be a lifelong passion, was able to develop freely. He cultivated the dangerous aspect of his taste; though homosexuality flourished at Eton it was against the school rules. It was also against the law.

Jeremy Wolfenden

Occasionally boys would be 'sacked' with a menacing fanfare that was meant to deter others; sometimes a boy would simply not reappear at the start of a new term. In his penultimate year, 1951, Wolfenden found himself in serious trouble over a scholar in the junior election. It had gone further than romantic posing and lewd comment, and Wolfenden narrowly escaped being expelled.

The masters at Eton were much occupied by the moral character of the boys, though their suggested remedies for laxity seldom went beyond a bicycling tour of Breton churches. Wolfenden was a cause for particular concern because he was so openly disrespectful. He was always in danger. While the other boys struggled with Hesiod, he read novels. The problem with his eyesight limited his usefulness at games, though he did his best. Eton's particular sport is the Wall Game, in which two teams try to move a small football along a wall through the crush of bodies and the suck of the mud beneath them. The small boys, known as 'seconds', go in on hands and knees to fight for the ball, while the larger ones mill around on top. If a boy is being suffocated he is allowed to shout 'Air', though this is considered an admission of 'weakness'. Wolfenden was a useful second, though quite crushable. He once cried 'Air' when he was buried and incapable of breathing: he lifted his head above the surface of the mud where it was mistaken for the football and fallen on by several eager bodies.

Jack Wolfenden had taken a sabbatical in 1941 at the request of the Air Ministry to be in charge of an urgent programme to train young men to be pilots. From Uppingham he was appointed headmaster of Shrewsbury, where among the visitors he and his wife received were Michael and Edwyna Hillary, parents of a distinguished old boy. After Shrewsbury he became vice-chancellor of the new Reading University, and the teenage Jeremy became more than ever restless at home. Although he despised much of what Eton stood for, he was more excited by what was going on there than by life in Reading, which he called 'a caricature of a university, consisting entirely of Agricultural Economy and Tennis.' He wrote dismissively about his mother –

unfairly so, perhaps, in view of how well she had looked after him, but her homely qualities were not ones that appealed to him. He was able to talk to his father on level terms, but he resented being his father's son and distrusted Jack Wolfenden's ambitions for both of them. He described his father as being 'surrounded by the aura of sanctity that is bound to grow on any Public School headmaster'. He told his mother that his father just wanted him to be another version of the Wolfenden success story.

In the school holidays he wrote letters to his friends that showed a precociously developed style, a self-consciously decadent attitude, a clear knowledge of himself and an obsession with the beauty of boys. Philip Howard was considered good-looking, as was Robin Hope, while Wolfenden was no more than average. He was of medium height, strong, but with sloping shoulders; his spectacles gave him a froggy look, for which the verve of his conversation worked hard to compensate. He did not really grow into his looks until his late twenties, when, with a heavier jaw, dark glasses and cigarette at an angle, he traded his gawkiness for a kind of louche glamour.

In the holidays he read D'Annunzio, André Gide ('a notorious homosexual'), Wilfred Owen (though it was not then well known that Owen was also gay), Naomi Mitchison's short stories about Sparta ('extremely reminiscent of the Boy Scouts'), various manuals on adolescent psychology ('all more or less pornographic, and all more or less inaccurate') and 'some of the more lurid bits of Walt Whitman', who was also 'a notorious homosexual'.

'I know I am not a good mixer,' he wrote to his close friend Robin Hope in the summer of 1950, aged sixteen. 'The essence of good mixing is lowering oneself to the level of those around you, a feat which you perform skilfully and seldom, and I only for some vast ulterior motive . . . Do you loathe teen-ager parties? All the girls here are very ugly, and all the boys ivory-headed (inside) Apollos. Which is very putting-off for a type like me. It is all I can do to control my natural – or rather unnatural – inclinations . . . My father, aflame with the Muse, is writing a tedious novel about education problems. It excites him but not me. All the helpfully enlivening suggestions I make are immediately quashed with the words. "This has got to be published by the Clarendon Press, you realize." '

The letters he wrote were dangerously frank, though in January 1951 he tried to reassure Robin Hope that they would not be intercepted. 'Neither you nor I are going to be compromised for some time yet. I am too clever and you are too cautious.' He also reflected on what he called 'the Wolfenden paradox' – by which he meant the tension in his character between a need to *épater le bourgeois* and an odd desire to please. It was in the question of family that this paradox was most evident. He had more or less concealed from his schoolfriends the fact that he had brothers and sisters on the grounds that the thought of himself as a 'family man' was something at which 'most imaginations boggle'.

In his last two years at School Wolfenden studied Russian, and this duly brought him the Newcastle Russian Prize in December 1951. He won various other school prizes, including the Rosebery History Prize twice, in 1951 and 1952. In his final term at Eton, Lent 1952, the Register shows him as listed behind Richard Layard, Kit Welchman, Philip Howard and Stephen Aris; but his reputation for brilliance was undimmed and unsurpassed. It was spectacularly confirmed when he was awarded an open scholarship to Magdalen College, Oxford in history – a subject he had perversely chosen against the wishes of his teachers who believed all scholars should read classics. He left a term early because he was bored and a danger to the younger boys; he was anxious to move on and discover what the world had next to offer.

This was in fact pretty clear: National Service. Wolfenden had decided to go on the new Russian interpreter's course in the Navy, but was too young to sign up in the spring of 1952 so went to live in Cambridge House at 131 Camberwell Road, London SE5, where he worked as a youth club helper. Being out in the world at last brought the expected dividends. 'My love life is seething with incident,' he wrote to Robin Hope. He kept close contact with various boys at Eton and made a flirtatious return visit. In London he showed a preference for heterosexual men, though not exclusively. He commented on all his affairs with a wry romanticism; he enjoyed the sensation of being in love, and was happy to lose his heart even to someone in whom he knew his interest to be superficial.

At this time he was exercised less about what he would do than about who he was. He clearly saw the difficulties. 'Where do we go from here? . . . I am not going to end up as Anthony Blanche arty-tarting around the art galleries . . . I am a queer; so much is physically evident. But I have a lot more important things to do than waste my time hunting young men. It is a charming hobby, and for the sake of physical and emotional well-being a certain amount of it is of course necessary. But it is not an essential part of my life, and the more "self-fulfilment" I achieve in my work and my thought and my writing, probably the less I shall need it. I may end up with an undemanding and unsensational ménage with a single boy-friend; I may end up unsatisfied except for an occasional Sloane Street tart . . . I may, I suppose, turn to heterosexuality; but if by a pretty mature (physically) eighteen I am not attracted by girls either physically or emotionally or aesthetically it seems unlikely. One can but wait and see, and not get too involved, or waste valuable time. Waste of time is the one mortal sin.'

It is hard to remember that this is written by a boy of eighteen at a time when all homosexuality was illegal. A few weeks later he predicted: 'I think I shall end up a mental acrobat with no physical life at all. Which might be a pity.'

Neal Ascherson, a scholar in the year above Wolfenden's at Eton, advised him to 'Be queer, but not *a* queer.' As schoolboys the two of them determined to 'travel light' and put down no roots; Ascherson felt that if Wolfenden became 'officially' homosexual it would inhibit his freedom of personal and intellectual movement. They were less concerned with achieving particular goals than about the kind of outsiderish but intellectu-ally honest figures they would strike in the world. They had absorbed the lessons of Sartre and Camus. Wolfenden said his 'formative' books were *Dr Faustus* by Thomas Mann, Heming-way's short stories, *To the Finland Station* by Edmund Wilson,

Bevis by Richard Jefferies, *The Grapes of Wrath, The Quest for Corvo* by A.J. Symons, 'and, alas, Tolkien'; but the French existentialists also had a bearing on the way he viewed himself.

At school Ascherson and Wolfenden had formed a 'People's Section' in the Cadet Corps, which elected its own corporal, saluted with clenched fist and moved in partisan single file. It reflected their adolescent respect for the Maquisard way of life: rootless, uncommitted, ready to move. Ascherson later wrote: 'At one level, [Jeremy and I] were just rebellious boys looking for an ideology of independence. But these were the years when Existentialism was powerful. Without realising what we were up to, we too were trying to identify and obey the laws of our inmost nature as individuals, to "do what we were" and act out our subjective identities.'

Wolfenden regarded his coming naval service with apprehension. There was one last fling with the Boys Club on their summer camp – 'The week was really made by the next-door camp: a glorious collection of pederasts funnier than anything in Evelyn Waugh. A terrific fat man with whisky breath and a bogus army rank, a funny little man with shorts like a bell-tent and a spotted bow-tie, and innumerable cadaverous young men in flowered bathing trunks. It was all enough to disgust me with pederasty, if I wasn't already' – and then it was off to RN Victoria Barracks, Southsea.

He was pleasantly surprised. The petty officers were sensible, the food was good and the others on the course were interesting. He most appreciated the men who had already been to university, but he also gave the public- and grammar-school boys high marks for intelligence and desirability.

Robin Hope and Jeremy Wolfenden in turn astounded their grammar-school colleagues on the course, with their *savoir-faire* as much as their brains. Wolfenden was not conceited about his abilities, but he was realistically arrogant. His friends from school, and those he was to meet at Oxford, told him he was the cleverest boy in England and he saw no particular reason to demur. The accolade did not make him happy; it was merely something he lived with. All this was dazzling to some of the eighteen-year-olds who were away from home for the first time.

It seemed to some of them that the flow of Wolfenden's epigrams was simply continuous. One of his fellow students was a very tall, angular young man called Robert Cassen, who appeared to have a surplus joint in his extended, awkward frame. 'The Anglepoise', Wolfenden called him; and when Cassen bashfully appeared in a new petrol-blue suit of which he was shyly proud he was met with the greeting, 'My God, Robert, you look like a Finnish power station!'

The Naval Russian course has gained a certain mystique in the years since National Service ended. From the outset it was seen, rather self-consciously, as the intellectual's option. It was a demanding course and those who failed any part were discarded. Although it was possible to study Russian in either of the other two services, only the Navy was sure to keep its linguists at their chosen task for the full two years, without at some stage moving them on to general officer training. When Wolfenden joined up in 1952, his was only the third quarterly intake since the scheme began. The course had not had time to develop a reputation, but its attractions were immediately obvious. There were only three weeks' basic training before they began to study Russian at a camp at Coulsdon, near Caterham in Surrey. This contrasted favourably with the amount of drill and boot-polishing required by the Army and the RAF.

In September Wolfenden went to Devonport Signals for a two-week cryptography course and by this time seven of the seventeen had already left. Devonport turned out to be a 'Nissen Nirvana perched on the hills behind Plymouth', while learning the codes was 'like playing "double the number you first thought of" with the Marx Brothers in four dimensions.' But, he wrote, 'being almost a mathematician, I am rather good at it, much better than anyone else, even the Petty Officer who teaches us.' Wolfenden found another homosexual in his group of ten, but he was 'sadly "camp" ' and Wolfenden preferred to seduce woman-isers. He and his new friend had an excursion one evening to 'a pub renowned as one of the "queer" centres of Plymouth' where they were bought drinks by a drunken Petty Officer with whom they managed to avoid going to bed. Wolfenden found the evening memorable chiefly for the fact that he was able to get drunk on an outlay of less than ninepence.

After Devonport came the sea itself, and HMS *Shipstone*. 'Afloat! Afloat!' wrote Wolfenden. 'I know I have queer tastes but I'm rather enjoying this.' It was particularly better than being in port, where the regulars laughed at the clueless young National Servicemen and they in turn were fed up with the endless hanging around: the general atmosphere was that of 'a Central European third-class waiting room . . . just like Ljubljana, but without the VD posters.' Aboard HMS *Shipstone* Wolfenden was taught more cryptography, but found his thoughts, as always, straying to romance: 'The fascinating thing about this lark is that one meets people, likes them a lot, perhaps falls in love with them, and then is swept away from them by sheer force of circumstances. It's a tip and run sort of life.'

In December 1952, while he was at Coulsdon, Wolfenden's continued playfulness with the lives of boys still at Eton led to trouble. On a visit in November he had been consulted by a boy about his violently erotic feelings for another. Wolfenden advised him to rely on his own conscience, and not to think he was abnormal. The boy consulted the chaplain, and, on this man's advice, decided to keep his friendship for the other boy on a 'pure' level. He then wrote to Wolfenden asking what he thought of his decision and how he should behave towards the boy in question. Wolfenden wrote back and told him he had come to the right decision (the two were not well suited) though for the wrong reasons (fear, prudishness). The Master in College, Stephen McWatters, acting on a hint from the leaky chaplain, made inquiries and managed to get hold of Wolfenden's letter. He wrote an explosive one to Wolfenden: 'I was foolish enough to trust you . . . absolutely intolerable that you continue to come down and make trouble . . . who are you to presume to advise . . . exhibit a malice and selfishness I had not expected . . . callous indifference to his welfare . . . little trace of anything but arrogance and self-interest.' McWatters banned Wolfenden from College premises and forbade him to communicate with any boy there.

There would be nothing to this schoolboy incident were it not for what happened next. McWatters contacted Jack Wolfenden, who reacted badly. It was his own fault, according to Jeremy, 'because he hates being out of anything yet complicates the issue by trying to act as a go-between. So I had to have a set-to with him out of which I emerged with honour, but little else, and all my cards on the table. With the result that between us now is a tense uneasy artificial peace that makes home intolerable.'

And so it was, as Jeremy Wolfenden laid his 'cards on the table', that the chairman of the committee whose report would lead to the decriminalisation of homosexuality in Britain learned about the sexual inclinations of his own son.

Jeremy Wolfenden was philosophical. 'On mature consideration it is a good thing. It forces me to do what I had long lacked the courage for – to distil what I want of Eton, abandon the rest, and proceed deracinated. And since at the same time he has heavily undermined my home life, I am more of an emotional nomad, a nationless, mercenary intelligence, than ever. So be it.'

Such phrases would, on the lips of almost any other eighteen-year-old, be merely self-dramatisation. In Wolfenden's case they were also accurately predictive. He passed the next naval interview and was sent to Sussex Square, near Lancaster Gate in central London. They lived two or three to a room, but quite comfortably compared to the average officer cadet, and were given a season ticket on the tube to Russell Square, where the real work began. Each student was given a stressed text of *Crime and Punishment* and told to prepare fifteen pages a day; failure to keep up meant relegation to the rank of 'coder special', return to uniform, and despatch to RAF Withall. Even clever young men found the work demanding, and had to stay up till one or two each morning. 'The amount of work one has to do here is over-rated,' Wolfenden wrote to Robin Hope. 'Of course we can't all be brilliant, but I find it helps.' In a later letter, however, he admitted that there was a 'hell of a lot' of work, and even he did not finish before midnight. 'We have had 350 words to learn in the last two days and I am exhausted. All Russian words are the same; some are grimmer than others, none are more attractive.'

Wolfenden nevertheless found it all a bit of a lark until a naval ophthalmologist told him his eyes were quite unsuited for study and he should take up pig-farming. Wolfenden told the story as a joke, but in fact it had serious consequences. A sensitivity to light made him attach fold-down shades to his prescription glasses, though his resulting resemblance to a *film noir* bandit was some compensation.

If he was not to be allowed to use his eyes in the evenings – no reading, no cinema, no writing – the question of boredom arose with some urgency. After study and young men, the passion of his life was talk with friends, though even the brightest of them could not entertain him all the time. He discovered that whisky dulled the anguish caused by his craving for intellectual stimulation and by the limits of even his most amusing friends. As an eighteen-year-old midshipman he developed the drinking habits of a storm-grizzled bosun.

Soon after arriving in London he saw a film of Cocteau's *Les Enfants Terribles*. 'Terrific. What is this book? It has not yet appeared . . . I am going to be a film director anyway.' Cocteau was the kind of writer who appealed to him. 'I dislike Jane Austen not only because I am bored by the unextraordinary social life and priggishness, but also because all the manifestations of love are such as can be observed, *mutatis mutandis*, and with a little speeding-up, any day in the suburbs of Reading. Of course it *is* a revolt. But my life is *all* a revolt.'

While admiring, consulting and above all listening to him, one or two of his naval colleagues did see even at this stage that beneath the fountain of amusement, somewhere at the dead centre of Jeremy Wolfenden's life, something was wrong. It seemed a serious defect of character that someone so clever should be so bored. Many of them assumed that his homosexuality made him anxious and was turning him towards drink, but the evidence of Wolfenden's own letters suggests that he was quite happy about his sexual feelings; in fact he complained of the naïve attempts made by Robert Cassen and others – who believed sexual preferences were a matter of conscious choice – to 'talk him out of it.'

Wolfenden did well on the Russian course, naturally, although his accent was far from perfect. 'I don't speak pure Russian,' he explained, 'I speak the language of the Moscow race track.' They raced ahead in their work, and within six months they were doing papers set for Oxford finals. Each day they had seven hours of classwork, twenty-five words of vocabulary to learn and two hours' homework. Wolfenden enjoyed examining the teachers, who were mostly *émigrés* attached to the School of Slavonic Studies. Their life stories seemed unimaginably tragic to the privileged boys they taught, who became aware of the fragility of circumstance: they understood how different their lives would have been had they been born a few hundred miles further east.

The interpreters' course also gave many of the young men, including Jeremy Wolfenden, a fascination for Russia. David Shapiro determined to be a Sovietologist, to know all there was to be known about Russia; Robert Cassen made an after-dinner speech in Russian of such virtuosity that even the most dubious interpreters were laughing. Wolfenden was already thinking of newspapers.

At the end of the year the Naval interpreters were sent to Bodmin in Cornwall where they joined those from the Army and the RAF, who had done their training in Cambridge under Dr Elizabeth Hill. At Bodmin they were given final instruction in the particular vocabulary and needs of their service. The Navy hoped to have a well-trained Reserve it could immediately call up in time of war. Such a war was to be fought – it went without saying – against the Russians. It was also assumed that it would be a 'conventional' war, something like the one that had ended a few years before.

At almost exactly this time the Russians detonated their first hydrogen bomb, rendering almost all the Navy's assumptions invalid. The Third World War was never going to need the kind of specialists in decoding shipping messages that the Russian Naval course had produced, though this was of no concern to those who passed a profitable two years on it. Their low-level introduction to military intelligence work meant that most of them received approaches from members of the Secret Intelligence Service (SIS – or MI6, as it was also sometimes known), though Wolfenden never mentioned contact at this time. He later told friends that he had spurned their advances in the Navy, but succumbed out of a bored curiosity while an undergraduate at Oxford.

Having done two years in the Navy, Wolfenden was twenty when he went up to Magdalen to read Politics, Philosophy and Economics in October 1954. Many undergraduates did national service after university: it is not difficult to imagine what a daunting figure Sub-Lt. Wolfenden in dark glasses, black shirt and OE tie ironically aslant must have appeared to an eighteen-year-old freshman.

When Philip Howard first saw his old schoolfriend Jeremy Wolfenden at Oxford he was shocked. Jeremy had always been dangerous company at Eton, but only in a small-time, schoolboy way. Now he looked as though a cloud had come over him. He was unshaved, he smoked all the time; his fingers were stained an oak-brown colour; there was something sinister about him.

When he arrived at Magdalen it was at a College where his father had been a fellow, to read a subject his father had helped to launch at Oxford, and to study under his godfather. There is no evidence that these were the wrong choices for him, but the self-avowed emotional nomad, the intellectual gypsy, the disembodied thinking machine must at least have been aware of the cosy connections.

He was taught logic in Magdalen by a man called Oscar Wood who gave three-hour tutorials in his over-heated room in College. Wood liked to place his hands flat against the wall or crawl about on the floor to help him think. Harry Weldon's technique was to ask the undergraduate to read an essay, then say: 'That's not a bad first move. Now, my move is this . . . What's your second move?' The conversation would then take in Descartes, Locke and the rest; but no name and no reference could upset Weldon: it was as though all stages had been mapped out in advance. He was prepared to go on for as long as necessary. 'Very well, that's not a bad fourteenth move. Now my next move is this . . .' By this time only Wolfenden would be hanging in there.

PPE was the dominant school in Oxford, and Jeremy Wolfenden was, from the moment he arrived, its fieriest star. Also in

Magdalen at the time were A.J.P. Taylor and his fellow-historian Bruce McFarlane. Wolfenden became friends with Taylor and sometimes spent all night drinking in Taylor's rooms; their friendship was not affected by Wolfenden's eerily precise imitation of Taylor's voice, in which he loudly held forth at dinner within earshot of high table.

The intensely competitive and destructive atmosphere of Oxford affected McFarlane and Taylor in different ways. McFarlane became so perfectionist and so frightened of the smallest footnote inaccuracy that he could never believe he was ready to publish. He brought out only one book, though his reviews of others' were enough to silence their authors for good. Taylor took the opposite line: he decided to defy the pedants by publishing pretty well everything – books, essays, BBC chats and 'why-oh-why' articles for the *Sunday Pictorial*. When Wolfenden went up in 1954 Taylor had just published his most admired book, *The Struggle for Mastery in Europe*. Taylor and McFarlane were responding to an environment that was bitchy, complacent and scared of itself; the tone was embodied in the character of the college president, Tom Boase. When David Marquand decided to go to the University of Berkeley in California for a year, his teachers suffered a seizure of affected ignorance along the lines of 'I believe, President, it is an establishment somewhere in the United States of America.'

The Magdalen fellows had driven the college up the Norrington league table of academic results while at the same time managing to look down on colleges, such as Balliol, that were too earnestly competitive. The Magdalen attitude was that people good enough to get firsts had to get them, but should do it languidly, giving the impression of doing the occasional essay only in their spare time. Wolfenden told his fellow-undergraduate Philip French, 'You can get a First between five and seven in the afternoon.'

Wolfenden was undoubtedly driven on by Weldon, but, as an undergraduate, was not badly affected by the small-mindedness of some of the dons. His enemy, as usual, was boredom; and work, whisky, friends and sex were the weapons with which he fought it. Wolfenden struck his fellow-undergraduates as not

Jeremy Wolfenden

only clever but extraordinarily even-tempered; he was never angry or even, at this stage, mildly out of sorts. This permanent amiability was a remarkable feature of his life. If he was bored, as he often was, he did not in the Oxford manner try to belittle the person who was boring him. He used his range of reference and reading to mock the circumstances he was in and to draw playful analogies, not to exclude or threaten those who were less erudite. This cheeriness was not necessarily a reflection of his moral character; it seems to have been more a matter of temperament: since his need for amusement was so all-consuming, it was a waste of time to sulk or to put down people who could not help him satisfy it.

He was happy to befriend people from different backgrounds, of which there were a good number in Magdalen. Two of his best friends, Mike Artis and Rod Prince, came from state grammar schools and had never met an old Etonian before; his contemporary Philip French found most of those he had met 'distressingly boring, snobbish and stupid'. National Service had increased the class discrepancies. Rod Prince, who had been a corporal in a Transport company, would have had to call some of his fellow-undergraduates 'sir' if they had met in the services. Wolfenden's position was that he was above all these petty distinctions: as a 'nationless, mercenary intelligence' he could make friends with anyone he chose; and his charm and *joie de vivre* allowed him to do it.

His closest friends in college were all committed left-wingers. Mike Artis used to wear black jeans and red socks with a jacket that looked as though it had graduated more than once from Oxfam. He cultivated the pinched, industrial pallor of a boy from some rickety slum. Colin Falck was a tall, unsmiling man who looked as though he might have been happier at a recruiting station for the Spanish Civil War. Rod Prince was a CND supporter who resigned from the Communist Party over Hungary. They were in the right place. Magdalen did not admit much of any changes in the world since 1937; the clock had stopped with the fall of Léon Blum's Popular Front. In love with the melodrama of fellow-travelling, the college turned out young men of impeccable left-wing opinions who were nevertheless trained to say the right things to the right examiners in Finals.

Or so it seemed to some of Wolfenden's Etonian friends. Artis, Falck and Prince were not in fact as solemn as they seemed. A long night in Wolfenden's room was lubricated by quarts of brandy; conversation was not always about new developments in Marxist theory, but more often full of gossip and lewd speculation. The background music might be Shostakovich, but usually Wolfenden set the gramophone arm to infinite repeats of Frank Sinatra singing *Songs for Swingin' Lovers*. He enjoyed the theories of the Left, but never gave the impression that he was truly committed. This annoyed some of his companions, particularly those who felt more passionately but were outflanked by him in argument. His own beliefs had to be refined to the accompaniment of flirtation and hard liquor.

At the same time he was drawn to the idea of journalism, and particularly to what he thought of as the 'hard news' side of it. As a reporter on the university paper *Isis*, Wolfenden met Philip French, who had somehow constructed for himself – improbably in the immature and sexually repressed Oxford of the early 1950s – a hard-bitten, journalistic persona. It suited Wolfenden to encourage French in these attitudes; French later came to believe that Wolfenden 'was re-inventing me as an image of his ideal self'. In the tough, no bullshit, foreign correspondent vein of journalism previously represented by Neal Ascherson and now also by Philip French, Wolfenden seemed to see something he might do for a living. His self-consciously 'intellectual' friends were alarmed because Jeremy, if he were to dirty his hands at all with journalism, should surely write commentaries, leaders or 'think-pieces'. But he had seen through all that. He told people that the *Guardian* was 'not a serious paper' because it had too much opinion and not enough news; the *Telegraph*, however, was 'serious' because it had extensive foreign news coverage. A newspaperman was a gritty, unintellectual thing to be – a gratifying way to *épater le bourgeois* yet, with due regard to the Wolfenden paradox, to stay just within the pale. What Wolfenden admired about his fellow-old Etonian Neal Ascherson was this: 'Neal travels light . . . he takes only a typewriter and a revolver.'

Writing in the *London Review of Books* 40 years later, French recalled Wolfenden's journalism for *Isis* in the summer of 1956: 'I think he wrote better than any of us, in a style we aspired to . . . I doubt if any Oxford undergraduate – and I include Peter Fleming and Kenneth Tynan – has written so wide-ranging, witty and intelligent a group of pieces as Jeremy wrote for *Isis* that summer.' These included articles on the homosexual in litera- ture, on T.E. Lawrence, on the right-wing journalist John Gordon and a presciently titled short story called 'So I Never Saw Paris'.

In 1956, at the end of Wolfenden's second year at Oxford, the National Union of Students sent twenty-five people on a tour of the Soviet Union. Among them were five graduates of the Naval Russian course: Robert Cassen, Rex Winsbury, David Shapiro, David Marquand and Jeremy Wolfenden. The tour was loosely organised: it was open to the first students who could raise the £100 or so required. Four or five interpreters were attached to the party in Russia: one was a genuine student, who spoke lamenta- ble English; three of the others were dull Soviet types in ill-fitting clothes, with dirty fingernails. The fifth was an altogether different character: smartly dressed, sophisticated, amusing. His name was Yuri Krutikov.

He took a special interest in the five Naval Russian graduates, who in turn assumed he was a high-grade KGB operative. David Marquand was preoccupied by a Dutch girl, but the others found Yuri congenial company. He was relaxed and clever; like Wolfenden, he was easily bored and constantly on the look-out for amusement. On a train journey from Yalta to Leningrad the two of them talked smut for several hours, trying to find appropriate translations for various phrases. However, Kruti- kov's family was from the heart of the Soviet establishment; and, despite his frivolity, Yuri never wholly neglected his work.

The students' itinerary took them from Moscow to Kiev and Odessa; thence to Yalta and Leningrad on the way back to Moscow. In Odessa they were taken by bus 50 kilometres on muddy roads to see a 'show' collective farm. Along the way they passed several desolate collectives that fell a long way below the required 'show' standard. When they reached the selected farm the contrast was so absurd that it was barely worth the journey.

Yuri was happy to join in the game, especially on the way back, when the party was incapacitated by a huge quantity of collective new wine.

In his sober and serious moments Yuri Krutikov's job was to look at the young Englishmen and see what use they might be to the Soviet Union. Marquand was unavailable, with his Dutch girl; Shapiro and Cassen were the sort of solemn right-wing social democrats who actually fought the Cold War; Winsbury was not much of a prospect. This left Jeremy Wolfenden. He was flirting with the Left at Oxford, but was no fellow-traveller. His intellectual arrogance, however, made him interested in totalitarian means and contemptuous of the niceties of Western liberalism. Krutikov would have seen some grounds for hope in Wolfenden's perverse originality, though Wolfenden could obviously not take state communism too seriously after what he and the other students had seen.

In any event, the KGB was at this stage not really looking for political sympathisers. The happy days when such men as Burgess, Maclean and Philby could be recruited because they actually believed in Communism were long gone. Wolfenden could not be persuaded, but he could be entrapped; and the way in which this could be done was through his obvious weak point: his homosexuality. Wolfenden of Eton and Oxford was already working at *The Times* (slogan: 'The Top People's Paper') during his vacations, and probably told Yuri in the course of their drink-assisted chats that his ambition was to be its Moscow correspondent. Yuri, like all KGB officers at the time, assumed all British correspondents in Moscow were working for SIS. If Wolfenden, as a Russian speaker, were to come to Moscow as a correspondent in the near future, then it would clearly be worth Yuri's while to pay him some attention. He was unlikely ever to have information in the course of his work that would be of much use. The nature of any entrapment would not in the first instance be practical; it would be mechanical: it would be done because it *could* be done. But if Wolfenden's career flourished as everyone expected then there could be long-term benefits. To have as editor of *The Times* a KGB agent of influence would be more than a coup; it could be useful.

Did Yuri Krutikov sleep with Wolfenden in 1956? If so, neither mentioned it to the other students on the course; but they in turn didn't rule it out. They put nothing past Jeremy, or come to that, past Yuri. In the room at Yalta where Churchill, Stalin and Roosevelt signed the Conference Agreement, Yuri put a flowerpot on his head and pretended to be a caryatid. Yuri kept in touch with his English student friends; his career flourished, though it had a hiccough when he was sent by one of the UN agencies to the new republic of Zaire (formerly the Belgian Congo) and had to be hastily withdrawn on the grounds that he looked 'too Belgian'. He was back in Moscow by the time Wolfenden arrived there as a correspondent in 1961.

While the NUS delegation was actually in the Soviet Union in 1956, Khrushchev made his denunciation of Stalin. It was the summer of the Suez crisis; in November the Soviet tanks rolled into Hungary. By the time the students were back at College for their final year, the post-war world had become a very frightening place.

Philip French and Jeremy Wolfenden both duly became editors of *Isis*. A curious custom meant that the outgoing editor became the subject of a profile in the next edition. On 25 April 1957 Wolfenden was depicted in the usual pose – cigarette dangling, dark glasses, wicked half-smile – above an anonymous article that mixed undergraduate bombast with remarkable insight. The author of the piece was Robert Cassen, his ex-Navy colleague. Without naming it as such, he quickly put his finger on what Jeremy had called 'the Wolfenden paradox':

> A desire to shock fights with an unwilling conformism which, through uncertainty or survival instinct, he has rarely abandoned publicly in the way that those who know him privately might have expected.

Such profiles appeared under the general heading 'Isis Idol', or in this case, 'Press Idol', and Cassen's account of Wolfenden was certainly, sometimes embarrassingly, admiring. In his estimation of Wolfenden's likely future, however, Cassen was acute:

There is no mistaking the value of the material . . . he has a gifted, fast-working intellect, an endless facility for coining epigrams, and a well-documented memory; on the job he is as reliable as concrete. All this, unfortunately some will say, is coupled to an emotional make-up which is not necessarily intent on making the best use of it . . . a deep contempt for most of the exterior things of life, like good food or clothes . . . he bristles at the mere mention of words such as 'simple pleasures' or 'taste' or 'gracious'; and an analogous contempt for the liberal ideas of the West – a similar effect is produced in him by the words 'democracy' or 'freedom' or 'love'. This is not an assumed outlook, a mask of 'toughness', an artificial cynicism; whether defensible or not, whether permanent or not, it is a genuine and consistent attitude: wherever else he may appear at ease, his true atmosphere is Paddington Station, a room in Ladbroke Grove, the self-service café, urban, rootless. If it were not for the intellectual dishonesty involved, one could imagine him happily employed by the Soviet machine; but for true contentment, one need only give him a supply of cigarettes, a few bottles of whisky, and a small war to run, or get killed in. And an audience.

Nevertheless it looks as though he will end up a journalist . . . he will sell his soul for less than its real price, or go away thinking that there is nothing for him to do but harden himself into a mercy-bullet for the sick conscience of the age.

Student magazines are not usually a reliable source of anything beyond sexual gossip and film listings, but in this case *Isis* may be an exception. Undergraduates who had done their National Service were more advanced than today's average student; Wolfenden was both sexually and intellectually precocious, thus closer to maturity at twenty-two than most. He would have enjoyed the bit about 'the self-service café, urban, rootless' and the 'mercy-bullet for the sick conscience of the age'; all that Cassen seemed to miss, or perhaps play down, was what fun he still was.

Wolfenden's circle included various female undergraduates, who spent as much time as possible in Magdalen because it was more interesting than their own austere institutions. His acknowledged but still illegal homosexuality added to his mysterious glamour in the eyes of these girls. Heterosexual male undergraduates looked on in despair as Oxford's few eligible young women were drawn away from them to this doomed cause. Wolfenden was inclined to lead people into relationships deeper than they had expected, and to mobilise in them feelings he had no intention of matching. While one young 'dish' was being lined for a 'bunnymoon' (his word for a weekend away) others were wandering around perplexed and cast off. In Anthony Page, later a theatre and film director, and in Kit Lambert, who became the manager of The Who, he had gay friends who were 'out' and with whom he joked about homosexuality.

It was a major liberal cause of the time because the police were active in prosecuting 'offenders'. John Gielgud was arrested after an incident in a public lavatory. Lord Montagu of Beaulieu and two friends were set up with two young airmen who subsequently gave evidence against them: all three went to prison. A novel called *The Philanderer* by Stanley Kaufman ran into trouble; the novelist Rupert Croft-Cooke was sent to prison. A discreet gay novel called *Finistère* by Michael Fitzpeters became notorious when its publisher, Victor Gollancz, took an advertisement on the leader page of the *Observer* to describe it as the best novel about homosexuality since Proust. Bookshops in the Charing Cross Road put up cardboard arrows saying 'Novels on a "Finistère" theme this way.'

One response to repression was simply to drink more. On the day before May Day Wolfenden determined to stay up all night drinking so that he could hear the choristers at dawn. At noon the following day he consulted his watch and found that he had been drinking for twenty-four hours. In dreary post-post-war Oxford everyone was more manic and more dissolute than today; no one had heard of jogging or health clubs; everybody smoked. But however dissolute they were, they could be sure that Jeremy Wolfenden would be a little bit more so.

Drugs were hard to come by, but he managed. It was the time of Aldous Huxley's books on his experiences in California, and Wolfenden succeeded in extracting some mescaline from the science laboratories, which he took on one occasion with his cousin Sally Hinchliff, herself an undergraduate, and two others.

Sally found she had lost the willingness to move and spent the night in Magdalen new building, marvelling at the 'profound' insights that the drug induced, such as Jeremy's apparent assertion that 'language is not horizontal.' She misheard him; what he actually said was 'Be careful, the landing is not horizontal.'

With the aid of Alka Seltzer (known to him in a phrase of Colin Falck's, after the rifle-cleaning cloth, as a 'pull-through') and the five-till-seven afternoon work stint, Wolfenden duly won a formal or congratulatory first. Its distinction from a normal first-class degree lay in the fact that when you went for your interview the examiners were supposed to stand up and applaud. Wolfenden was given straight alphas throughout his papers, though they were not altogether happy about his attitude. One examiner made the frightening comment: 'We had to give him straight alphas, but frankly I didn't enjoy doing it. He wrote as though it were all beneath him; he wrote as though it were all such a waste of his time.'

Wolfenden's reputation was at its height. It was more substantial than that of bright graduates at other times because he was older. One or two of his more astute friends began to worry about his recklessness and lack of any instinct for self-preservation. His life, his attitudes and his intellect seemed to embody their own aspirations in some dazzling form; his existence seemed to demonstrate what happens when a rage for the life of the mind is taken to the limit. It was magnificent, but it was frightening. What would become of him?

Other killjoys noticed that while Jeremy was undoubtedly brilliant, he didn't have an aptitude for anything in particular. The word 'brilliant' recurs in all contemporary descriptions of him, but it is not an adjective of unlimited admiration; compare Proust's biographer George D. Painter on the fantastic Comte Robert de Montesquiou: 'He invented and kept his own astonishing rules of life: he was ... by far the most remarkable and original person in the empty milieu of the Faubourg St Germain; he was witty, and brilliantly though not profoundly intelligent.' Substitute any one of the closed English institutions in which Wolfenden lived for 'Faubourg St Germain' and the limiting description works for him too. He could take in philosophy, music, art, Greek, theatre, maths, history, any subject you might care to mention, with astonishing ease and virtuosity, but he didn't, for instance, have anything that you might call a *talent*.

Two months after leaving Oxford, Wolfenden had found himself a job on *The Times* as what he described as a 'general apprentice-cum-dogsbody at £5 a week'. This had been secured by his impressive work for the paper during vacations and by the support of a journalist called Peter Nichols, for many years the *Times*'s correspondent in Rome. 'However,' he wrote to Robin Hope, 'it's all a great victory ... especially as JFW [Jack Wolfenden] had no part in it – and gives me something to go on for the future.' He planned to keep his academic options open by sitting the All Souls exam in due course.

He moved from Cheyne Walk in Chelsea to Arundel Gardens in Notting Hill, but the gallery of exotic characters – 'A. had sex last night with a transvestite sadist from Reading clad entirely in black, including a crash-helmet' – stayed the same. Wolfenden's own intrigues were usually with respectable types who needed to be smuggled through the *Cage aux Folles* atmosphere of his various flats. One such object of desire was 'rather like Bamber Gascoigne only a bit butcher (Imagine!)', though when Wolfenden got him home he found Kit Lambert and a friend called Roger halfway through a four-hour conversation about each garment they would be taking with them on holiday to Greece. After two and a half hours of 'solid camp of a rare vintage', the dish in question was 'so tired that we could only play teddy bears'.

Kit Lambert was almost as dissolute as Jeremy Wolfenden, but at this stage a close ally. He was the son of Constant Lambert, with whom Christopher Wood had had his unfortunate cooperation for the Russian Ballet. Constant Lambert held no grudge, however. Four years after Wood's death his son was born and he needed to find a name; and so it was that Jeremy Wolfenden's friend was named after Kit Wood.

'Meanwhile,' Wolfenden wrote, 'I work for this aged newspaper, which creaks in every joint, accept all the drinks I'm offered by Public Relations Men ... I'm the smallest office boy here really – which makes me think I should have an affair with the smallest office boy – but it would really be too difficult. The place is full of dishes, but they would really be *so* much more use to me any place else.'

Newspaper foreign desks stay open late into the night in case stories come in from parts of the world in different time zones. It is expensive to remake pages and move stories around, and was especially so at this time, when printing was done on site using hot-metal presses. Although more advanced technology was available, the British print unions had successfully resisted it; when the linotype machines that set the print went wrong the management sometimes had to look for spares in Victorian museums. An organised racket in the print room meant that many printers on the payroll never turned up for work; some were paid under imaginative aliases such as 'Mickey Mouse'. Many of the scams had been written into the contracts by a blackmailed management, desperate not to lose a night's production. One of the most hilarious was an agreement by which linotype operators were paid to correct mistakes in the typesetting for which they were responsible. Proofs therefore seldom arrived on the editorial floor without their quota of 'errors'. The expense and the hostility meant that as few editorial changes as possible were made between editions and that journalists who stayed late on the night shift had time for drink and intrigue.

Wolfenden, even at the height of his promiscuity, declined to have affairs in the office. He enjoyed danger but always seemed to know how far he could go. He was almost thrown out of Eton, but he survived; at Oxford he never quite, as Cassen's piece for *Isis* noted, made his public life into the full-scale revolt that those who knew him privately expected. It was the apparent loss of this sure instinct later in his life that so perplexed his friends.

While Jeremy Wolfenden's sexual life in London and Oxford was reaching its rackety peak, his father was chairing a Committee on Homosexual Offences and Prostitution. The Home Secretary, Sir David Maxwell Fyfe, outlined two problems. The first was that there was too much brazen soliciting by prostitutes in London: innocent passers-by had to be protected. The second was the feeling that homosexuality was on the increase and that something should be done to stop it. The Government thought that the two subjects should be considered by the same committee and were ready for the same treatment. The homosexual problem was not, like soliciting, thought to threaten the public directly; it was said by the Home Office to be an 'unnatural vice' that degraded the individual and society. It also led to crime in the shape of blackmail.

According to Jack Wolfenden, most people were unaware that homosexuality existed. Of the few that knew about it, most thought it distasteful, and only a handful were tolerant. Buggery was illegal anyway, whether the second party was a man or woman. Lesbian activity had never been against the law, while the Act that made any gross indecency between men an offence was a legislative accident – a spin-off from a hastily passed bill introduced by Labouchère in 1885 and designed to protect women and girls. Certainly the law was due for reform; though whether trying to stamp out the practice altogether was the Home Secretary's best response was open to doubt.

Jack Wolfenden never found out why he had been chosen for the job. At first he worried about his children. 'What,' he wrote in his memoirs, 'might they have to put up with in comment from their contemporaries if their father got involved in "this sort of thing"?' What indeed? Jack Wolfenden was being disingenuous, since he had known for sure for at least two years (longer if he was informed of the incident with the first year scholar) that his elder son was devotedly homosexual. But he accepted the Home Secretary's offer and set about forming a Departmental Committee (it was not a Royal Commission, because such commissions publish all evidence, and the Wolfenden Committee felt it might lose the evidence it wanted if it was not 'off the record'). It says a great deal for Jack Wolfenden's personal ambition that he was prepared to risk it. It is difficult to imagine more than forty-eight hours lapsing in today's press before the first story – 'Vice Man's Son is Gay' – appeared in print. Jeremy had never made a secret of his sexual life; he was a famous figure in the small world of Oxford, and an active one in the larger sphere of London: his preferences were known about by hundreds, perhaps thousands of people. Either Jack Wolfenden had an overmastering desire to chair the committee or a deep trust in the tact and voluntary discretion of the British public.

Jeremy Wolfenden used to say that his father wrote him a letter at this time which went roughly as follows: 'Dear Jeremy, You will probably have seen from the newspapers that I am to chair a Committee on Homosexual Offences and Prostitution. I have only two requests to make of you at the moment. 1) That we stay out of each other's way for the time being; 2) That you wear rather less make-up.'

The Vice committee met, like Winston Smith and his rats, in Room 101. Their deliberations took two years and the Report was not published until 3 September 1957. Its main recommendation was that homosexual behaviour between consenting adults in private should no longer be a criminal offence. There was outrage in the press: John Gordon in the *Sunday Express* called the report 'The Pansies' Charter'; the *Daily Express* called it 'cumbersome nonsense'; even the *Evening Standard* thought the recommendations 'bad, retrograde and utterly to be condemned.' The Government, which had commissioned Wolfenden from a feeling that homosexuality ought, in its own words, 'to be curbed' was now in difficulty. In November 1958 Rab Butler, then Home Secretary, opened a debate by saying that any change in the law regarding homosexuality might be regarded as conferring some sort of tacit approval; on the other hand he was happy to implement Wolfenden's tame new legislation for fining prostitutes more heavily, and this became law the following year.

As for the homosexual law reform, the Government did what it did best: it did nothing. Labour friends told Jack Wolfenden they would have done the same. In 1960 a free vote on an Opposition motion to implement the recommendations of the report was heavily defeated. In 1965 Lord Arran set the business in motion again in the Lords; in 1967, on the initiative of Leo Abse MP, the Commons did the same. In the summer of 1967 the Sexual Offences Act came into effect, almost ten years after the Wolfenden Committee reported.

Jack Wolfenden personally abhorred homosexuality: he thought it was a disgusting abomination. However, he viewed the recommendations of the Committee as a philosophical exercise. He could not find any respectable reason for a government to interfere with the private behaviour of its adult citizens. His suggestion that homosexuality be decriminalised was a victory for intellectual process over personal distaste; it was a vindication of the disinterested mental disciplines of Oxford PPE.

By the time the law was passed in 1967 Jeremy Wolfenden was dead. For the whole of his adult life his father's report was either in progress or lying in a heavy pile, ticking powerfully, on a shelf in the Home Office.

Meanwhile, there was the All Souls exam. As the candidates stood waiting to go in Wolfenden remarked to David Marquand: 'You realise I've been competing with these people all my life, since I was seven.' He didn't mind competing, though, because he always won. Most of the candidates had flu, but contrived to make it a reasonably pleasant social experience.

Wolfenden sent a ripple of panic through his fellow-competitors when he strode out of one exam after half an hour. He handed in a single sheet of paper only two-thirds full. The question was 'Liberty, equality, democracy – three beautiful but incompatible ideals.' Wolfenden did not write an essay, but merely jotted down a string of aphorisms. He won a prize fellowship.

All Souls gave Wolfenden a base in Oxford with few teaching obligations in return. He would go back to Oxford at the weekends and hold soirées long into the night. It was on one such occasion that Colin Falck noticed that the conversation had taken a peculiar turn. Beneath the banter Wolfenden apparently had a serious purpose: he was attempting to recruit Falck to the Secret Intelligence Service.

Both of them were drunk and the approach was made obliquely, but Falck was quite certain what Wolfenden was suggesting, and quite certain that he was serious: even when drunk he had an inner mental gyroscope that kept him balanced. The man that Falck should go and see, said Wolfenden, was Robert Zaehner, someone to whom he had already gone to considerable lengths to introduce Falck. He was Professor of

Eastern Religions and Ethics·and a fellow of All Souls. Born to Swiss parents but raised in England, he was a short, fair-haired man with very thick glasses who, despite his myopia, had managed to join the Army as a press attaché and had been in Teheran from 1943 to 1947, returning to be acting counsellor in 1951–2, before settling in at All Souls for the rest of his life. Falck understood that Zaehner had been Wolfenden's own Oxford conduit to SIS, even though initial contact had been made in the Navy. Falck declined, and nothing more was said of it. His impression was that Wolfenden thought it all a game: he had himself signed up as an anti-boredom measure and because he was quite certain he could keep two steps ahead of any plodder from British Intelligence.

He was fascinated by a man called Whitaker Chambers, a Communist agent who left the Party to become a writer on *Time* magazine and later named Alger Hiss to the House Un-American Activities committee. Wolfenden saw playful applications of such duplicity to university life and was drawn to the idea of 'respectable' (frequently Old Etonian) diplomats playing a double game. It was connected to his feelings about his homosexuality, which had required him to assume to some extent a false role in society, and to his pleasure in walking the fine line of acceptable revolt. His enthusiasm for espionage extended to the novels of Ian Fleming, of whom he was an early admirer.

Meanwhile younger undergraduates such as Brian Wenham and David Murray, a handsome Canadian Rhodes scholar, joined the inner circle and enjoyed the combination of drink, flirting and shocking conversation. Wolfenden never seriously contemplated a career in Oxford. He was too impatient to live a life like Bruce McFarlane's; something like A.J.P. Taylor's might have been within his grasp, but there was the question of his homosexuality, which he neither wanted, nor knew how, to conceal.

In London *The Times* appointed him Night Foreign News Editor, which he enjoyed because '*The Times* is nicer when there aren't quite so many old men in the building, and when it is actually in the process of being a newspaper, and not just an institution, which is what it is in the daytime . . . I'm doing so much work one way and another, what with *The Times*, and teaching, and two books I'm supposed to be writing (which don't get anywhere very fast) . . . I must say I rather look forward to going abroad, if and when I get the chance . . . The attractions of England are strictly limited, especially when half the people in it *aren't* in it, because they've gone abroad, or else are in a state of congenital depression (usually justified).'

Of many London addresses, 27 Oakley Street in Chelsea was the longest lasting. It was a flat inhabited at various times by Kit Lambert, Philip French and his Swedish wife Kersti, Michael Sissons, Godfrey Hodgson and his first wife Alice Vidal, Sally Hinchliff, Michael Connock, a *Financial Times* journalist later caught in a 'honey trap' by Polish secret police, and a respectable but high-living lawyer called David Edwards. On quiet days Wolfenden would return from *The Times* at about midnight and would do the crossword in the next day's paper with his cousin. The days were seldom quiet. The drinking was riotous and so was the sex; Wolfenden often came home with a black eye or bleeding lip from some rough encounter. Anthony Page would use the house to rehearse John Arden's *Live Like Pigs* when there was no room at the Royal Court.

Gay life in London revolved around well-known clubs, such as the Rockingham or the Arts and Battledress, which was situated in an alley between the Strand and St Martin in the Fields. They were essentially pick-up joints that would be especially crowded on Friday and Saturdays nights. Compared to the defiantly 'out' discos of London today, or the bars that sprang up in Manhattan in the 1970s, these were genteel places: there were no shaved heads, nipple rings or dungeons, but men dressed in suits, cavalry twills and cravats. Attached to this scene was a more sardonic, queeny world that did not appeal to Wolfenden – 'the shallow emotions and the casual, treacherous, cynical sort of love I now associate with the homosexual underworld in London . . . an atmosphere in which sordid homosexuality is the only practic-able form of self-expression . . . the catty cynicism of the queer bars and camp little flats in Earl's Court Road.' He always wrote of his own sex life as though it should be, however anguished or sordid, a source of entertainment and laughter – a major bulwark against the tide of boredom.

Wolfenden's work in the office was well regarded and in 1960 he was sent to Paris as number two to *The Times*'s main correspondent Frank Giles. He had an apartment in the Avenue Kléber in the grand but dreary sixteenth *arrondissement*, between the Etoile and the Eiffel Tower. It could have been comfortable, but he never bothered to furnish it. He wrote in September:

> So here I am, working in Paris. There is, especially under the present régime, a great deal of rather silly and chauvinistic *panache* – Gardes Républicaines on every staircase, huge invitations for the slightest function, and more unnecessary bits of paper with photographs on them than I have ever seen. But the police are on the whole friendly and even cynical about all this (provided you do what they say . . . otherwise they just hit you), and the natives, though pretty arrogant, and speaking French in an intimidating sort of way . . . are on the whole better disposed than their rulers.
>
> For the last three weeks I've been working like a black, because my boss [Frank Giles] chose this time to take his holiday, quite regardless of the fact that the French were all coming back from theirs, and everything was starting to liven up . . . Otherwise my life has been full of people passing through on the way south, fugitive sex, and then the Gare de Lyon the next morning; followed by the same people coming through a couple of weeks later on the way north, horribly brown (I'm beginning to feel positively *green* after looking at all my friends), spending a night telling me all about the sex they've been having in the meantime, and then the Gare St Lazare the next morning . . .
>
> Had an extraordinary lunch with Nancy Mitford the other day; I was rather tired and preoccupied, and in one of my most savage Angry Young Man moods, so did not take at all kindly to sipping a single glass of Dubonnet for twenty-five minutes while she and three other queens analysed in minute detail the seating plan for the General [de Gaulle]'s dinner for Lord Gladwin.
>
> I live a very quiet life, if only because if one lives and works on the Right Bank there is no real reason ever to go to the Left Bank, and vice versa.

Jeremy Wolfenden

This is a peculiar, in fact a ridiculous and self-destructive, attitude for him to have taken. The Left Bank of Paris was between two of its great periods. The heyday of Sartre and de Beauvoir was over; the Left had split and crumbled over the Soviet invasion of Hungary; Existentialism, which had had such a bearing on the way Wolfenden saw himself, had also passed its fashionable high point. But while it paused to gather itself for the revolutionary activities of 1968 the Left Bank was still a place of genuine intellectual excitement as well as of conversation, posing and drink: it is hard to think of anywhere that should have appealed more to Jeremy Wolfenden. But he was not interested. He worked long hours in the office, which was in the rue Halévy, beside the Opéra, then went back to his flat to drink. David Murray, the former Rhodes scholar from Oxford, was living in Paris at the time and used to force Wolfenden out to a play or a film in the evening, but this only postponed the drinking. Wolfenden did not speak particularly good French and showed little interest in the place or the culture; nor was he journalistically stretched. Murray, who had known Wolfenden well at Oxford, believed that he was depressed.

He was right. In January 1961 Wolfenden wrote: 'For the last week or so I have been suffering from an emotion which is difficult to describe – a sort of cross between regret for lost youth, sheer sentimentality, and a sort of jealousy of those who are not suffering from this. It all started in the [Café] Flore a few days ago, seeing a couple of American boys pretty obviously in love with each other, and has built up into a sort of feeling that if I had gone to different places or different people at different times, I would not now be in the position I am . . . I do more and more often feel that the way I live, both administratively and sexually, cuts me off from people more than it need, and leads to a sort of formalized life which is the last kind of thing I want to lead.'

Perhaps this black epiphany in a famous Left Bank café was what persuaded him to cross the Seine no more. In Paris he was separated from his friends, and, to some extent, from his audience. They were beginning to get married: Sally Hinchliff married Owen Humphreys; Godfrey Hodgson, Michael Sissons and other friends from Oxford were engaged. Hodgson, a fellow-

Yorkshireman, had known Wolfenden as a child; he had gone as a scholar to Winchester and thence to Oxford. Although Wolfenden, somewhat to Hodgson's disappointment, refused to engage in intellectual competition, he was aware of Hodgson's life and early achievements as a journalist. There had been a lull after graduation when many people found reasons to prolong their stay in Oxford (research; or 'research' as Wolfenden called it) while those that came to London continued to live a student-Bohemian life. But by 1960 they had begun to find jobs, spouses, ways of living; and Wolfenden, in his stuffy Right Bank apartment, was no longer at the centre of their admiring world. He had the congratulatory first, and the All Souls fellowship, but so what? Residence in college 'would mean that I never had any sex except with John Sparrow [warden of All Souls] which would be a grim prospect.'

He had done everything he could do, and he had done it with vigour and unfailing style. Now in Paris there seemed to be a question of 'What now? What is it all for?' and a sense that for the first time he was starting to lose the thread.

The *Daily Telegraph*'s man in Paris was the genial Ronnie Payne. He was immediately charmed by Wolfenden and thought him a first-rate reporter. However, Wolfenden's drinking excited comment, even in this milieu. At the *Standard* correspondent Sam White's Christmas party in 1960 the police were called after complaints from the concierge about '*tapage nocturne*', particularly the crash caused by a pot of flowers falling off the balcony.

Whatever inner doubts he may have been feeling, Wolfenden's journalistic performance was impressive, and soon attracted the interest of the *Daily Telegraph*, then edited by Colin Coote. The identity of the editor was not in fact that important to *Telegraph* foreign correspondents since he had no say in the news operation, home or abroad. By a curious *Telegraph* tradition, the editor ran only the comment and leader section of the paper, while all news came under a Managing Editor who reported direct to the paper's proprietor, Lord Hartwell.

Ronnie Payne received a call from the Managing Editor, a man called S.R. (Roy, but known as 'Pop') Pawley. He asked Payne if he would sound out Wolfenden about the possibility of his going to Moscow for the *Telegraph*. The conversation went like this:

PAYNE: Certainly. He's very good journalist. But . . . Moscow. You do realise, don't you, that he's an active and busy homosexual and, well, as is well-known, horrid things tend to happen to such people in Moscow.

PAWLEY: Are you sure? Isn't he Sir John Wolfenden's son? Didn't his father write the Report?

PAYNE: Yes, that's right. Perhaps that's *why* Jeremy is. I don't know. I'm just telling you.

PAWLEY: Well, anyway, Lord Hartwell's very keen for him to go there. But . . . well, I'm told he drinks a bit.

PAYNE: Do you know any foreign correspondent who doesn't?

PAWLEY: I see what you mean. Anyway, go and sound him out, will you?

Payne met Wolfenden at the Crillon for drinks, something that was not difficult to arrange. Payne put the Moscow idea to Wolfenden, who was thrilled. 'God, yes, I'd love to. But aren't there . . . you know, objections?' Payne told him what Pawley had said: Lord Hartwell was very enthusiastic. Wolfenden said he would think it over and let Payne know after Christmas. He duly contacted Payne and said, Yes, he was very interested.

Shortly afterwards Pawley again telephoned Payne and said that Wolfenden had been in touch. 'The odd thing was,' Pawley said, 'he sounded as though he had been drinking.' Payne did not wish to stand further in the path of a fellow-journalist's career and made no comment. The decision in London had been more or less taken. 'Anyway,' Pawley concluded, 'Lord Hartwell's very keen.'

And so the disastrous appointment was apparently made because no one wished to displease or disabuse the *Telegraph's* proprietor. The *History of The Times* ('Struggles in War and Peace, 1939–66') recorded: 'Jeremy Wolfenden who was in Paris after being in the foreign news room . . . in 1960 joined the *Daily Telegraph*, partly because the *Telegraph* was ready to send him to Moscow; he had long hoped *The Times* would send him there.'

There is a more conspiratorial explanation of how and why the

Telegraph hired Wolfenden, though it would not have been clear to him at the time.

Meanwhile, on various return trips to Oxford, Wolfenden had been conducting a new sort of romance: with a woman. One of his tutors at Magdalen, Frank Burchardt, had a daughter called Susie, who was an undergraduate when Wolfenden was at All Souls. Wolfenden paid court to her in Somerville, though in his distinctive way: on one occasion he arrived in her room awash with ouzo and collapsed on the bed. The Burchardts were European, but Susie had been brought up in the United States: she combined a serious intellectual background with a New World exuberance. She danced tirelessly and sang at parties; she was what Eileen Wolfenden called a 'fizzer'.

Susie Burchardt was initially drawn to Jeremy Wolfenden, like everyone else, because he was a fountain of brilliant amusement. But, having grown up in the sarcastic, destructive world of post-war academia, she particularly valued the fact that Wolfenden did not use his wit to put people down: it was not just his own voice that he wanted to hear; he would draw people out and listen to them.

She represented to him the possibility of order and a family life and she was good company into the bargain: the 'Wolfenden paradox' found its most acute expression yet. Her friends told her she was being ridiculous, that Jeremy was a confirmed homosexual who could never be happy in a conventional marriage. But it was not quite a conventional marriage that she had in mind. It turned out that Wolfenden was not wholly homosexual, and in any case she was prepared to be open-minded about his predilections if she felt the relationship gave them both enough in other ways.

The thought of Moscow kept him going in Paris. 'It will be nice to be back in Moscow again,' he wrote, 'even if I have to work seriously this time: taxis with their checkered sides, the smell of diesel exhaust, the chandeliers and the ambiguous telephone numbers, Russian cigarettes and the barley-sugar on top of St Basil's.' From the NUS visit he knew where all the pick-up places were; he told David Murray that he fully expected to be caught and blackmailed within the first two weeks. The prospect didn't seem to worry him. His employers also appeared unconcerned. Perhaps Roy Pawley had disbelieved Ronnie Payne when he told him Wolfenden was busily homosexual, but the belief in Fleet Street was that Pawley was briefed by the SIS. Wolfenden's own arrangement with them appeared to contain no specific brief at this stage; everyone seemed happy to let events take their natural course.

He left London on 11 April, a beautiful spring day. There was a single ragged cloud visible from the window of the plane; the sky and the sea seemed otherwise clear reflections of each other. Then came the caviar and the vodka, as much as he could drink. He woke up in deep cloud, bumping over pine forests and unmelted snow. The taxi from the airport drove through a heavy snowstorm to deposit him at the Ukraina hotel, a skyscraper of the most uncompromising Stalinist design. He had a single room, number 865, with bathroom. At the end of the corridor sat an old crone who noted his movements with the all-seeing gaze of the Paris concierge but with more sinister intent. From the instant he arrived in Moscow, he was under pressure, and for the rest of his life the cloud never truly lifted.

Wolfenden, mercifully for the rest of the world's traffic, had not learned to drive a car. To escape from the atmosphere of the Ukraina hotel he depended therefore on the Reuters correspondent John Miller for lifts; if Miller was busy Wolfenden faced a long wait for a taxi, shuffling around in the bitter cold. For some reason he would not wear the full Russian hat that protected the ears, but only an Astrakhan cap on the side of his head.

What they could do as reporters was limited. Although censorship had officially been lifted, it was understood that newspaper correspondents would impose a degree of self-regulation. They were not allowed to report on crime, food shortages or Khrushchev's difficulties. Many organisations, including the BBC, were refused a correspondent; and even when a paper was allowed to send someone, the authorities were choosy about who it was. The obvious man for the job at the *Telegraph* was David Floyd, its Communist affairs expert, who had been in Russia during the war; but he was refused a visa. He may have been viewed as too implacable a cold warrior, while Wolfenden was thought more biddable: Yuri Krutikov had made his report on the students five years earlier.

The whole of the British press corps (at this stage only the *Telegraph, Mail, Express* and *Observer*) relied on Reuters. They had radio and television; they were supplied with a wire from Tass, the Soviet news agency. They also had – a wondrous thing in stone-age Moscow – a teleprinter, that had come to them through 'Lease-Lend', the American system of patronage to its wartime allies. Every morning Wolfenden would take a taxi to Reuters headquarters where he would be given the file of the latest developments. His early morning visits were interrupted by a period of asylum in the lavatory where he could be heard coughing and retching his way clear of the previous night's excesses. The journalists gave each other code names: when the florid Martin Page arrived to take over the *Express* office he became Mr Pink; the self-effacing Mark Frankland of the *Observer* was Mr Grey; but right from the start the bilious Wolfenden was Mr Green.

On a typical day the correspondents met at the Reuters office, took the file, then went home to rewrite the stories in their own way, though they agreed the angle among themselves and put no great effort into giving the story an individual spin. A system of open and intense collaboration developed on the basis of a feeling that in this implacable place the journalists must survive together or not at all.

The press was prohibited from talking to Soviet citizens; all questions had to be put in writing and sent to the Foreign Ministry press department, which frequently didn't bother to reply. Even going to interview the Bolshoi Ballet posed a tense bureaucratic problem. Reporters could not travel more than 25 miles from Moscow without permission, which was usually refused. Trips to Leningrad were encouraged, though the press saw it chiefly as a lunching opportunity: they could be back in Moscow by four – two o'clock London time – and at least have had a change of scene.

Although the conditions in which the journalists worked were dismal, there were some interesting stories to report. Russian-speaking correspondents like Wolfenden and Mark Frankland were able to supplement their news agency diet by cultivating semi-official and official intellectuals and – much more cautiously – ordinary people. Change was in the air. The Gulag had been opened; there were grounds for a modest optimism. Khrushchev himself was a perpetual drama. He never gave press conferences, but he could be seen at some of the receptions the Western press attended and was, if in the mood, approachable. In September 1962 he declared that any aggression towards Cuba by the United States would lead to nuclear war. On 22 October President Kennedy revealed that Russia had missile sites in Cuba and imposed an arms blockade on the island. Since the huge American arms build-up under Kennedy and the aborted invasion at the Bay of Pigs the Russians had had some reason to be nervous. For a week the two men gazed into each other's eyes. Kennedy seemed to know more than his opposite number; he knew not only about Cuba, and had the photographs to prove it: he seemed to have information about the likely outcome of any large conflict. On 28 October Khrushchev blinked: he promised that the Russian missile sites in Cuba would be dismantled; Kennedy in response lifted both the blockade and the threat of invasion.

In Moscow the Western press asked Khrushchev at a Christmas party whether he would be the president of their club. He agreed, and was presented with a tie. A few weeks later it was pointed out to him that it was normal in such circumstances for the president occasionally to *wear* the tie. 'I will wear it,' Khrushchev replied, 'at my next press conference.'

In the week of the Cuban missile crisis a 38-year-old Admiralty clerk called John Vassall was jailed in London for eighteen years for spying for the Soviet Union. While on a previous posting to the British Embassy in Moscow, Vassall had been set up by the KGB in a homosexual trap. He was photographed in compromising circumstances, then blackmailed. This was a routine piece of work for the Second Chief Directorate, the internal security service, which was the Soviet equivalent of MI5. What was unusual about Vassall was that the KGB was able to continue its hold on him when he returned to London; this appeared to have been achieved by annually paying him the equivalent of his Civil Service salary of £700.

The espionage aspect of the Cold War was at its height. The British Embassy in Moscow had not only its regular SIS officer in diplomatic guise; in the wake of the Vassall case, M15 was also an active presence, trying to create tighter security against Soviet penetration. Much of this was mechanical: both sides liked to entrap citizens of the enemy and enjoyed the embarrassment it caused. However, the Vassall case showed that from such mundane manoeuvres real results could occasionally spring.

Although Wolfenden, like the other correspondents, relied on Reuters for his daily stories, he made some headway on his own. His most notable contact was with Guy Burgess, by then near the end of his life. The KGB had provided Burgess with a guitar-playing boyfriend and a pleasant flat near Novodevichy monastery where, in blue silk pyjamas from Fortnum and Mason, he was drinking himself to death on Armenian brandy. Wolfenden was the only person who appeared to have a real rapport with Burgess. Sometimes the old traitor would come to the Ukraina hotel where Wolfenden had now been moved to the Siberia of the twenty-seventh floor, with no fire escapes but a mass of bugging equipment. The two would put on their Old Etonian ties and get drunk together. When Burgess decided to give a full interview about his feelings for England and about his life, it was Wolfenden he summoned to his flat. Wolfenden asked John Miller of Reuters to go with him and his great exclusive thus went round the world as an agency story on the Reuter wire. He may have asked Miller just because he needed a lift, but he may also have been anxious about intelligence repercussions: he was not sure how friendly he was supposed to be with Burgess.

The British Embassy, itself involved in the longest of games, encouraged Wolfenden to keep in touch with Guy Burgess, and at his worst moments Wolfenden had much in common with the pathetic spy. 'In his own disreputable way Guy Burgess is very amusing,' he wrote, 'but he has to be taken in small quantities . . . apart from anything else, to spend 48 hours with him would involve being drunk for at least 47. He has a totally bizarre, and often completely perverse [idea] of the way in which the outside world works; but he makes up for this with a whole range of very funny, though libellous and patently untrue, stories about Isaiah Berlin, Maurice Bowra and Wystan Auden.'

One morning in the summer of 1961, quite soon after he had arrived in Moscow, Wolfenden was standing at the bookstall in the lobby of the Ukraina, smoking furiously and hitching up his trousers, which didn't fit properly. He was approached by a pretty nineteen-year-old English girl called Martina Browne. She thought he looked English and vulnerable; she thought he needed cherishing and feeding up. They fell into conversation and she found herself at once captivated by the Wolfenden charm. They went off together and ate ice-cream; presumably this was what Wolfenden thought what he called 'teen-ager girls' liked to do.

Martina Browne was a mother's help to Roderick (known as Ruari) and Janet Chisholm and their three small children. Ruari Chisholm was from a working-class Scottish Catholic family and was Visa Officer at the British Embassy. He spoke German and Russian and had begun his career by doing translations at the trials in Berlin after the War; he had been in the Far East before being posted to Moscow. Janet Chisholm came from a refined English family and had also worked as a diplomat. She was a` Russian speaker who had previously been in Hungary; she had met her husband in the service and it was in every sense a diplomatic marriage. Ruari Chisholm was worried that the children would not receive a proper Catholic upbringing in Communist Moscow; before they left England he and his wife advertised for a mother's help at the Roman Catholic Challoner Club in Pont Street in Knightsbridge. Diplomatic staff in Moscow was supplied by UpDK, a domestic agency run by the KGB; it was not unusual for a diplomat to tolerate UpDK drivers and handymen, but no one wanted to live with a Russian nanny. Many therefore recruited adventurous nineteen-year-olds from various parts of Britain and Western Europe. These pleasure-loving young women arranged their baby-sitting duties so the greatest possible number could be free for any given party; they were known to Wolfenden as the Corps of Moscow Nannies.

Martina Browne successfully applied for the Chisholms' job and began work in July 1960. One of her duties in Moscow was to take the children to services conducted by an American priest in the apartments of other Catholic families in the diplomatic blocks. It was not a case of being a formal nanny and having sole charge of the children; Martina was supposed to help the family in all its domestic life and be a friend and support to Janet Chisholm. She also had a whole day and two mornings of free time each week. Ruari Chisholm's other job, as Martina Browne slowly discovered, involved rather more than visas: he was the Secret Intelligence Service officer in Moscow.

Martina Browne herself came from a poor family in Greenford, Middlesex. Her Irish father, when employed, was a sheet-metal worker; at home he was a drunk and a tyrant who used to beat his wife. Martina left her convent school at fifteen and did a variety of jobs, including tracing in a draughtsman's office. She wanted to escape from her parents' home, where she still lived; she wanted 'to travel'. It did not occur to her that Moscow might be a complicated place to live at this time in its history; there were different parties to go to every night and she enjoyed the gossip and intrigue of the small diplomatic community. Once she had met Wolfenden it was easy to keep in touch; in this closed world she could barely avoid meeting him two or three times a day. Sometimes he would go over to the Chisholms' apartment in Sadovo Samotechnaya and would often end up staying the night, drunk, on the sofa.

Wolfenden enjoyed Martina's company. 'I am being aided, but confused,' he wrote, 'by a nice "nature girl" who has, lunatically, got herself employed as a nanny to one of the diplomats here and seems to be in a state of rebellion against the diplomatic world (not surprising) and in fact almost everyone except me . . . it all looks rather sweet and fills a gap.'

Meanwhile, there was drink. The drinking was prodigious and the alcohol itself was dangerously, disastrously cheap. Whisky could be bought for about four shillings and sixpence a bottle; Stolichnaya vodka was so cheap that some official drivers would put it in their radiators in place of anti-freeze. There were endless national days and cocktail parties; as a journalist you could cruise from one embassy reception to another: you could drink for free all day, and if you wanted more you could get it dirt-cheap from the commissary of the British Embassy on Fridays. Jeremy Wolfenden was drunk from midday to midnight every day. There was no social stigma attached to being a drunk in Russia, he pointed out to his press colleagues, and, so far as the Russians were concerned, he was right.

Lunch would often be at the first floor restaurant of the National Hotel, overlooking the old Tsarist Cavalry School. It would habitually take at least two hours. First there was vodka, then smoked salmon; then there might be crab in cheese sauce and a main course of shashlik, chicken Kiev or baked sturgeon. It was a little like Colonel Narishkin's establishment in Paris in the 1920s, but was patronised by foreigners, not Russians. Wolfenden's order seldom varied: 100 grams of vodka to still the shaking hand, some clear chicken soup to soothe the stomach and then a skirmish with an omelette. The food was not as important as the drink. Georgian wine would follow the vodka, and Armenian brandy was served with the coffee; Wolfenden drank wine only as a sluice between spirits.

In the late afternoon he would have to book a telephone call to the office in Fleet Street. The line was always bad and was frequently lost in mid-flow; the copy-taker at the other end would ask 'How are you spelling Khrushchev?' twenty times in each story. The *Telegraph* demanded that news stories be written in a flat, bald style, shorn of adjectival decoration or fancy punctuation marks. Full stops, and plenty of them, were advised; commas were permitted; semi-colons were banned. The style was based on an original idea that a newspaper reader might be struck down, or have to get off his train, in mid-story. If this should happen, it was thought, he ought still to know what the story said. Therefore all the important facts went into the first paragraph, or 'nose'; subsequent paragraphs supplied further, but subsidiary, information and 'quotes' from people involved. Skilled reporters could turn this odd form into a minor art; in less adroit hands it became an inferior concerto, with the later paragraphs no more than rococo variations on what had been said at the beginning. It was a long way from All Souls. Wolfenden was easily able to adapt to the demands of the style: because he could write well, he could write any way they wanted. His account of Yuri Gagarin's first manned space flight – which took place only one day after he arrived in Moscow – read like the work of a veteran *Telegraph* man.

In the evening there was sometimes a visit to John and Brenda Miller's flat in Sadovo Samotechnaya ('Sad Sam' to the British), one of the foreigners' compounds where Wolfenden was at least provided with a proper meal and some ordinary human contact. He was good at playing games with the Millers' three small children. The eldest, David or 'Dodik', regarded his young twin siblings with caution and was particularly demanding of the vodka-breathing visitor he called 'Wuff'. Wolfenden in turn was genuinely amused by the Miller children. Sometimes there would be a game of 'Moscow Mexican', a crude variation of poker. The house rule said a player could only lose ten roubles before he had to retire, but the Uruguayan ambassador, Leslie Close-Pozo, who occasionally joined the games in his MCC tie, asked to be allowed to lose as much as he liked.

The journalists had so little idea of what Muscovites were talking about that they discussed the London stock market; Wolfenden and Keith Morfett of the *Daily Mail* even dealt on it. Wolfenden did not take to Morfett in the way that he had to his predecessor, John Mossman – 'Mossy', a man of small culture but colossal drinking capacity. Another favoured topic of conversation at poker evenings was the ideal foreign posting. It was not Moscow. Peking and Washington were favourites, though there was a feeling that London would be a good place to be. All of them assumed that an incoming Labour government would usher in a long future of social democracy and that England would be a place of refreshing intellectual ferment while this benign revolution took place.

At night Wolfenden would return to his incarceration in the Hotel Ukraina. In good weather he could see over the gold domes of the Kremlin right across Moscow to the Komsomolskaya skyscrapers; the huge shadow of the Ukraina was cast across the river and on to the further bank, where it appeared to move no more slowly than the barges that nosed through the broken ice on their way upstream – or was it down? He never could make out which way the river flowed. But in bad weather, you could see nothing: he would look from his window and see only fog; he couldn't even make out the ground below.

He was lonely. Susie Burchardt was by now his more-or-less formal fiancée, but she was in Oxford. There was the mother's help from Greenford to think about, but he told her, 'I can't be in love with you. You're too young . . . you're just a teen-ager.' She was also a Catholic virgin who had no intention of sleeping with anyone until she was married. For him there were no 'dishes', none of the romantic or intellectual intrigue that had previously helped him keep the killing tide of tedium at bay. As he wrote to Robin Hope: 'There are one or two dishes among the British students here in Moscow, which is more practical good to me personally, or rather might be if they knew the facts of life and I didn't know only too well the facts of Moscow hotel life [ie bugging].' What there was, in vast inexhaustible quantities, was liquor. Sometimes in the morning Wolfenden would sheepishly admit to one of his colleagues, 'I'm afraid I did a bad thing last night. I must have lit a cigarette when I got into bed. I fell asleep and . . .' More than once he woke up in flames.

Even his hardest-drinking colleagues, in awe of Wolfenden's intellect, humour and fluent Russian, were embarrassed by these pathetic lapses. In the dismal tension of the Ukraina hotel, kept at a constant pitch by the apparatus of the totalitarian state, the exuberant brilliance of his life was starting to fail.

In July 1962 Ruari and Janet Chisholm left Moscow in a hurry. Janet managed to get two of the children out with her, but the youngest, Alistair ('Ali-boy') was put on to Martina Browne's passport and came out with her on a later flight. The couple's activities had led them into deep trouble with the Soviet authorities. The extent of the damage was not apparent until the following year, and their departure did not cause undue comment at the time: it was quite common to see people from the Western diplomatic community heading speedily to the airport with no explanation. As Wolfenden himself remarked in a later newspaper article (for the *New York Times*): 'There is only one airport for international flights, and if an embassy employee is sighted there leaving out of turn, it is guessed at once that he has been compromised and is being hastily shipped out.'

On her return to England Martina Browne was no longer required by the Chisholms and took a job in a Mexican restaurant in Knightsbridge. She moved to New York in March 1963 and found work with an advertising agency; she continued to write to Jeremy Wolfenden in Moscow throughout this period.

Then on 2 November 1962, in an incident connected to the Chisholms' departure, a British electrical goods salesman called Greville Wynne was arrested in Budapest by Soviet counter-intelligence officers. He was taken to Moscow where he was charged in December with receiving military secrets from Oleg Penkovsky, a colonel in Soviet military intelligence. It was a case that bore powerfully on Jeremy Wolfenden's life.

Wynne was a stocky, dapper man with a pencil-line moustache who liked to wear a curly-brimmed Alpine trilby, a sheepskin car coat and a bow tie. He liked to claim (and did, at length, in a book called *The Man from Moscow*) that he had worked for military security during the war and had then been reactivated in 1957 with the task of making contact with Oleg Penkovsky, a colonel in Soviet military intelligence. In fact Wynne was recruited as part of the SIS 'directed travellers' scheme. For a couple of years he pottered round the Balkans in his car coat with a caravan full of electrical gadgets in tow. Eventually he found himself in the Soviet Union, which he thought a thoroughly disagreeable and backward place: the petrol stations were infrequent and the restaurants were grubby; the women wore no make-up and, Wynne complained, had yet to discover the brassière.

In late 1960, at a meeting of the Scientific Research Committee which he attended as British trade delegate, Wynne spotted a Russian who was quite different from the other Soviets, with their unshaven, blackheaded complexions, their nylon shirts and their nicotine-stained coalminer's hands. This man wore a silk shirt, he had manicured fingers and a plain, dark tie; he seemed – like Yuri Krutikov on Wolfenden's NUS trip in 1956 – to be of a different pedigree. His name was Oleg Penkovsky and he asked Wynne to pass a message to the CIA.

Back in London Wynne reported the meeting to the head of the SIS station, Dickie Franks. SIS set up a joint operation with the CIA, who at that stage had no one in Moscow. It was agreed that Wynne should act as the go-between because he was not, like Ruari Chisholm, obviously a suspect. In the spring of 1961 he befriended Penkovsky and acted as his courier; he brought back large quantities of information and eventually, on an April trade mission, he brought back Penkovsky himself. In room 360 of the Mount Royal Hotel near Marble Arch in central London, Penkovsky was pumped up with benzedrine and ravenously debriefed by two SIS and two CIA officers. There was a direct line to Washington so that the Americans could simultaneously share the spoils that tumbled out into the spinning tape-recorders. The CIA had initially rebuffed an approach from Penkovsky because they thought he might be a plant; he was too good to be true. This time they were convinced; and their difficulty was in dealing with the demands of Penkovsky, who was disappointed not to be introduced to the Queen. His SIS interrogators thought he was deranged by vanity and by the hugeness of what he had done.

It was certainly important. The United States had been humiliated at the Bay of Pigs invasion of Cuba; Gagarin had been the first man in space; the West believed the 'missile gap' was in the Soviet Union's favour. Now there was this excitable Russian colonel telling them that Khrushchev had been bluffing; that the West had more weapons and that many of those the Soviet Union did possess were unusable. They gave him a Minnox camera and sent him back to Moscow, telling him to concentrate on what mattered: 'Only the top-secret stuff, Oleg, forget the plain secret material.'

Further meetings between Wynne and Penkovsky took place in the autumn at a trade fair in Paris; also on leave in Paris were Ruari and Janet Chisholm. Janet was to work with Penkovsky in Moscow when Wynne could find no plausible 'trade' reason to be there. Although all the operational procedures were gone through carefully, Wynne believed Penkovsky was uneasy about the change of contact by which Janet Chisholm became the main recipient of his largesse. SIS in London was also worried about the Chisholm connection: Janet and Ruari had both known George Blake in Berlin and their files were accordingly marked. Dick White, the head of SIS, chivalrously believed that the KGB would not suspect a lady: he could not use Ruari Chisholm because, thanks to Philby and his friends, the Russians could always work out who the SIS officer was.

SIS decided to get Wynne back into the Soviet Union with instructions to bring Penkovsky out with him for the final time in one of his caravans. Luckily the vogue for 'trade fairs' – which seemed to exist principally for the benefit of frenzied espionage activity – was still on: the next was to be in Helsinki in September 1962, and the idea was that Wynne would slip along to Leningrad for a private exhibition soon afterwards.

Through the summer of 1962 Penkovsky continued to cooperate with the Chisholms. He used dead-drop boxes, but also passed film concealed in boxes of sweets, which he gave to Janet Chisholm and even to her children in the park. It was appallingly risky. Wynne, meanwhile, was having trouble with the chassis for his new mobile caravan: various British industrial relations problems and restrictive practices meant that they were out of stock. Wynne wanted to have the thing made in Europe; but SIS patriotically insisted that it be made in Britain – no Soviet defector was coming out beneath the floorboards of any foreign-built rubbish.

Then on 2 July Wynne flew to Moscow, ostensibly to smooth the official way for his Leningrad visit. He was by this time under suspicion: he had not been sufficiently well documented about his forthcoming 'trade delegations'. Penkovsky had also become disenchanted with Wynne: he drank too much and boasted of his affairs with women.

In a room in the Hotel Ukraina Penkovsky and Wynne exchanged a large quantity of film and talked about plans for Penkovsky's escape. By now Wynne was being followed; after dinner one night he found his room in the Ukraina had been searched. SIS had been greedy. Although both men had been willing to carry on, they should have stopped the operation at least six months earlier. At this stage Ruari and Janet Chisholm made their undignified exit, with Martina Browne following close behind.

In late September Greville Wynne's giant Mobile Exhibition hit the road. The chassis problems meant he had missed the private trade fair in Leningrad, but luckily there was one in Bucharest. In the plains of Rumania Wynne saw vast mobilisations of troops with long wobbling columns of tanks and armoured vehicles. The Cuban Missile Crisis was at its perilous height and the Soviet bloc was preparing for world war. What Wynne did not fully understand was that the information he had carried out in the pocket of his sheepskin car coat was enabling Kennedy to win the staring match. Ray Cline, then deputy director of the CIA, said Penkovsky's intelligence 'allowed the CIA to follow the progress of the Soviet missile emplacement in Cuba by the hour.' It also helped Washington grasp the extent of America's strategic advantage in nuclear missiles.

Wynne was arrested by Soviet counter-intelligence officers in Budapest, where he had driven from Rumania, on 2 November. He was taken to Moscow and imprisoned in the Lubyanka to await trial the following May. Penkovsky was arrested in Moscow. The KGB had recordings of their conversations in the Ukraina, they had tapes and photographs; they had everything they needed.

The KGB initially acted only on suspicion in following Penkovsky; they had no evidence of his treachery until they found the Minnox camera in his apartment. Once he was arrested, SIS made no attempt to rescue or exchange him. This enraged Joe Bulik, the CIA case officer, who suggested that the British release the Soviet spy Gordon Lonsdale, then in prison in London, in a swap. SIS refused, and in the end Penkovsky was left to the mercy of the gentlemen in the Lubyanka.

Life in the press corps continued in its bizarre, anxious, drunken way. Once Chisholm had gone, those who had had anything to do with him came under increased scrutiny. Wolfenden was watched more closely than ever by the KGB: he had been a friend of the Chisholms; he had liked playing with their children; he had been close to their young mother's help. He had also met

Greville Wynne at various parties and was more vulnerable than any other Western correspondent. Martin Page was also single, but he was clearly heterosexual; he lived in his own flat and was given protection from the KGB by virtue of working for the *Daily Express*. Lord Beaverbrook was favourably regarded in Moscow because of his support for two Germanies; he had procured British warplanes for the Soviet Union and his correspondents received favours in return.

The *Telegraph*, on the other hand, was implacably anti-Soviet. Its managing editor S.R. Pawley was believed by many people to be friendly to, if not actively involved with, SIS. During the General Strike in 1926 Pawley helped produce the anti-union *British Gazette*, edited by Winston Churchill; in the Second World War he served with the Buffs before being appointed Public Relations Officer to General Eisenhower. He was given an OBE and awarded the Croix de Guerre and the United States Bronze Star. In 1945 he returned to the *Telegraph* to organise its foreign news department, which was to be a separate entity for the first time. He visited eighty-two countries in twelve years and used up five passports.

In December 1968 John Miller, Wolfenden's successor for the *Telegraph* in Moscow, reported that the Russian weekly newspaper *Nedelya* had published an exposé of the connections between the British press and the intelligence services. Among those journalists it said were linked to Intelligence were the two *Telegraph* men who had hired Wolfenden: its proprietor Lord Hartwell and its managing editor S.R. Pawley.

This in itself proved nothing; but the Russians were always good at knowing who the spies were. Dick White, head of SIS, did not even consider it worth trying to conceal the fact that Ruari Chisholm was the SIS officer in Moscow because, as he told a colleague, 'they have our complete order of battle.' SIS had been so often and so comprehensively betrayed from inside that Ted Heath, then a junior foreign office minister, told White in the wake of the George Blake case that he might as well start again on the grounds that the Russians knew the identity of every single SIS officer. Although the various diplomatic expulsions from Moscow over the next twenty-five years contained some

innocent people (including a subsequent *Telegraph* correspondent), the real spooks were always in there too.

During the Second World War there was a close liaison
between SIS and senior newspapermen. The connections sprang
from a patriotic desire to help the Allies and give no inadvertent
comfort to the enemy. The links, however, survived the change
of conditions: an unspoken assumption of a common interest and
a greater good underlay dealings between SIS and some editors
for at least twenty-five years after 1945. The egregious example is
David Astor, the liberal-minded editor of the *Observer*, who was
persuaded to offer cover for the SIS agent Kim Philby as a
journalist in Beirut. (Neither Astor nor the SIS then knew that
Philby was also working for the KGB). Sometimes a 'journalist'
would ask an editor for a foreign job without revealing what his
true purpose was. Frank Giles, Wolfenden's former boss in Paris
and a man with impeccable training in diplomatic and intelligence ways, helped Harold Evans, the editor, sniff out one such
bogus applicant at the *Sunday Times*. The role of 'stringer' (a
part-time, non-staff overseas reporter) was a cover much favoured by SIS. A whole section of SIS – the BAQ department –
was given over to cultivating these contacts, and another to giving
regular off-the-record briefings to correspondents close to the
front line of the Cold War. The ethics of these briefings were
unclear. The journalists were free to discount what they were
told, but their independence was tarnished. As a correspondent
in Germany, Neal Ascherson believed it was a duty to treat all
information emanating from the West as sceptically as that
which came from the other side. He found Jeremy Wolfenden's
failure to do so one of several reasons why his journalism was
disappointing.

Even without such complications the pressure on a journalist was
intense. No one could leave the Soviet Union without an exit
visa, which might be denied at an official's whim. A Swedish
correspondent and his wife suffered nervous breakdowns
because they could not make love beneath the hidden gaze of the
KGB camera. Martin Page's successor for the *Express* took an
overdose within a week of arriving; Page, who was still in

Moscow, complained to the Foreign Ministry that he was having difficulty getting his man home. They replied that a Soviet Embassy chauffeur in London had developed schizophrenia and was still in an English hospital after eighteen months: the British press took this to be a warning that if they cracked up they would be sent to a Soviet mental institution.

The 'Moscow twitch' was a common phenomenon in the reserved diplomatic blocks in which Western journalists lived. The Western press was continuously denigrated in Soviet newspapers, and the lives of Soviet citizens who talked to any foreign correspondents were made unbearable. The cleverest instrument of anxiety developed by the Russians was their legal definition of 'intelligence', which was not restricted to the obtaining or relaying of secrets, but included any systematic analysis of printed matter. Thus a background feature article that innocently drew, for instance, on figures of agricultural production to try to give an overall picture of farming life in the Soviet Union could be termed espionage. All reporters lived with the knowledge that if the Cold War took a wrong turning, the Soviet authorities could legally arrest and convict them. The legitimate sentence for carrying out their jobs could be years of hard labour.

There were also provocations. An official might leave a file marked 'Secret' on a table while he left the room. The telephone would ring and a female voice would offer herself for company. Frequently such women operated in threes. The *Newsweek* correspondent Pat Ferguson was unwisely tempted; within an hour he found himself with three naked Russian women dancing in his flat and three men in raincoats hammering on the door, saying they believed he was ill-treating Soviet citizens.

Drunk, lonely and banged up in the Ukraina hotel, Jeremy Wolfenden was an absurdly easy prey. In his life, sex had played not just a prominent part, but a part that was associated with laughter, romance and intrigue. He still also had the conviction that he knew how far he could go; his self-confidence and judgement had never previously deserted him.

Although Wolfenden was regarded by others of his generation as a leader and a man of distinct individualism, it is possible to argue that his life was excessively influenced by fashionable writers. He and Neal Ascherson had clearly been thrilled while at school by the outsiderism of Camus and Sartre; Camus's *The Myth of Sisyphus*, which took it all a step further by discussing suicide as a rational option, appeared in 1955, when Wolfenden was at Oxford, and was enthusiastically received by him. By this time Ionesco's plays and Beckett's *Waiting for Godot* were also widely known, giving further moral respectability to an absurdist or nihilist point of view. In 1962 Allan Sillitoe published *The Loneliness of the Long Distance Runner*, the story of a Borstal boy who refuses to win a cross-country race against another institution because to do so would be to accept the terms of the authorities who have imprisoned him. This tale also interested Wolfenden, who for some time had been developing the idea of deliberate under-achievement as the only honest response to a society whose own idea of 'achievement' he believed to be false.

While all these writers in their way gave intellectual credibility to pessimism, a fellow-old Etonian, Cyril Connolly, had given sloth and despair a modish justification in *Enemies of Promise*, on which Wolfenden had been pretty well suckled, while the baleful influence of Connolly's *The Unquiet Grave*, with its *angoisse des gares*, scholarship Latin and afternoon *cafards*, also surfaced in Wolfenden's letters from Paris. Guy Burgess offered the worst living example of degenerate old Etonianism, but was a unique and patently inimitable disaster; Cyril Connolly, on the other hand, preaching privileged gloom from within the pale, may well have been an actively damaging influence.

There are several versions of what happened next, but they all mean the same thing in the end.

One day Wolfenden took up to his room in the Hotel Ukraina a waiter from the Praga restaurant, and in the middle of their love-making two men sprang from the wardrobe with flash cameras . . . Wolfenden had fallen for the barber at the Ukraina and it was with him – or perhaps with his son – that he was compromised . . . Wolfenden came back one night to find a Polish boy sitting naked in his armchair, but was too drunk to do anything . . . Wolfenden was set up with a Polish boy called Jan and they went to bed. 'He was gorgeous,' Wolfenden claimed, but he was so drunk he could not remember whether he had done anything or not. Nothing happened for a few days . . . He was immediately taken to a KGB office situated, conveniently, within the Ukraina.

Given Wolfenden's vulnerable situation and the remorseless methods of the KGB it is possible that these are not all versions of the same story but in fact versions of two different incidents: first, a Polish boy followed by a functional failure through drink, then a more successful encounter with an employee of the Ukraina. Whatever happened, he was trapped. Next came the blackmail. Wolfenden tried to pass it off in Wildean style (he was so pleased with the prints that he asked for enlargements); but he knew that if the truth of his activities were made public he would lose his job. A man of his talents could easily have found other employment, but that was not really the point. Being a foreign correspondent, travelling light 'with a typewriter and a revolver', was something he had thought of for himself; he didn't want to be a civil servant, a lawyer or a university teacher: he didn't want to do one of those things his father might have advised or had already done himself.

Homosexuality was not embarrassing to Jeremy Wolfenden, but it was illegal. The Soviet penal code decreed a lengthy prison sentence, and although it was unlikely that the courts would imprison a British journalist, it was a worrying prospect. Meanwhile, the reason that the law had not been repealed in Britain was that Jack Wolfenden's report was still lying in a fat, explosive bundle somewhere in the Home Office. If it were to emerge that its author's son was homosexual the credibility of the report would be destroyed; the liberal reforms it proposed would be set back by a decade or more. Jeremy Wolfenden was open to blackmail not only on his own account but on behalf of the civil liberties of millions of British men. The KGB may have been slovenly, cynical and tired; but they were not that stupid.

Nor was the Secret Intelligence Service. Wolfenden's relationship with the service was informal: he did not want to do anything that would compromise his work, but he was intrigued enough to keep a line open. After the incident in the Hotel Ukraina his position was considerably weakened.

He decided to report what had happened to the Embassy, and their response was soothing. They told him to do nothing: to go along with what the KGB asked him. Then, when he was on leave in London, he could call at the address in Whitehall and have a chat with M15. And so it was that both British Intelligence and Security were able to use the man they wanted. He had been delivered to them by the KGB. It was almost too good to be true.

And probably it wasn't. SIS, especially after the Vassall case, was aware of the vulnerability of homosexual men to blackmail. The only reasonable inference is that they wanted Wolfenden to be set up, and in S.R. Pawley they had the man to help. He was prepared to send Wolfenden where *The Times* would not because he was doing what he was told. SIS hoped to learn more about the KGB by having someone on the inside, like Wolfenden, than through their own officers. They wanted him to tell them what the KGB was thinking, even though all the KGB was thinking, as it turned out, was: how can we embarrass more Western visitors?

Wolfenden's colleagues, visitors and friends were surprised that the Embassy let him stay. David Shapiro, who visited Wolfenden in Moscow, discovered a sense of shock, of outrage, as though something unfair were being done. The standard procedure when someone had been compromised was to tell them to leave at once, but SIS believed Wolfenden could be of more use to them if he stayed. They gambled that any information he gave to the Soviets could only be of trifling use because he had no access to military or other secrets – unless they gave him some for the purpose of disinformation.

Wolfenden did some work for the KGB. He wrote articles for the Novosti Press Agency on the nature of British Institutions. This was standard low-level stuff. Wolfenden told John Miller that he was writing the articles and Miller told him he must be out of his mind. Wolfenden ignored Miller's advice and did what he called 'a few bits'. The main task the KGB asked of Wolfenden was to inform on his colleagues in the press. In an emotional meeting in Martin Page's apartment, Wolfenden warned Page never to tell him anything that he would not want the KGB to know. When Page escorted Wolfenden to the lift he was weeping; as the lift came, he said goodbye and kissed Martin Page on the lips.

A British journalist called Douglas Botting, who was in Russia making a film for the BBC, had to leave Moscow to go on location. He discovered on his return that Wolfenden had been reading his mail. Botting also saw the payment that Wolfenden received from the KGB: he was told such things as the composition of the new Politburo before it had been announced and would discuss them loudly over vodka with his colleagues. They were embarrassed by this evidence of his situation but had too much affection for him to make anything of it.

It was the end of an era, but even what had gone before had not been simple. Both Wolfenden and Page were used to operating with the Soviet authorities for their day-to-day business. Wolfenden had a minder called Vladimir Pozner and Page was looked after by Yuri Vinogradov. Their role was to tell the English correspondents about Soviet foreign policy, or a version of it, and to portray the domestic situation in an optimistic light.

Pozner and Vinogradov were both cultured men, like Yuri Krutikov and Oleg Penkovsky; Pozner was in fact part Jewish and had been brought up in the United States. He had had an affair with an Anglo-American writer called Sally Belfrage and had told her many things about the Soviet Union that she subsequently used in a book called *A Room in Moscow*. Although Pozner may not have been a serving officer, this indiscretion put him in hock to the KGB. He was in any case a believing Communist who went on to become one of the great propagandists of the Brezhnev era. In one of the remarkable transformations of the late twentieth century he went on to present a talk show on American television.

Other more crude KGB types occasionally tried to bully the correspondents, and Wolfenden was by this time so trapped that he was unable to fend off pressure of any kind from any side. All he had left with which to defend himself was his wit and his arrogance. These now became not social manners but qualities on which he depended for survival.

In the autumn of 1962 Wolfenden was on leave in London and

saw a good deal of Susie Burchardt, to whom he was supposed to be engaged. Things did not run smoothly between them. Wolfenden's drinking had reached colossal proportions and his fiancée found the brandy at breakfast increasingly hard to tolerate. However, she was still enchanted by his exuberance and by the fact that he seemed to understand how difficult the relationship must be for her. The engagement went off and on, according to the high spirits and optimism of both parties. He told her that he was 'debriefed by the Foreign Office' when he was in London, but she assumed that all correspondents went through a similar experience.

Then, on 7 May 1963, Greville Wynne and Oleg Penkovsky were put on trial. It was an astonishing story of microdots, dead-drop boxes, photographs taken with the smuggled Minnox camera, bugs, recordings, double-bluff, fear, farce and appalling drama. For all the inclination of journalists to mock the dreary men of the intelligence services and the 'games' they played, the information that Wynne took out from Penkovsky did change the course of the Cold War. At the intelligence level it enabled Britain to regain a little of the reputation it had so disastrously lost in American eyes with the Philby, Burgess and Maclean affair; more importantly, it helped the West face down the Russian threat in the knowledge that Khrushchev had fewer weapons than they did. Though some, including Wolfenden, feigned apathy, only those who believed that Soviet totalitarianism was morally the equal of Western capitalism could be quite indifferent to the outcome of such events.

At the trial both men pleaded guilty, though Wynne did not accept all the charges. The idea, prearranged with Penkovsky, was that he should present himself as an innocent dupe who had been drawn further into the business of espionage than he understood. His room for manoeuvre was limited by the fact that his captors had given him the answers they expected to hear. He was supposed to recite thousands of words from memory, though in the end they allowed him to read from a concealed text; by vigorous head movements and eye-rubbing he tried to indicate to the Western press that this was what was going on.

Jeremy Wolfenden was given the front and back pages of the

Telegraph to write about the trial, with further coverage inside. Most of this in fact came from Reuters, who occupied the only two seats in court that had been allocated to the British press. The 'pool' system was working at its best: the years of cooperation, kept secret from the newspaper offices in London, paid dividends in a masterfully smooth operation. Every half an hour or so either John Miller or Peter Johnson of Reuters would telephone into the Reuters office an account of what had happened. One of the newspaper correspondents would then sub-edit the story for the Reuter wire and provide 'blacks' or carbon copies for all the other papers. No reporter had a different story; and, best of all, no reporter was left exposed to the wrath of a Fleet Street foreign editor telling him to 'match' the account that had appeared in the Daily Other.

The Wynne they described was not the hard-eyed poker player of his own subsequent account. He came over in court as petulant and afraid; he spoke bitterly of the various 'foreign office officials' in London who at first led him on and then, when he understood the magnitude of what he was doing and tried to escape from it, threatened to cripple his electrical business. Wynne claimed that these recriminations were part of an agreed text which was to pave the way for his mitigating speech of repentance. In any event he gave the impression of being a man who was floundering. The *Daily Telegraph* editorial column took the line that Penkovsky was probably a double agent and that Wynne was his toy. It spoke with alarm of the prospect of exchanging him at a later date for the imprisoned Soviet spy Gordon Lonsdale: such a swap would be a 'sprat for a shark'. The *Telegraph* line was the line that SIS would most have wanted it to take: Wynne not really an agent, Penkovsky tarnished goods, no hope for Lonsdale . . . The *Telegraph* could not have done better if the editorial had been dictated by SIS itself.

Considerable damage was being done to SIS by the trial. Ruari and Janet Chisholm had been named in court, along with other embassy staff, John Varley, David Senior and Felicity Stuart, all of whom had been ordered out of Moscow. The *modus operandi* of a Western spy ring had been laid open to the public for the first time (it had been known to the Soviet authorities for many years, thanks to the Cambridge spies). In a brash damage-limitation exercise, the Chisholms welcomed *Express* photographers to their home in Sussex with a magnificent display of baffled innocence. 'It's a pantomime,' beamed genial Ruari on his sofa, drink in hand: 'Do I look like a spy?' asked busy 'housewife and Mum' Janet, as she tucked up little Ali-boy in his pyjamas.

Then on 8 May Greville Wynne dropped Martina Browne in the mire. The *Daily Express* had clearly had a tip that her name was going to come up, because they managed to take a picture of her in New York. On page 15 of the paper on 9 May the story ran:

> Martina Brown [sic], former nanny from Greenford, Middlesex, was mentioned for the first time at the trial yesterday.
>
> 21-year-old Martina looked after the three children of British diplomat Robert [sic] Chisholm while she was in Moscow.
>
> Wynne said in court: 'I was told that there was a young English nursemaid who slept in the next room where I was given the packets by Mr Chisholm.
>
> 'She used to go out with Russian civilians. Besides, I was told that there were microphones hidden in the apartments of foreign diplomats in Moscow.'
>
> Martina now works in New York, where she is pictured yesterday.

That was all, but it was embarrassing. It is not quite clear what Wynne is suggesting, but the impression is that he was talking in general about the conditions of secrecy in which he operated with Chisholm. Extra care was needed because there was a nanny who might overhear what was said, and this nanny had Russian friends to whom she might inadvertently let something slip: this would land him and Chisholm in trouble. The use of the word 'Besides' seems to indicate that Wynne saw Martina as being in the same category as a microphone: you wouldn't want to be overheard by either.

However, it is possible that Wynne believed that any leakage from Martina Browne to the Russians would not be inadvertent; it is possible he thought that she was actually working for the KGB. The Chisholms' other domestic staff certainly were. All their 'maids' were university-educated linguists. There was a wardrobe in Ruari and Janet's bedroom with a mirror on the back of the door; if both bedroom and wardrobe door were open, it was possible to see into the bedroom from the front doorway of the flat. A quiet and unexpected return often revealed the sight of a Russian 'maid' rifling through the waste-paper basket.

On 11 May, to the loud applause of the court, Penkovsky was sentenced to death. Wynne was given three years in prison and five in a labour camp.

On 18 August Jeremy Wolfenden wrote to Martina Browne in New York:

> They were rather beastly to your Big Boss, weren't they? Did the newspapers pick up all the bits about us – for instance the bit where Ruari was alleged to have said to Wynne: 'You mustn't talk because we have an English girl sleeping in the next room, and we don't want the press to hear all about it'? This must have seemed a bit mysterious to most people, though it made John [Miller] and me chortle a bit. Having sat through the whole wretched trial, I found it difficult to take the whole thing seriously, or to keep my temper with it in general. But at least there were some nice newspaper photographs, especially in the *Daily Express*. There was one of Janet and Ruari sitting on a sofa and Ruari expansively smoking a cigarette and saying how absurd it all was – and then there was that funny one of you from New York – which I must say still looked very like a rather smudgy picture of you and not at all like a rake, or a Nanny who has stopped wearing her nanny's hairdo. How did they get hold of you? Was the wicked Harper [Stephen Harper, former *Express* Moscow correspondent] to blame for putting them on to you? I must say the quotes sounded quite convincing . . . or at least what I would have invented if I had been going to invent quotes from you about Ruari.

Wolfenden's interpretation of Greville Wynne's reference to Martina Browne was that Chisholm warned Wynne to keep his voice down in case Martina heard something and told her boyfriend (ie Wolfenden), who was a journalist. This was what made him and Miller 'chortle': they knew that he and Martina saw each other a good deal. However, Wolfenden must either have misremembered what Wynne actually said (he made no reference to the 'press' or to 'English friends', but to 'Russian civilians') or Wynne must have said something else about Martina that was not reported. Where in the *Express* story are the 'quotes' that she is supposed to have 'invented' about Ruari Chisholm? The third possibility is that the paper got it wrong. Perhaps Wynne did mention 'British press', not 'Russian civilians'. Perhaps the *Express* misquoted him. It's not impossible; after all, in their references to Martina Brown and Robert Chisholm they managed to get the names of both protagonists wrong.

On 2 July Wolfenden finally escaped from the Ukraina hotel and moved to an apartment in Sadovo Samotechnaya. He described his new flat in a letter to Martina:

> It consists of a huge long corridor and a huge kitchen and a huge whisky bottle and three very small rooms : . . I sit out on my balcony and watch all the nannies coming and going from my Captain's Cabin on the eighth floor. Or else pour beer on John Miller who also has a captain's bridge from which he controls the traffic in the yard from the third floor. Or just shout at everybody . . .
>
> It does feel funny, having a flat of my own after all this time. I keep wandering from one room to another, not being able to remember where I put things now there is more than one room to put them in. But I went to Copenhagen and in one and a half hectic days bought all the things that I'd seen other people buy . . . The bed almost entirely fills the bedroom (but this is not a bad thing . . . one really has to decide whether one hates the people one is living with more when they are horizontal or when they are vertical . . . whether one would rather have them in the bed to avoid them, but keep bumping into them when one is dressing, or the other way round. My answer is: only bed, no manoeuvring.) And there are also lots of blue and white sofas and things, and a special Apricot room which is my office, with apricot curtains and a black and apricot lamp. It's all very snazzy and is going to cost the *Daily Telegraph* a lot of money.
>
> I am still very frightened of Sadovo geysers, and the hot water makes a lot of volcano noises, but I expect I shall get used to that in time as well. I also keep losing the key to the door, so that string men have to come with pick axes to break it in, and the

commandant reads me a long lecture . . . But it's so nice to wander up and down, and even to be able to cook for oneself a sort of meal (usually consisting of a tin of Individual Steak and Kidney Pudding from the Embassy). The only trouble is that since I am so near the Reuters office all the people come and drink my Scotch, instead of my going and drinking theirs. But after two and a half years, this is only fair.

Some of the 'self-assembly' furniture he had bought in Copenhagen never did assemble itself, but lay around the apartment in unopened flatpacks. Wolfenden's contempt for the material world was so complete that he could not be bothered to drive or buy clothes: he was certainly not the man to pass Sunday morning with bradawl and spanner. The ready-made Embassy pie was as far as he could go in preparing food, which in any case he seldom ate. This was partly a doctrinaire position: food was bourgeois and boring; it was partly an alcoholic's revulsion; and it was made worse by the fact that opening a can represented the height of his practical abilities. Other correspondents bought Wiltshire pork sausages, English tea and Heinz beans from the commissary in the British Embassy; they placed orders for fresh food with O.Y. Stockmann in Helsinki and would receive regular deliveries of meat, cheese, beans and even salad. The only meals Wolfenden ate were the ones Brenda Miller cooked him or the bits and pieces he might pick out in the restaurant to accompany his lunchtime drinking. His colleagues despaired of watching him try to force down a plain omelette. Like Guy Burgess, he had a motherly Russian housekeeper who would try to make him eat soup, but with little success. He hated breakfast, and fought against the idea of food at that time of day. The daily retching and heaving in the Reuters office was the convulsion of an empty stomach.

Sad Sam was arranged about a courtyard in which, weather permitting, the Embassy wives would sit knitting or sewing for the bazaar run by the ambassador's wife, Lady Trevelyan. No secrets could be kept from the *tricoteuses*, who provided a more effective, if more friendly, security screen than the KGB men who hung around outside. Once a year a team would be sent out from the Ministry of Works in London armed with chisels and metal detectors. They would attempt to remove from the walls the various wires which had no right to be there. In the Chisholms' flat they were helped by little Ali-boy whose repeated hammering of the wall with his plastic tommy-gun had revealed a suspiciously hollow area.

Microphones were reinstalled as fast as they could be taken out. Russian workmen came hammering on the Chisholms' door almost every day with unreported gas leaks to fix, plumbing to be checked, draughty windows to be rehung. On one occasion, as Wolfenden himself recounted in an article for the *New York Times Magazine*, 'The British Embassy was doing a plaster job on the apartment of their security officer when they located a hollow spot in the wall. Digging into it, they found what they had expected, a microphone. But when they tried to pull it out of the wall, they felt an answering tug on the other end of the wire. Three or four Britons joined in the tug of war, but the forces at the other end seemed to have been reinforced to the same extent. At last the Russians gave up, and the Britons fell backwards, with a microphone and some strands of hastily clipped wire in their hands.'

Sad Sam was where the Chisholms' flat had been: a busy place where Wynne had unloaded the goods and Wolfenden had paid court to the teenager nanny before passing out on the sofa. When Wolfenden moved into the block the Chisholms' flat was unoccupied. Chisholm's successor at the Embassy, Gervase Cowell, had gone the same way – expelled by the Soviet authorities on 13 May 1963 in the immediate wake of the Wynne-Penkovsky trial. By this time the walls were so hollow that the rooms were echoing.

In a letter dated 18 August 1963 Wolfenden told Martina Browne, 'I shall probably be here for some time yet . . . now I've at last got the flat and furnished it, I feel very reluctant to get out and hand it over to someone else . . . I haven't been very well recently, and the *Daily Telegraph* are apparently thinking that I've had about enough (which annoys me a bit). But I reckon I'll be here until April at least . . . it would be unfair to send someone in just at the beginning of the winter.'

Whatever he wrote – and he may not have wished to be fully

honest about his feelings, for a variety of quite innocent reasons – Wolfenden was by now sweating under the pressure of the demands being made of him. He took a BEA flight to London that summer with Martin Page and demanded two large vodkas before take-off. He told Page he was going to see his boss to ask for a change of posting. When they met again in Moscow, he told Page that his request had been turned down; he appeared crestfallen and desperate. One of his Russian minders was heard by Douglas Botting to comment: 'I think we're going to have to get Jeremy out. I don't think he can take much more of this.'

In the autumn of 1963 Guy Burgess died. He had been a considerable collector of books, specialising, though not exclusively, in stories of himself, Philby and Maclean. He left to Wolfenden the first pick of his library; Wolfenden was in Yugoslavia when the news came, and by the time he got back to Moscow the KGB had been through Burgess's flat. All that was left were cloth-bound uniform editions of the works of Jane Austen and Thomas Hardy. Wolfenden had been close to Burgess; he may even have been his lover, though given the physical state of Burgess by the time they met no one could imagine much serious activity. The two men were alike in style – drunk, clever, epigrammatic. But in Wolfenden's manoeuvring between the competing intelligence services there was a feeling of bravado and superiority to both. It was a long way from the idealistic fight against Fascism undertaken by the Burgess generation; it had neither the glory of Spain nor the squalor of subsequent treachery.

Wolfenden was a pallbearer at the funeral, where Burgess's brother told him that most of his estate had been left to Kim Philby. At about this time Susie Burchardt came to visit Wolfenden in his flat in Sad Sam. He made an effort to amuse her by taking her to a series of exotic places and drunken parties. She had the impression that he was not wholly approved of at the Embassy: he was impatient at the protocol but still seemed to know, just as at Eton, how far he could take his rebellion. When she said she could not be bothered to attend a certain function he emphatically told her she had no choice. He took her to Georgia and to the Ukraine. Outside Moscow he seemed less desperate and less drunk; back in town he seemed to suffer a mixture of boredom and fear which only ever-increasing quantities of alcohol could assuage.

Susie Burchardt took back an alarming picture of Jeremy Wolfenden's life to his friends in London. David Edwards, with whom he had shared the house in Oakley Street and later a flat in Gray's Inn, heard the story with alarm. He had often suggested to Wolfenden that he should at least try to eat a steak before going out for an evening's drinking, but soon recognised that there was very little he could do. He believed that Wolfenden drank and smoked to excess because that was how he thought he ought to behave; it was part of the idea of a foreign correspondent as a cross between Humphrey Bogart and W.H. Auden. Even at the time it seemed childish, but there was little that his friends could do: if they tried to remonstrate they would wither under the superior fire of Wolfenden's wit.

There was still some desperate fun to be had from life in Moscow. At Christmas there was a visit to a diplomatic hunting lodge at Zavidovo on the Volga river north of Moscow, where the Foreign Ministry invited the British journalists to go on an elk-hunt. It was agonisingly cold, even by Russian standards, and Wolfenden in his flapless Astrakhan contracted frostbite in one ear. Part of the lobe came off, and the pain was soothed by gargantuan quantities of vodka. Owing to a shortage of implements the Christmas turkey had to be carved with an axe. Although the other journalists knew of Wolfenden's compromised position, the group survival instinct made them disinclined to be critical. So many people in so many different occupations were involved in one way or another with intelligence that even those who had kept aloof were forced to accept it as part of the background to their daily lives.

Eventually the management of the *Daily Telegraph* relented. Things had not been going well. Wolfenden made a show of being able to dictate grammatically correct sentences, ad lib, while drunk, but on occasions the foreign desk's calls had gone unanswered. For periods of four or five days Wolfenden would have to lie low and give his traumatised system time to rest. The telephone in the apricot room would thunder on ignored and the paper would have to whistle up John Miller to fill the ever-hungry foreign columns. Perhaps these lapses in such a young correspondent convinced his superiors of the strain he was under. At any rate they finally reached an agreement by which Wolfenden was to be allowed to swap jobs for one year with Ian Ball, the correspondent in New York, on the understanding that he would return to Moscow when the twelve months were up.

Wolfenden was out of Moscow. In January 1964 he left the Soviet Union and went via London to New York. It was a watershed. He had escaped from the demands of both the KGB and the British; it was possible that he could put his life together again. He did not have career ambitions in quite the same way as his old friend Godfrey Hodgson, who had been for eighteen months the *Observer*'s Washington correspondent. Hodgson was tall, good-looking and startlingly young for the job; it was assumed that he too would do 'great things' – a slightly more realistic assumption, perhaps, given his greater sense of self-preservation (everyone had a greater sense of self-preservation than Jeremy Wolfenden). What Wolfenden wanted more than office promotion was somehow to realise the fantasy of his life. This ambition certainly involved being in the right places, on the right stories and dazzling all the right people by his reckless brilliance; but it did not include the kind of orthodox achievement that could be measured in published books or honours lists. He had won the honours, and they had bored him. His driving wish was to be the emotional nomad whose nonaligned intellectual integrity would somehow be a rebuke to the small-minded.

However, he had also been deeply disturbed by the Moscow experience, and he arrived in New York in a chastened mood: although his essential aims for himself had not changed, he did hope to live in a different way. If he was to flirt with danger he would like it to be on his own terms and not those dictated by any secret service. It was in this state of mind that he renewed his acquaintance with his pen-pal, the teen-ager nursemaid.

Martina Browne was working for an advertising agency and living with a girlfriend in a brownstone on West 83rd Street. She had been in love with Wolfenden in Moscow, but he had at that time been engaged to Susie Burchardt and had considered Martina too young. Their intermittent correspondence in the eighteen months since Martina had left Moscow had been based on a quality that was unique in Jeremy Wolfenden's relationships: sentimentality. This was the bridge between these two disparate characters.

Martina liked the way Jeremy had played with the Chisholm children. When she had left for London and then New York, Wolfenden told her stories of the Millers and their new twins ('the girl nondescript and the boy exactly like Lord Beaverbrook'). He called himself Jeremy Fisher and drew pictures of frogs; there was a fantasy by which a flat was a lily-leaf on which a frog squatted. The Miller boy's name for him, Mr Wuff, was also taken up in the letters. Part of this was a manifestation of a simple kindness in Wolfenden's character: for all that he had suppressed the existence of his siblings while at Eton, he had come to be truly fond of children and – like his father – something of an expert with them. He used baby-talk in his letters to Martina and cast himself as the naughty boy/Big Bad Wolf and her as the forgiving mother/Little Red Riding Hood. He pretended both to fear her displeasure in the first role and, in the second, to be on the point of gobbling her up in his big strong jaws.

Like most relationships, it was shaped by the needs of its participants. Martina Browne was drawn to damaged and unhappy men in the hope that she could make them whole again; the life of her drunk and aggressive father acted more as a challenge than a warning. She was flattered that a man of Wolfenden's intellect was prepared to put his gifts at her service in dreaming up games and fantasies for them both. They may have been at a rather different level from those he might have shared with John Sparrow, but in a sense that made them all the more wonderful.

For his part, Jeremy Wolfenden was not just charmed by Martina Browne's good looks and oddly forceful 'nature-girl' personality; he saw in her some hope of domestic redemption and safety. His life was in crisis, and demanded critical measures: a heterosexual romance with an almost uneducated mother's help was a suitably drastic expedient. Two months after he arrived in New York they were married.

Many of his friends assumed that Martina's close association with the Chisholm spy-ring and Jeremy's involvement with British and Russian intelligence was a factor in their marriage. They assumed, to put it bluntly, that it was a put-up job. What better control could SIS exert over Wolfenden than by having their own officer run his life from the marital bed? Even if she genuinely loved him, she would have had to ask permission from her boss, whoever that now was. As far as Wolfenden was concerned, the marriage was a bold move in his determination to free himself from the demands of the KGB. To marry the Chisholms' nanny, to wed into the family who had smuggled out the nuclear secrets of the Soviet Union . . . it was at the very least a gesture of defiance to his Soviet persecutors. To many of Wolfenden's friends there seemed no other explanation. The twin pivots of his character were his intellectual brilliance and his homosexuality: he was the last person in the world to marry a woman who had left school at the age of fifteen.

Yet it was, naturally, more complicated than that. The affair may have been based on sentimentality and expedience, but it developed into something tougher: a desperate kind of love, that was given poignancy by the fact that Wolfenden was already killing himself, and his wife knew it. David Edwards, his most level-headed friend, believed that Wolfenden was heading for his ultimate fate before he even set foot on Russian soil; and Martina Browne was aware of a destructive anguish inside him that was based on the knowledge that he was not going to live a complete life.

The wedding took place on 6 April at the Holy Trinity Church at 213 West 82nd Street. It was a small and hasty affair attended by none of the parents. John Miller, who had been posted by Reuters to New York, gave Martina away; Godfrey Hodgson came up from Washington to be the best man. A cine-film was shot, but the cameraman, like everyone else, was drunk. They stood on the steps of the church, Wolfenden in a suit but with a cigarette already burning, Martina looking up at him with unfakeable devotion, her childlike features framed by dark hair

Jeremy Wolfenden

cut in a Helen Shapiro bob. As they drove to the reception on
East 51st Street Wolfenden had to be restrained from calling into
the *Telegraph* offices to wire over an account of his own wedding
in time for the London first editions.

The honeymoon was spent in Jamaica. While they were away
Greville Wynne was surprisingly released from prison and sent
back to England in a swap for Gordon Lonsdale. The months that
followed in New York provided Jeremy Wolfenden with a period
of calm and relative happiness. There may have been an element
of play-acting for him, as the wandering gunslinger had a go at the
role of domestic husband, but it was an act that amused him.
Martina took the home seriously and tried very hard to reform
her drunken, wayward man. She was delighted by him. When
the paper man came with his little son and asked to be paid,
Jeremy couldn't be bothered to find out how much he owed or to
look for the right change. He would just give him a ten-dollar bill
and get down to the serious business of talking to the boy. His
expense accounts for the office posed a chore too tedious even to
contemplate. To some extent Martina did control his drinking;
she even managed to make him eat from time to time, though she
was discouraged when he pushed aside her roast chicken,
describing it as 'dead hen'. They were absorbed in one another.
They had front row seats at Carnegie Hall when the Beatles came
to New York, but couldn't be bothered to leave the apartment.

The year passed too quickly. Ian Ball was hating Moscow and
had no intention of staying an hour longer than was necessary.
Wolfenden was frightened of going back there himself; in fact he
believed it was impossible for him to return. At some stage in the
course of 1964 he managed to persuade his superiors at the
Telegraph that he was too deeply compromised to continue as
Moscow correspondent. He also told them about his wife's
involvement with the Wynne-Penkovsky case. John Miller's time
in New York for Reuters had not been a success, and Wolfenden
suggested to the *Telegraph* that they should hire Miller in his
place. After some consultations, the *Telegraph* agreed to take on
Miller in Moscow and to relocate Wolfenden at a junior level in
their Washington office. The deal was done, but with a worrying
proviso: Wolfenden would have to go back to Moscow for a

'hand-over period' between Ian Ball's return to the United States and John Miller's installation.

It was the best deal he could do. He discussed it with Martina and she had a feeling of doom about his return. She wanted to go with him, and applied to the Russian Embassy for a visa. Her action provoked a severe response from the British Embassy in Washington: the SIS head of station came to see her and told her that on no account was she to return to Moscow; if she did, she could assume she would be arrested and imprisoned for the rest of her life. He told her that Wolfenden would be arrested too. The Russians not only felt vindictive towards the Chisholm spy-ring; they would view her as a newsworthy swap for one of their spies, probably George Blake, who was then in Wandsworth gaol. The SIS man made it clear that the British would not be interested in any such exchange and would make no effort whatever to free her. They were prepared to allow Wolfenden to go alone, if he wanted to risk it.

It says something for Martina Browne that even this terrifying warning did not fully convince her. She went round and round the problem in her mind, wondering if she could find a way to help her vulnerable husband. He was also extremely worried about the trip, but felt a strong if curious loyalty to the newspaper that had done so little to protect him in the first place. He argued that he couldn't let the paper down: there was to be a hiatus before Miller could extract himself from Reuters and he didn't want the *Telegraph* to be without a correspondent in Moscow for that time. Martina argued that he should just look after himself; after all, that was what Ian Ball had done: it was his prompt return that was causing the interruption to the Moscow service. She said she was sure Ricky Marsh, the foreign editor, would understand the position if he explained it. Wolfenden was stubborn: he told her he couldn't allow the paper to suffer, but Martina was so worried about what would happen that she was prepared to risk going with him.

The Russian Embassy granted her a visa, as the British had feared they might. It was almost as though British Intelligence actually knew the Russians would grant the visa; and this was the most worrying aspect of it. Right down to the day of departure

Martina toyed with the idea of going with him; but at the last minute she went to London. While he was in Moscow, she stayed in Iverna Court, just off Kensington High Street, which was as close as she could safely be to him.

Moscow was even worse than Wolfenden had feared. He was very, very frightened. From the minute he arrived, they were after him: who 'they' were he did not explain either to Martina or to John Miller, who landed in Moscow soon afterwards. Miller was shocked by the state of his friend 'Wolfie' (he never had managed to pronounce his Christian name); he believed Wolfenden was daily expecting some revelation or denunciation. Miller did not know about the various warnings given by British Intelligence in Washington. What was frightening Wolfenden more than any denunciation was the thought that he was going to be arrested and imprisoned indefinitely in a Soviet gaol. To deal with his fear he relied on the usual specific of neat vodka, but this time with the addition of various benzedrine mixtures.

He counted the days. The chances of a safe escape were slowly growing until matters took a turn that surprised the world. A meeting of the Politburo summoned Khrushchev back from holiday in the Black Sea and deposed him. With the backing of the KGB, they accused him of wilfulness and haste; Khrushchev appealed to the Central Committee, but they had already had their cards marked. Since Kennedy had, with the aid of the information brought out by Greville Wynne, humiliated Khrushchev over the Cuban missile crisis, his time as leader had been limited. The committee voted him out of the leadership of the Communist Party in favour of the coffin-faced Stalinist Leonid Brezhnev. The story was broken to the world by the *London Evening News*, whose flamboyant Moscow stringer, Victor Louis, was a Soviet citizen. The *Daily Telegraph* naturally wanted Wolfenden to stay and report this huge event, which, in the most difficult circumstances it is possible to imagine, he did.

However compromised, drunk and scared he was, Jeremy Wolfenden's famous charm had secured him many Russian friends. Sophisticated men like Vladimir Pozner and Yuri Vinogradov were fond of him and sought out his company; the babushkas in Sad Sam worried about his welfare; even the lift girl in the Hotel Ukraina asked wistfully after him. He was in his wayward fashion a great spirit; and the Russians, however crushed and duped by their totalitarian world, could still respond to that. Shortly before the hand-over period was due to expire, he was tipped off by a Russian friend. Do not wait, said the friend: leave now, not tomorrow or the day after, but go to the airport now.

It was not difficult for the man with no roots to get going, but he arrived in London in an appalling state. He was exhausted by drink and drugs, frightened almost beyond endurance, and pursued by terrible dreams that he had recounted nightly down the fizzing telephone line to Iverna Court. But he had made it. Whatever it had cost him, he had not let the paper down and now, at last, he was free.

Or so it seemed. The Wolfendens went on holiday to Tangier, where they stayed in bed late, drank, lay by the pool and were generally tired enough to enact the life of the brochure. No smiling Arab boy who ferried out the fizzy drinks could guess at the peculiar stresses they had endured, at the way their white bodies, stretched out beneath the winter sun, had been such busy little conduits for the continental movements of the Cold War. Wolfenden did not want to talk about what had happened to him in Moscow; all he wanted to do, in his wife's company at any rate, was to play the part of the young husband, to give the fullest possible rein to the small conventional side of him that had never quite cut loose from the tangle of the 'Wolfenden paradox'. She didn't press him to talk in detail about things he wished to put behind him; she encouraged him to forget.

For his part, Wolfenden showed no interest in the detail of his wife's involvement with the Chisholms' work. It was now three years since the height of espionage activity and eighteen months since the trial. They had been on opposite sides of the world when it took place and a great deal had happened to both of them in the mean time. Martina believed that Jeremy assumed she was as deeply involved with the spy-ring as Ruari and Janet Chisholm themselves, but that it did not deeply concern him. Her appearance in the *Daily Express* had severely limited any future activity. Since the only people who knew what Wynne was going to say – or rather read out from his prepared text – were the KGB (who had written it), it is fair to assume that they were, indirectly, the source of the *Express* tip. It suited them to embarrass SIS further: whether the mother's help was a serving officer or merely an accomplice they could at least make sure she never got up to any funny stuff again.

So a writ of silence ran between them. The subject of espionage was fit only for joky captions in the family photograph album. Perhaps when you came to think of it there wasn't all that much to say: whatever they had done was past and seemed linked to a place they could never revisit and to an extraordinary set of circumstances that would never be reproduced. Whatever happened now was to be about them, and their new apartment in Washington, and his new job, and their pussy cat called Pooskat, and her new job working for a photographer, and their baby talk, and her red VW Beetle called the Flying Flea, and their happy new life of regular meals, and even breakfast, and only social drinking, and maybe one day babies, and not spying, only happy families . . .

The head of the *Telegraph*'s Washington bureau was Vincent Ryder; his number two was David Shears, and the *Sunday Telegraph* was served by Stephen Barber. Wolfenden's arrival on 27 December 1964 made it a four-man operation, which, even by the standards of the day, was lavish. Jeremy and Martina had a modern duplex apartment on G Street in the south-west part of town. Stephen Barber and his wife Deirdre were their near neighbours and they saw more of them than of anyone else, including his old friend Godfrey Hodgson and his French wife Alice. Hodgson was surprised by this; he felt it was as though Barber had been told to keep an eye on Wolfenden and, perhaps, to keep him from his old friends.

Wolfenden told Martina he was happy at last: he used to be unhappy, he said, but not any more. She saw him full of spontaneity and joy; his reputation went before him, and everywhere they travelled people flocked to hear what he would say. He never short-changed them: the fountain of epigrams was once more in flow, albeit fitfully, and edged with a sentimental tenderness. The Martinis in America, he remarked, were twice the size he had been used to at home; the Martinas, on the other hand, were only half the size of European ones. And she saw the shadow side of him; she could see even in the moments of domestic happiness that he knew he would not reach old age; inside he was on fire with some unquenchable misery.

He never stopped drinking. He had interludes of drinking less, but not long ones. David Shapiro, his old friend from the Naval Russian course, stayed for five days over Easter and it was clear to him that things were not good. Wolfenden was drinking huge quantities from breakfast onwards; he was not the reckless but essentially humorous pleasure-seeker of old: he was sullen and morose.

In April Wolfenden wanted to go to the Dominican Republic, but encountered difficulties with flights from Puerto Rico until eventually he persuaded Vincent Ryder to let him charter his own plane. He was introduced to a smart Puerto Rican with captain's stripes on his shirt who was to fly the plane and to a second, scruffy man with no uniform at all who sat next to the pilot. Wolfenden and his suitcase took up the other two seats in an interior that was about the size of Martina's Volkswagen.

The little plane bumped along the coast of Puerto Rico, then over to the Dominican Republic, where the second crew man woke from a deep slumber and radioed the ground. Inside the Arrivals building the man suddenly put on a uniform and demanded to see Wolfenden's passport: part of the charter deal had apparently been that he should bring his own immigration officer. When he went through customs the same man popped up again, stamped all his papers and shook him warmly by the hand. Wolfenden told the story with delight. He was interested in the Dominican Republic, but feared to stay too long in case he should end up, like other journalists, by thinking the story was important. He wanted to be back with his wife and with the more significant events of the United States. He enjoyed his trips around the country, but part of him was reluctant to leave home:

Jeremy Wolfenden

it was almost as though he felt superstitious about it and couldn't quite believe it was still going to be there when he got back.

In the early summer Martin Page went to the United States to publicise a book he had written about the fall of Khrushchev. Martina picked him up from the airport in the Flying Flea and Page travelled happily into town to see his old friend Mr Green, who, according to the gossip, had made a new and sober start to his life. He was dismayed to see the state of him – drunk, depressed, and unamenable. At dinner that night there was a naval physician from Bethesda who, in a 'spontaneous' move prearranged with Martina, urged Jeremy to go into hospital for some tests. Wolfenden shrugged off the suggestion and poured more drinks.

At breakfast the next day Page picked up a glass of what he thought was water. He spluttered to discover it was neat vodka. 'I thought all journalists started the day with vodka,' Martina told him. At lunch time Page went with Ross Mark of the *Express* to fetch Wolfenden from his office. The atmosphere was extremely tense and Wolfenden was incoherent. They took him to the Terrace Restaurant of the Willard Hotel, where, after two large vodkas, he rallied a little, though his condition remained deplorable. Later, at the National Press Club bar, which was full of beer-bellied journalists shouting at each other through a fog of cigarette smoke, Wolfenden told Page his life had been ruined by British Intelligence.

Each year on the day of the Queen's Official Birthday the British Embassy in Washington gave a large reception on its lawns with champagne, strawberries and other traditional 'English' fare. Wolfenden duly attended for the *Daily Telegraph* and was in the middle of doing what he did best, drinking and talking, when a familiar and deeply unwelcome face came into view. It was, he later told Martin Page, his old control from MI5 in London. 'Hello, Jeremy,' he said, 'it's good to be back in business with you.'

It was beginning again. He had not escaped. This time there was to be a further complication: the Americans wanted a piece of him. For the next six months Wolfenden was required not only

(289)

to report to his British contact at the Embassy; he had also to have regular meetings with a man from the FBI. When he returned from these encounters he was in a desperate emotional state: it was so bad that Martina even suspected he might be having an affair with his mysterious contact. Wolfenden would never say who this person was or what he wanted. He began to drink even more and the passages of relative sobriety were forgotten. All the good that his loving wife had done was being destroyed; she saw the empty bottles going downstairs in brown paper bags, and this time she could do nothing to stop it.

Wolfenden's friends had started to notice an unpleasant smell about him, as though his internal organs were not functioning. At a press conference in September he passed out. He was sure it was just because the room was overcrowded or too hot; nevertheless, in October Martina at last persuaded him to see a doctor for a complete physical check. He had had hepatitis in Moscow and had never gone 'dry' to give his liver a rest; there was the possibility, the doctor thought, that the disease was still lurking in his system, but he could find no indication of jaundice. He advised Wolfenden to drink less, slow down, and avoid stress: otherwise, he said, there was nothing wrong with him.

Wolfenden continued to meet his contacts in the Embassy and in the FBI. He continued to do his work for the *Daily Telegraph*, but after a second trip to the Dominican Republic at the end of September he did not leave Washington. Christmas cast its long shadow. Wolfenden, ever since the day he had locked himself in his bedroom to avoid the children's party, had hated such forced festivities. Everything was shut; there was no one to play with; there were no newspapers to read – and, significantly, no newspapers to work for. In those days, depending on how the festivals fell, the *Telegraph* might go for four or five days without publishing. With no prospect of being telephoned by London, some correspondents liked to take advantage of their freedom by indulging, uninhibited, their passion for alcohol. Wolfenden went for broke.

What happened next is known only to Martina Browne.

When I began to write the story of Jeremy Wolfenden it was clear

Jeremy Wolfenden

to me that I had to track down his widow. Whenever I
interviewed his friends and contemporaries, which was usually
easy enough to arrange – many of them could not understand
why no one had written about him before – I always asked about
Martina and if they knew where I could find her. They had
peculiar and inconsistent memories of her. She was sometimes
described as forceful, sometimes quiet, and often, with a lift of a
fastidious eyebrow, as 'not an intellectual'. Estimates of her
physical attractiveness varied from plain to beautiful. That was
not surprising since some remembered her as blonde, some as
dark, some as red-headed. Then there was her accent – variously
described as Irish, Scandinavian and Midlands.

Friends such as David Edwards could not fathom why Jeremy
had married at all, since what made him happiest was chasing
men. The consensus, no doubt affected by a glancing reference to
her in a book about espionage by Phillip Knightley called *The
Second Oldest Profession*, was that she was a spy, and that her
marriage to Jeremy had been 'arranged'.

The path to her door was a long and discouraging one.'Find the
nanny,' Knightley told me in El Vino, the Fleet Street bar where
Wolfenden drank with Ricky Marsh on a panicky return trip from
Moscow. 'If you could get to the agent . . .'

But where was she? Most people seemed to think America,
where she had lived before, escaped, and successfully reinvented
herself after the Chisholm débâcle. Only Martina would know
the truth about Wolfenden's last days; and it was the mysterious
circumstances of his death which had done so much to increase
his reputation.

After many months of dispiriting struggle with American
telephone directories I finally tracked Martina Browne to the
Republic of Ireland. There was some checking and vetting first,
but she agreed to see me. She met me at the airport. She looked,
unsurprisingly, unlike any of the descriptions I had been given:
handsome, bright-eyed, well-dressed. She had charm and presence, but life seemed hard. We went to her house on a small
estate. She is a social worker, specialising in grief counselling, but
the Republic has had to suspend such programmes until it

receives more money from the European Union: grief is temporarily unassuaged.

Martina has a teen-ager daughter, to whom she introduced me. She also has a son by her second marriage. She called him Ruari after her old boss in Moscow, but the second marriage had ended in separation.

After she had made some tea she gave me Jeremy's letters to her and showed me the monochrome cine-film of their wedding, which she had had transferred that morning to a video cassette. There they were on the steps of the church. It was all out of focus and trembly. I could vaguely make out young, smudged versions of Godfrey Hodgson and John Miller at the reception. In the final shot Jeremy turned, smiling, to the camera, knelt down on the floor, cigarette in mouth, drink in hand, and danced with a small girl. It was heart-rending.

I asked her about his final day. This is what Martina said:

'I woke up late on the morning of December 27th, about ten am. We had been at home the night before and he had been drinking very heavily. We had a row and he passed out on the sofa. I got up and went to the bathroom. The door was locked. We *never* locked the door. I called out but there was no answer. I could hear the extractor fan going inside. I went and got a beer-can opener and opened the lock with it. He was lying across the room with his head up against the bath. I thought he had fallen. He was moaning and breathing. I put my arm round him and called out, "Jeremy". I touched his face. His eyes were closed. Then they opened, looked round, and closed again. I went out and rang Stephen Barber and told him to come round immediately. I rang the doctor who had given him a check-up in October. He wasn't helpful. He told me to ring an ambulance. So we got him to the hospital.

'I had a sense of impending doom. I tried to get him to talk. He was making sounds, but nothing came out. In the hospital they kept shouting at me. "What happened? Where were you?" They didn't know what to do with him. I was in the waiting room with Stephen Barber. I think they gave him a lumbar puncture. I decided I had to go and ring his parents. I rang them and woke them up. I went back to the hospital and as they came along the corridor I knew.

'I went into his room and he just looked so peaceful. I sat with him. I was numbed. I wanted him to be alive. I think I tried to say a prayer. I wanted him to sit up. I rang his parents and told them. I was glad I'd warned them. Then Stephen Barber had to go off and ring the office. He had to get the news of Jeremy's death into the first edition.

'The front page of the paper the next day said he died "suddenly" and this may have led to the mystery. By the time the autopsy was done and the death certificate had been issued he was not news any more. I met someone in Washington who said he had heard Jeremy shot himself. The official cause of death was "fatty liver". The doctor said it was "like hepatitis", so Lady Wolfenden wouldn't be too upset. He had had hepatitis badly in Moscow and never stopped drinking afterwards.

'The following March when I was in London I had a call through Ruari Chisholm to go in and see M16 to talk about his death. They were thinking that the death might have been suspicious. It was part of the mystique around Jeremy that people would assume there had to be odd causes. The longer it goes on the more I ask myself: Did I miss something?'

I said: 'Was he dressed when you found him in the bathroom?'

She thought for a long time. She said nothing. Her little sitting room had some framed religious texts on the walls. She had been crying, but now she seemed bemused. I looked at some photographs on the sideboard. In one of them Martina was blonde with thick mascara: she had gone from Helen Shapiro to Dusty Springfield.

Eventually she said: 'Isn't that incredible? I can't remember . . . He was either wearing clothes or pyjamas. He wasn't naked. But the locked door bothered me . . . Unless he sensed that something was going to happen and he didn't want me to find him . . . Did he take just one more drink knowing that it was going to kill him?'

Then she showed me the death certificate and the autopsy report. The Coroner's Office pathology report showed a blood/alcohol level of 0.06 per cent. This is not in itself remarkable (the breathalyser limit is 0.08), but for a reading taken perhaps thirty-six hours after he had had a drink it is very high. The autopsy was done at 1 pm on 28 December. He was six feet tall and 135 pounds; the pronounced time of death was 11.55 pm on 27 December 1965. The report read:

> Police report is not available at this time. The physician who had been treating the patient called to state that during the short hospitalisation before death the patient had a carbon dioxide combining power of 0 and that to his knowledge the patient had not had massive gastrointestinal bleeding.
> Anatomical diagnoses:
> 1. Fatty liver
> 2. Ruptured esophogeal varices with haemorrhage from the nose and mouth
> 3. Apneumatosis of left lung
> 4. Bilateral pulmonary congestion and pulmonary edema of right lung
> 5. Chronic fibrosing and calcific pancreatitis.

Numbers three and four are normal post-mortem changes. Numbers one, two and five are consistent with chronic alcohol abuse and death from liver failure.

A more detailed narrative reported:

> The sclera are moderately jaundiced but no jaundice is seen on the skin. There is no evidence of trauma on the scalp, face, trunk, or extremities. The oral cavity does not show any evidence of injury . . . The cut surfaces of the lungs show marked congestion and edema in the right lung and the left lung is almost completely airless and has a dark purplish congested appearance. There is no evidence of consolidation, pulmonary embolism or aspirated material.
> The liver is enlarged to six finger breadths below the right costal margin and the edges are rounded. The liver has a bright yellow colour and appeared to be extremely fatty. Cut surfaces of the liver show a yellow fatty appearance . . . The pancreas is extremely firm and throughout shows small focal areas of scarring and cut with a gritty sensation, indicating focal calcification. The kidneys are pale, suggestive of haemorrhage.
> CAUSE OF DEATH: Fatty liver.

It was signed by Dr Marion Mann, Mr Compton attending.

These are a classic set of symptoms for death from excessive alcohol consumption. The pancreatitis was typical, so was the liver damage and the ruptured esophogeal varices, which are like burst varicose veins in the abdomen caused by blood being unable to go on its normal course through the liver.

Unless I was being defrauded on a magnificent scale it appeared that, at the astonishing age of thirty-one, the most brilliant Englishman of his generation had drunk himself to death.

Everyone in the Chisholm household had been involved in spying: even the children had been given boxes of sweets by Penkovsky in the park. What about Martina Browne? How come she was so handy at prising open doors with a bottle-opener?

SIS did not usually busy itself recruiting among working-class fifteen-year-old school leavers; nor was an advertisement on the noticeboard of a Catholic social club a promising manoeuvre. Martina herself denied being an SIS officer, though she made ambiguous remarks about her role. She had dinner with Greville Wynne and formed the impression that he was too nervy to take the pressure. She once referred to her own job as 'looking through keyholes', but told me that that was just a 'throwaway remark'. Even if she was not telling the truth, it did not seem important as far as Jeremy Wolfenden was concerned. What mattered in his life was whether the marriage had been a fake, a security front; and his surviving letters to her – 'Darling Mina-Wife' – proved that it had been based on love.

Martina Browne was known to Jeremy Wolfenden's friends as a romancer. When she arrived in London after his death her Greenford accent had become 'pure Sloane Square'. She would invent stories about her childhood and her past; the one she told you in the evening contradicted in several respects the one with which she had enthralled you at lunch.

It is possible that Martina felt humiliated by the fact that all this activity was going on in the Chisholm flat without her being involved. The West was saved by information carried out by Janet and Ruari – even little Ali-boy was said to have helped; and she had just peeled the potatoes from O.Y. Stockmann and

washed the children's faces. It is possible that, far from conceal-
ing anything, Martina Browne had actually exaggerated her
involvement.

Everyone who saw her in the days following Jeremy's death
was struck by the depth of her grief and the dignity of her self-
control. This was more than could be said for Jeremy's father.

Jack Wolfenden made a dreadful impression on Jeremy's
friends and colleagues when he and his wife arrived in Washington for the funeral. 'How are you?' he had written in a postcard to
his son a few months earlier. 'And how behaving?' His line was
that he would not visit Jeremy in America unless he could make it
fit in with a lecture tour or some more serious purpose. The
Wolfendens were shown around by Jeremy's *Telegraph* colleague
Stephen Barber and his wife Deirdre. The funeral was in
Washington Cathedral. Eileen Wolfenden did not cry; she felt it
was a question of somehow enduring it. Martina was distraught
but brave. Afterwards, they all went out to dinner. Martina sat
slumped and stunned at the table while Jack Wolfenden made
the others play word games. No one who knew him doubted that
at a deep level his love for Jeremy remained intact, but at times he
seemed more concerned to make sure everything was done
properly than to inquire how his first-born and prodigious son
came to be dead at the age of thirty-one.

Eileen Wolfenden thought they should at least see the doctor
who had treated Jeremy in hospital, but he was away for the New
Year holiday. Stephen Barber told her that everything possible
had been done, and after a while, Eileen Wolfenden felt she had
better accept it. Her husband's attitude was the Evangelical
'Where they fall . . .' He felt that his son had been given a chance,
a great chance, and that now there was no more to be said. He was
not what his wife called a pry-er; he was a man who knew better
than most how to take a tip over brandy in a Pall Mall club, and if
SIS had wanted to warn him not to ask too many questions he
would have known how to read between their lines. Eileen
Wolfenden meanwhile had to face the bitter fact that never again
in her life would she know the sense of wonder and possibility
that Jeremy had given her.

Within hours of Wolfenden's death, John Sparrow, the

warden of All Souls, asked Jack Wolfenden if the service of commemoration could be held at the college. He agreed, and the memorial service took place at All Souls on 5 February 1966. The *Telegraph* was disappointed that the service was not in Fleet Street, that the soul of Jeremy Wolfenden was finally claimed by the world of scholarship, not journalism; but the paper had done little to deserve the honour.

It was a dismal day. A train arrived from Paddington bearing many of the young men and women who had been inspired by the hope and ambition that Jeremy Wolfenden had given them. Their sense of what was possible in their own lives contracted with his death. Some say that they never recovered it.

John Sparrow gave an address in which he compared Wolfenden to a comet with a long orbit.

'Two words recur insistently when I think about him,' said Sparrow: ' "brilliant" and "lovable". Brilliant he certainly was. He came here with a fine record as a scholar of Eton and then Magdalen; he got his First with an alpha in every paper; had he wanted an academic career, the way lay open to him. But he was a dedicated professional, and the call of Fleet Street was strong. He wanted above all to be a foreign correspondent – "to roam the world with that wild brotherhood" – and that meant that "he came to Oxford with his friends no more". Those who knew tell me that he would have risen to the very top of his chosen profession, and I do not doubt it.

'But in that unfulfilled promise lies less than half the tragedy of his early death. That was his loss, and his profession's.

'The real tragedy is our loss. For if he was brilliant, he was lovable too. He had a gay manner, a lively mind, an affectionate nature, and an open heart. Those who knew him have lost a friend, and those to whom he was closest have lost much more than that.

'I should say too that until recently he was a wayward and a restless spirit; then, a year or so before his death, he seemed to find himself; and he found himself in the best way – by finding someone else. In one of his last letters he told me without sentimentality how happy his marriage had made him. He was not fated to enjoy that good fortune for long. If that adds

poignancy to our sorrow, let us at least be thankful that before he
died he knew what it was to give such happiness and to receive it.'

Jeremy Wolfenden's ashes were scattered beneath the trees of
Addison's Walk in Magdalen, but his friends still mourned him.

That was the end of Jeremy Wolfenden's life, but there is a sense
in which his story is likely to remain incomplete. In spring 1966
SIS officers visited All Souls and Magdalen. They were unhappy
about his death, but if they found out anything from his former
colleagues they kept it to themselves.

The end of the Cold War has meant that intelligence services
admit their own existence and provide press officers. This is a
significant development. What has not changed is this: they still
reveal nothing. It is not so much that, in the dispiriting phrase of
James Jesus Angleton, we are in a wilderness of mirrors; it is more
that we are through the looking-glass.

One person who is occasionally helpful to writers is a man
called Gervase Cowell, who has the title 'Advisor to the S.O.E.
Archive'. He was, funnily enough, Ruari Chisholm's successor at
the embassy in Moscow and his expulsion by the Russians, for
spying, was reported by Jeremy Wolfenden in the *Daily Telegraph* on 14 May 1963.

Anyone can ring Gervase Cowell and ask for his help.
Unfortunately, he told me, he was not allowed to reveal anything
at all about British citizens. 'Of course,' he said, 'you are entitled
by the Citizen's Charter to write to MI5 if you think he was also
involved in security work. I can give you their address.'

There are always the tactics of the side-door. Friends of friends
can make discreet inquiries of retired officers and they in turn . . .
One such man replied that indeed Wolfenden's name rang a bell,
but he didn't hold out much chance of anything coming to light:
it was all a bit recent. Something pre-War would stand a better
chance of an answer.

From Yuri Kobaladze, chief of the Press Bureau of the Russian
Intelligence Service (KGB), came this fax:

There are two aspects to your request which have to be explained.

First, the Russian Intelligence Service is responsible only for foreign operations ie outside the territory of Russia (the Soviet Union in the past). And second, irrespective of the person in question it is to be borne in mind that the existing law prohibits to reveal operational information. So we keep to the rule adopted by secret services throughout the world not to comment on the questions of attribution of any person to Soviet/Russian Intelligence Service.

Give or take a verbal construction, this could have been written by Gervase Cowell himself.

The Soviet double-agent Oleg Gordievsky confirmed that the seduction and blackmail of Wolfenden would have been a routine job for the Second Chief Directorate, or Counter-Intelligence Service. 'But,' he said, 'it is almost impossible to get anything from the domestic service.' Many weeks later a reply finally emerged from its office in Moscow:

I regret to inform you that no record of the Counter-Intelligence Service concerning the dealings with Jeremy Wolfenden was found in our archives. In addition to this I must certify that Mr Wolfenden is unknown to the Service. As a result of the matter I can't give any documentary evidence of the case to you.

Yours sincerely Alexander Mikhailov.

Vladimir Pozner, Wolfenden's link to the Russian establishment, who now lives in New York, made no reply to a request for information. Both the FBI and the CIA, however, are bound to answer questions under the American Freedom of Information Act. The FBI said that the large number of applications meant that there would be a delay of up to two years in dealing with new inquiries.

The CIA wrote as follows:

I must advise you that in all requests such as yours, the CIA can neither confirm nor deny the existence or the non-existence of any CIA records responsive to your request. The fact of the existence or non-existence of records containing such information – unless, of course, it has been officially acknowledged – would be classified for reasons of national security under sections 1.3 (a) (4) [intelligence sources and methods] and 1.3 (a) (5) [foreign relations] of Executive Order 12356. Further, the Director of Central Intelligence has the responsibility and authority to protect such information from unauthorized disclosure in accordance with Subsection 102 (d) (3) of the National Security Act of 1947 and Section 6 of the CIA Act of 1949.

Accordingly your request is denied on the basis of FOIA exemptions (b) (1) and (b) (3). By this action, we are neither confirming nor denying the existence or non-existence of such records. An explanation of the FOIA exemptions cited above is enclosed.

The letter was signed by John H. Wright, Information and Privacy Co-Ordinator. The attached explanation of exemptions included the two relevant paragraphs:

(b) (1) applies to material which is properly classified pursuant to an Executive order in the interest of national defense or foreign policy;

(b) (3) applies to the Director's statutory obligations to protect from disclosure intelligence sources and methods, as well as organization, functions, names, official titles, salaries or numbers of personnel employed by the Agency, in accord with the National Security Act of 1947 and the CIA Act of 1949.

Many of Jeremy Wolfenden's friends, including his cousin and confidante Sally Humphreys and his former fiancée Susie Burchardt, were ignorant of his involvement with the intelligence services. Those who knew of it had their own theories. Some believed that Yuri Krutikov, his first KGB contact on his student trip in 1956, later ran him as an agent in Moscow; others believed that he was switched from Moscow to Washington by the *Telegraph* at the request of SIS because a former Russian lover had been posted to Washington and they were consequently hoping for a klondike of new information through Wolfenden.

The extreme theory of Wolfenden's death ran as follows: that he was murdered, probably by the CIA. Furious at SIS's indifference to the fate of Penkovsky, whom it left to be tortured and killed by the KGB, the CIA determined on revenge. They reasoned that the only person who could have known both what was going through Ruari Chisholm's flat in Sad Sam and who was in regular contact with the KGB was Jeremy Wolfenden. Against the argument that Wolfenden would not have wished to blow Penkovsky's cover, the conspiracists had the answer that it was not deliberate: the man was drunk for twelve hours a day every day. The KGB had nothing on Penkovsky until they searched his room and found a Minnox camera; his meetings with Greville Wynne and Janet Chisholm had not been observed: someone must have tipped them off. Given a chance to redeem himself in America through contact with the FBI, Wolfenden failed. He was killed, or pushed into suicide, and his wife, herself an agent, was squared by SIS.

This is an attractive theory, not least because it answers one of the great mysteries of the Cold War: who shopped Penkovsky, the Man Who Saved the World? However, it cannot be true. The CIA did not plot to kill people like Jeremy Wolfenden, white Old Etonians, in Washington. They plotted to kill people like Patrice Lumumba in the Belgian Congo. Nothing in Wolfenden's private letters to Martina Browne suggests any degree of knowledge or culpability in Penkovsky's fate. The theory also depends on Martina Browne's being an SIS officer who married Wolfenden under false pretences. But although she may have helped in the Chisholm household she was not herself working for SIS; and, despite everything his friends believed, Wolfenden married her for reasons of sentimental love.

Wolfenden drank himself to death. His involvement with the intelligence services increased his self-destructive desperation and made his life shorter, but the spies did not kill him. His gift for self-preservation, of knowing just how far he could go, deserted him in the end because he underestimated the doggedness of the intelligence services and believed that, drunk or sober, he could use them merely to amuse himself.

In fact they used him. SIS had their eye on him in the Navy and recruited him at Oxford. He was not trained by them, but felt formally enough attached to attempt to recruit one of his best friends, Colin Falck.

His ambition to go to Moscow was thwarted at *The Times* because his superiors saw the risks. S.R. Pawley of the *Daily*

Telegraph, however, was more responsive. Senior *Telegraph* men had retained wartime connections with intelligence, and though such contacts were considered louche at 135 Fleet Street, they were regarded as acceptably patriotic. A degree of cooperation with 'the Embassy' was the price Wolfenden was asked to pay for getting posted to Moscow in the first place. It did not in the first instance seem much to ask. Wolfenden knew he was likely to be blackmailed by the KGB, but he did not mind. He thought it would be amusing.

SIS did not mind either; in fact they preferred it that way. A double agent was more useful to them than a loosely sympathetic journalist. Wolfenden resented having to work for either side, largely because what he was required to do – open mail, write articles, report on Keith Morfett's sex life – was boring. He also took his journalism seriously and felt compromised.

By then it was too late. His father's reputation and the civil liberties of millions of homosexual men in Britain were at stake. When Ruari and Janet Chisholm turned out to have been connected with the greatest flow of information ever received by the West, his position became more tense. Both sides took a closer interest in him. By the time he married the Chisholm nanny – a woman who had been named by Wynne at the trial and who was warned by her own country's Intelligence service that she faced a lifetime of incarceration if she so much as set foot in the Soviet Union – he had become enmeshed beyond any hope of escape.

The United States provided no relief. Because the Penkovsky-Wynne connection had been run jointly by Britain and America, both SIS and the CIA assumed there was a legitimate continuity in his commitment. Suspicions about the shopping of Penkovsky did not help.

In 1965 the Americans were extremely agitated about Soviet penetration in the United States. Wolfenden was thus asked to advise the FBI on the bona fides of Russian diplomats, business-men and other visitors. The FBI also, in his wife's belief, made further, tougher demands of him. British intelligence and security continued to maintain an interest.

There was no amusement any more to be had from these

flirtations; there was desperate pressure with no end in sight. The man who had impressed his Oxford friends not just by his brilliance but by the sweetness of his temper, had been worn down. There were no more 'dishes', no parties that he cared for, no more excitement. There was only drink, and that by now had a self-destructive purpose.

Martina Browne felt that in Jeremy's dealings with the FBI there was the suspicion of some love affair; the utter misery they caused him could not otherwise be explained. She assumed the affair was with the FBI agent, which seems unlikely, but her instinct may have been right. Sex and spying were intimately connected in Wolfenden's life, and somehow, somewhere, with some person, it may have continued in Washington. No one knew the details. His wife knew only that 'something was going on'. This final emotional twist provided the leverage that broke him.

All this I had pieced together without any official help or confirmation from the intelligence or security services. Then, when this book was with the printer, one of the many side-doors I had been trying swung open a few inches. I was not disabused. Wolfenden was on SIS's books, and although nothing more was 'confirmed or denied', I was offered a likely outline of what might have happened in such circumstances. It tallied in almost every respect with the story Jeremy Wolfenden's friends had put together for me and which I have told here. The role of the FBI was considered plausible, that of the KGB almost inevitable. Why Wolfenden was allowed to go to Moscow remains unclear, though dangers revealed by a routine MI5 defensive security briefing would not necessarily have been shared with the *Daily Telegraph*.

None of the four Wolfenden children 'achieved' anything in the sense their father would have understood. This would not matter if they had seemed happier or more fulfilled in other ways. Was there a trauma in childhood? Or since such relative 'failure' is the norm of human life, is it naïve to look for a single cause? Jeremy Wolfenden would certainly have laughed at this biographical enterprise (he referred mockingly to 'my biographers' in a letter);

but he might have laughed less if he thought it was offering a complete psychological theory or 'solution'.

He would have died anyway, even without the intelligence complications; his liver would have killed him. It was not for any spying activities, anyway, that his friends mourned or remembered him, but for the reckless way he burned away his life for their edification and amusement.

His death left them all diminished and uneasy. They wondered if they could have helped; they wondered what they were supposed to learn from his existence. They missed him because they had known no one like him and a part of their sense of what life could be had died with him. The Allies had won the War, England had in the phrase of Wolfenden's one-time drinking partner A.J.P. Taylor, 'arisen'; now it needed thinkers of Wolfenden's brilliance to shape the peace – to form the new, post-Beveridge world of social justice and universal education, to inspire the country whose values had supposedly been 'stamped for ever on the future of civilisation' by the deaths of hundreds of thousands of men like Richard Hillary. It never happened.

Wolfenden's friends lived their own lives, the majority of them in the disappointing country Britain became. With the education they had, most of them have done well by the standards of the world, though their ideas of what that world might turn out to be have, over the years, been modified.

More than thirty years after his death, they puzzle over him, one or two become damp-eyed when they recall him, some shake their heads and smile.

Mike Artis, who appeared to Wolfenden's Etonian friends as though he were starving to death from a cocktail of industrial diseases, is now Professor Michael Artis and lists his hobby as 'eating out'. He and Robin Hope both live in Italy. Sally Humphreys and Colin Falck teach in America. Philip Howard, Neal Ascherson, Philip French and Godfrey Hodgson have been among the most prominent journalists of their generation. Susie Burchardt, under her married name of Susan Watt, runs the London publisher Michael Joseph.

Stephen McWatters, the Eton Master in College, is long retired, but remembers the schoolboy he taught: 'He admitted to having homosexual inclinations and he was critical of society's attitude to the question and the school's policy that reflected that attitude.'

Wolfenden's own views survive – for instance, in a letter to Michael Parsons, an Oxford friend, from Paris, January 1961: 'There is just no such thing as anyone's real personality. Personalities are the product of the initial feelings or attitudes someone takes up and the needs of the situation they find themselves in . . . and, for that matter, the initial feelings themselves are the product of earlier conflicts of that sort. There is a dialectic of personality, just as there is a dialectic of history (and it's just as unpredictable).'

There are other voices whose words stick in the memory:

Sally Humphreys: 'Martina said an extraordinary thing after he was dead. She said, "Why was he always so unhappy?" This surprised me, because I felt in general that the opposite was true.'

Eileen Wolfenden: 'When I heard that he was dead I thought, Never again can I have a marvellous boy who turned out to be everything to us . . . It was not until I had had three normal children that I understood how extraordinary he was.'

Robert Cassen: 'I felt it was a defect of character that someone that brilliant should be so bored.'

Jeremy Wolfenden himself in a letter from Moscow, January 1962: 'Personally I'm becoming more and more anti-political; the gap between the fascination of political theories and dreary actions which people take in their name is getting me down.'

His Finals examiner at Oxford, after giving him eight alphas: 'He wrote as though it were all beneath him; he wrote as though it were all such a waste of his time.'

David Shapiro in his letter of condolence to Martina Browne: 'I was for a long time frightened of him, at first by his sheer brilliance, but then, even after one felt the kindness of his wit, by the deep unhappiness of his life.'

Martina Browne: 'And then in Washington, with the FBI, *something was going on*, and he died, and we're never going to know.'

David Edwards, his friend in London: 'Jeremy was on course to meet his fate before he even set foot in Moscow.'

Philip French: 'Turning recklessness into a philosophy and a style, he behaved as if life truly was absurd, as if suicide was a serious option, and nothing really did matter beyond a certain point. What others see as the proper subject for a book or play, he made the improper subject of a life.'

Colin Falck: 'His inability to find a way to live and be happy seemed not so much a personal failure as somehow a failure of all the English structures and systems that had produced him.'

Martin Page, his colleague in Moscow: 'The intelligence services pursued him for information that was so trivial it was of no account to them. Yet they were willing to see this extraordinary man of such brilliance collapse as a human being, to the point of death, apparently without remorse. So much of the Cold War seemed to be like that.'

When I left Martina Browne's house in Ireland I drove to the airport in thick snow and flew back to London. The news on the radio at home was that the Prime Minister, John Major, was facing criticism on two fronts. The Opposition told him that his party's education reforms were failing the country's schoolchildren, while a group of Conservative MPs had criticised his foreign policy: they believed that Britain must fight to stay further aloof from the European Union.

That evening I switched on the tape of Martina Browne's melodic (slightly Irish, as it turned out) voice and thought about Wolfenden. Compared to Christopher Wood or Richard Hillary he had 'achieved' almost nothing. Despite being far cleverer than they were, he was more deeply and horribly flawed. Apart from the memory of his brilliance, he had left nothing behind – no paintings, no book, only some newspaper articles now lost by the paper in question. Yet, like the other two, he had touched a nerve; in some minor way he had represented a generation. How? Was it that like Hillary, the pilot, the epitome of the 1930s private figure forced by calamitous events into a public role, he had been a victim of sinister global forces? Was there something exemplary in his life, like Wood's, or in his death, like Hillary's? Wolfenden's was a murkier, more sordid story, replete with internal contradictions and dead ends. In fiction one would be obliged to harmonise the dialogue, themes and actions of the narrative into a more artistic whole. In fact it presented a puzzle that I could not fully solve, though I felt that Colin Falck had been getting close when he talked about the failure of the institutions that produced him.

When I went downstairs the next morning, still thinking of all that bright promise wasted, I found a letter from Wolfenden's old Oxford friend, Rod Prince, who had seen an advertisement I had placed in a magazine asking for information. His letter talked about the great days of political hope at Oxford, of their aspirations for the new Elizabethan age. He concluded:

'Jeremy was a strong influence, of course, and *still is*. I can only say how very much I appreciate having known him.'

ACKNOWLEDGEMENTS
AND SOURCES

CHRISTOPHER WOOD

The main source is Wood's letters to his mother, copies of which are held by the Tate Gallery Archive. I am grateful to the trustees and staff for allowing me to consult these and related papers.

I would also like to thank Winifred Reitlinger, Christopher and Sabrina Penn, Teddy Kennedy, Maurice Dirou, Douglas and Madeleine Johnson, Nigel Stewart at Malvern, Jill Thomas, Euan Cameron, Julian Turton, John Sheppard, Toby Eady, Matthew Gale at Kettle's Yard, Françoise Steel and Marie-Claude Martin of the Hôtel Ty-Mad.

Richard Ingleby's *Christopher Wood: An English Painter* (Allison and Busby) had not been published when I wrote my life, but I read it while mine was in proof and was able to compare notes with him on dates, spellings and so on. Richard Ingleby's loan of various papers also spared me hours at the photocopier. It is not gratitude, however, but admiration for the result that makes me able to recommend his biography unreservedly.

Wood was a terrible speller and was not well served by the typist who transcribed his letters. I cannot guarantee that I have corrected all their errors, particularly in proper names. Most of the translations from the French are my own, so a similar doubt must hang over their accuracy.

RICHARD HILLARY

The principal sources are: *The Last Enemy* by Richard Hillary, Macmillan, London, 1943; *Richard Hillary: A Biography* by R.

Lovat Dickson, Macmillan, London, 1950; *Mary and Richard* by
Michael Burn, André Deutsch, London 1988; documents in the
Richard Hillary Trust archive at Trinity College, Oxford.

Arthur Koestler's essay 'The Birth of a Myth' was published in
Horizon, April 1943 and reprinted in *The Yogi and the Commissar*.
Middleton Murry's essay appeared in *Adelphi* in July 1944 and
was reprinted in *Looking Before and After*, 1948. Eric Linklater
wrote an essay on Hillary in *The Art of Adventure*, 1947.

I would like to thank Dennis Burden, Clare Hopkins and the
Hillary trustees for allowing me to consult the archive; Michael
Burn, whose reconstruction of Hillary's last year in *Mary and
Richard* I have confidently followed on the few occasions where
the archive was silent; Tony Gould, John Coldstream, David
Woodrow, Godfrey Carter, Barry Brigg and Air Chief Marshal
Sir Christopher Foxley-Norris. I have also drawn on reminiscen-
ces by former fighter pilots Brian Kingcome and Paddy Barthrop
published in the *Independent on Sunday* in September 1990.

My particular thanks to Captain A.B. Sainsbury, archivist
extraordinaire, and to Denise Patterson (née Maxwell-Woosnam) the dedicatee of *The Last Enemy*.

JEREMY WOLFENDEN

The source was interviews, with the addition of some letters, to
Robin Hope, Martina Browne, Neal Ascherson and Michael
Parsons. All Wolfenden's work for the *Telegraph* was destroyed in
the move from Fleet Street to Canary Wharf, though his mother
and his cousin Sally Humphreys have some cuttings.

I would like to thank Lady Wolfenden, Daniel Wolfenden,
Martina Browne, Sally Humphreys (nee Hinchliff), Godfrey
Hodgson, Robin Hope, Philip Howard, Christopher Parsons,
Stephen McWatters, David Pryce-Jones, Neal Ascherson; Joe
Spence, Matthew Wilson and Penny Hatfield at Eton; Susan
Watt (Susie Burchardt), David Shapiro, Robert Cassen, Jeffrey
Gray, Philip French, David Marquand, Colin Falck (twice), Rod
Prince, Natasha Burchardt (Edelman), Anthony Page, Michael
Sissons, David Edwards, David Murray, Brian Wenham, Michael
Parsons, Norman Dombey, Ronnie Payne, Chris Dobson, David
Floyd, Colin Welch, Ricky Marsh, Phillip Knightley, Martin

Page, Oleg Gordievsky, Mark Frankland, Douglas Botting, Marcus Warren, Charles Alexander, John Miller, David Shears, Stephen Dorril, Simon Barber, Deirdre Barber and Donald Anderson.

BIBLIOGRAPHY
I read more books than I intended in the course of writing this short one, but did not keep a list of them. To two of them, however, I have incurred a debt I should acknowledge.

The first is Francis Steegmuller's biography *Jean Cocteau* (Constable, London, 1986). The second is Samuel Hynes's celebrated trilogy *A War Imagined, The Edwardian Turn of Mind*, and *The Auden Generation* (Pimlico, London, 1992). I have borrowed, without feeling the need to double-check, some factual detail from both authors and was often encouraged by Professor Hynes's, to me, congenial belief that 'a close relation exists between literature and history, and . . . this relation is particularly close in times of crisis, when public and private lives, the world of action and the world of imagination, interpenetrate.'

I would finally like to thank Richard and Elizabeth Dalkeith, J.W.M. Thompson, James Fergusson, Malini Maxwell-Hyslop, Sue Freestone and Gillon Aitken.

London, 1996

POSTSCRIPT TO PAPERBACK EDITION

When this book was first published in April 1996 I read from it at the Assembly Rooms in Edinburgh and was afterwards fortunate enough to meet Archibald McIndoe's sister, Elizabeth Mason. She gave me a letter that Richard Hillary's mother had written to McIndoe's mother. When I had read it, I thought of trying to incorporate a little of it into the narrative, but in the end decided it was better given complete, as an afterword; for every *puer aeternus* after all, a mother must stand and watch.

26 Rutland Court   April 24 1943
Rutland Gate
Knightsbridge SW7
London

Dear Mrs McIndoe

Thank you so much for your letter to me about my son Richard and for your loving sympathy.

He insisted on returning to the active list – knowing what it meant, he still insisted. I do not think I have ever known such courage, courage of mind and soul and an almost super-human bravery. He had so much to live for and yet he gave it all away with both hands – a truly great and gallant man.

He told me he would never know any peace within himself if he did not try to return, so I watched his return with an aching heart and some sadness, but this he would sweep away with his gay laugh, telling me all would be well . . .

Death held no terror for him; we had so often discussed this. I therefore know he met 'The Last Enemy' as gallantly as the first and as undefeated in spirit. He was to me the most amazing companion, so gay, gallant and witty. I am so humbly grateful for being allowed his companionship for 23 glorious years and know that my life has been tremendously enriched.

Richard had a great understanding of and liking for your son Archie, for it was thus he always spoke of him. I am busy with voluntary war work and am so glad to have this to do. Richard was always so amusedly proud that I could work – Again thank you from the bottom of my heart for your understanding sympathy.

With all kind thoughts always

Yours sincerely

Edwyna M. Hillary

The work pioneered by Gillies and McIndoe continues at the Blond McIndoe Centre, Queen Victoria Hospital, East Grinstead, Sussex RH19 3DZ. The hospital treats people suffering from accidents or from disfiguring birth defects and is grateful for donations.

S. F.
London, February 1997.